Scriptwriting for the Screen

'An excellent resource for students and teachers alike'

In the Picture

'...a valuable addition to every screenwriting bookshelf'

Screentalk

'this is one of the best guides to help screenwriters think visually that I have ever read'
Creative Screenwriting

'The inventive exercises in Scriptwriting for the Screen give it the potential for revitalizing the experience of even experienced scriptwriters. Moritz's book brings a new perspective to discussions about scriptwriting'
'Scope' Online Journal of Film Studies

Scriptwriting for the Screen is an accessible guide to writing for film and television. It details the first principles of screenwriting and advises on the best way to identify and formulate a story and develop ideas in order to build a vivid, animated and entertaining script.

Scriptwriting for the Screen introduces the reader to essential skills needed to write effective drama. This edition has been updated to include new examples and an entirely new chapter on adaptation. There are examples of scripts from a wide range of films and television dramas such as *Heroes*, *Brokeback Mountain*, *Coronation Street*, *The English Patient*, *Shooting The Past*, *Spaced*, *Our Friends in the North* and *American Beauty*.

Scriptwriting for the Screen includes:

- advice on how to visualise action and translate this into energetic writing
- how to dramatise writing, use metaphor and deepen meaning
- tips on how to determine the appropriate level of characterisation for different types of drama
- practical exercises and examples which help develop technique and style
- a section on how to trouble-shoot and sharpen dialogue
- a guide to further reading

Charlie Moritz has worked as a writer for theatre, television and film. Alongside work as a scriptwriter, storyliner and script editor he has taught screenwriting and scriptwriting to undergraduates in both the School of Film and TV and the School of Theatre at Manchester Metropolitan University. He has also taught postgraduate writing students at Sheffield Hallam University and at the RITS School of Film and Television in Brussels, and trained young writers of television drama in Skopje, Macedonia.

Scriptwriting for the Screen

Second Edition

Charlie Moritz

 Routledge
Taylor & Francis Group

LONDON AND NEW YORK

First published 2001
by Routledge
2 Park Square, Milton Park, Abingdon, Oxon OX14 4RN

Simultaneously published in the USA and Canada
by Routledge
711 Third Avenue, New York, NY 10017

Second edition published 2008

Routledge is an imprint of the Taylor & Francis Group, an informa business

© 2008 Charlie Moritz

The right of Charlie Moritz to be identified as the Author of this Work has been
asserted by him in accordance with the Copyright, Designs and Patents Act 1988.

Typeset in Goudy by Wearset Ltd, Boldon, Tyne and Wear

British Library Cataloguing in Publication Data
A catalogue record for this book is available from the British Library

Library of Congress Cataloging in Publication Data
Moritz, Charlie, 1952–
Scriptwriting for the screen / Charlie Moritz. – 2nd ed.
p. cm.
Includes bibliographical references and index.
1. Motion picture authorship. I. Title.
PN1996.M66 2008
808.2'3--dc22

2008014189

ISBN13: 978-0-415-46518-2 (hbk)
ISBN13: 978-0-415-46517-5 (pbk)

Contents

Illustrations

Preface

This book is about how to start out telling stories for the screen, and then how you can set about complicating and enriching your scripts. It is also about finding and keeping your own voice while you build and put together all those moments, scenes and sequences in a vivid, animated and entertaining way.

Over the last fifteen years, I've worked with lots of people just starting out with their screenwriting. Many of them have had little or no experience of creative writing in any shape or form, and some have felt frightened of chancing their arm at all, feeling sure screenwriting was something beyond them. It is both the progress some have made and more importantly perhaps, the obvious enthusiasm many have gained for the activity, which has persuaded me that some of the principles and ideas I work with could be of wider interest.

What I'm setting out here is a graduated, practical guide for beginners. This is not a manual all about writing a feature film or a short film, scriptwriting for a popular series or penning a one-off television drama. You will find examples drawn from all these forms and comment passed on aspects of their differences, as well as their similarities. Along the way I'll indicate other books which focus on different specialised aspects of screenwriting and which obviously go into more detail. This book offers you some strategies towards dramatising for the screen, applying them right across the board. It approaches the huge field of screenwriting like a geologist taking a core-sample: looked at carefully, that sample should reveal useful information about the deeper terrain, and suggest the relationship to the bigger landscape.

Many books on screenwriting seem to gloss over or take for granted the important little matter of being able to write drama at all, let alone put it onto the screen. In this book I try to pay special attention to that essential skill, supporting your journey with examples, exercises and suggestions for useful further reading. Books alone will not develop your imagination, skills or awareness. I cannot overstate the importance of trusting instinct and passion, and of finding good teachers, courses or writing-groups. Writing itself has to be a solitary and dedicated activity. Partly because of this I think there can be great value in joining or forming a group of like-minded enthusiasts to share your development as a scriptwriter. Although most of the exercises included in the book will be useful to you if you do choose to go it alone, many are designed with collaboration in mind.

There is nothing accidental about a good script. Nor can that first tingle of recognition, the feeling that a character, a moment, an event has the makings of a good drama ever be translated onto the page effectively, without a lot of application, craftsmanship, and critical awareness. Every outing with the pen or cursor presents a new learning curve, and if drama is to come off the page with conviction and energy, there can be no short cuts.

Nobody gets there straightaway, but stick with the challenge and you could be well rewarded. Writing scripts can be tremendous fun and also hugely fulfilling. I hope *Scriptwriting for the Screen* reflects that spirit and proves to be a trusty companion on your journey.

Acknowledgements

My thanks are due to Trea Smallacombe and Granada TV for permission to include the excerpts from the *Coronation Street* script and storyline; to Peter Flannery for kind permission to include the unpublished excerpt from *Our Friends in the North*; to past students Ian Mayor, Joanna Smith and Joe Tucker for letting me include examples drawn from their work; to Omar and Adam Sattaur for their help with the graphics.

I'm grateful to Wout Thielemans of the RITS for inviting me to teach in Brussels, for many valuable conversations on the subject of screenwriting and for continued advice with this book. Thanks also to Christopher Cudmore at Routledge for initially sponsoring and gently guiding the project and to Aileen Storry for her enthusiastic support and sensitive advice with this second edition. I also want to acknowledge the late Geoffrey Sykes, Director of the Manchester Youth Theatre, who did so much to inspire a passion for drama and to encourage my writing when I was starting out.

Heartfelt thanks to Sue Hampton for her care and support, and to my good friend and mentor Andy Logan, for unflagging encouragement to do my thing.

And finally to students past and present at Manchester Metropolitan University, the VOSS post-graduate scriptwriting course in Belgium, and elsewhere, my sincerest thanks for the privilege of teaching you, and along the way learning a lot.

Extracts from the following books are used throughout the book.

Story by Robert McKee, Methuen 1999. *Adventures in The Screen Trade* by William Goldman, Warner Books 1983. *The Fisher King* by Richard LaGravenese, Applause Books 1991. *The Art of Dramatic Writing* by Lajos Egri, Touchstone Books 1960. *Writing The Character-Centred Screenplay* by Andrew Horton, University of California Press 2000. *On Directing Film* by David Mamet, Penguin 1992. *Some Mother's Son* by Terry George and Jim Sheridan, Grove Press 1996. *My Left Foot* by Shane Connaughton and Jim Sheridan, Faber 1989. *Shallow Grave* by John Hodge, Faber 1996. *Collected Works of Paddy Chayefsky – The Screenplays*, Applause Books 1981. *The Poetics* by Aristotle, translated by Malcolm Heath, Penguin 1996. *American Beauty* by Alan Ball, FilmFour Books 2000. *The English Patient* by Anthony Minghella from the novel by Michael Ondaatje, Methuen 1997. *Casablanca: Script and Legend* by Howard Koch, Overlook Press 1992. *Our Friends in the North*, reproduced by permission of The Agency (London) Ltd © Peter Flannery 1994. *Brokeback Mountain, Story to Screenplay* by Annie Proulx, Larry McMurtry and Diana Ossana, Harper Perennial 2006. *Nurse Betty* by John C. Richards and James Flamberg, Newmarket Press 2000. *The Birds and Other Stories* by Daphne du Maurier, Virago 2007. *Truly, Madly, Deeply* by Anthony Minghella, Heinemann 1991. *Encounter* © Roy Jacobsen 1989. English translation by Frankie Shackleford. Reprinted with kind permission from Roy Jacobsen and Cappelen Damm Agency. Screenplay of *Encounter* by Joe Tucker, based on the short story *Encounter* © Roy Jacobsen 1989. Screenplay reprinted with kind permission from Joe Tucker, Roy Jacobsen and Cappelen Damm Agency.

1
Scripting stories: some first principles

Writing can feel like a very risky business, and any newcomer to the craft of scripting for the screen takes on numerous challenges simultaneously: there's turning ideas into stories, creating moments and scenes, building those into sequences or acts, animating characters and making them behave engagingly and convincingly. It is all too easy to be discouraged by the various tasks facing you: it can also be rather tempting to ignore paying these tasks the close attention they do indeed deserve, choosing to believe that the thing about writing is it's all a gift anyway, and what's more you've definitely got it. That way, when you do manage to get something which looks like a script down on paper, with action which moves and characters who speak, you can convince yourself there's really nothing to this business of juggling pictures, sound, characters, action and dialogue whilst incorporating them into structured scenes and sequences which will hold themselves together and also hold an audience! Perhaps you are one of the very few for whom this is true. For most of us, it can be helpful to simplify the process, juggle with fewer elements to begin with, and in so doing really notice what it is we are attempting to do.

Mainly, and most often, what we're attempting to do in scripting drama for the screen is to formulate stories. Through this ancient art we tell tales which will involve our audience, evoking their thoughts and feelings while they get in touch with our thoughts and feelings as expressed through the drama. It's a universal tradition, and humanity's way of trying to make sense and meaning out of our experience of being, and of then sharing with each other both those outer adventures and the innermost journeyings they provoke.

GETTING HOLD OF YOUR STORY

Here's a very broad working definition of what is generally meant by story in classical narrative:

For a story to occur, something extraordinary must happen to so upset the balance of a chosen character's life that he is then impelled to pursue a goal generated by the change in his life. In doing so, he will face obstacles and antagonistic forces until he does or does not get what he wants, reaches a point of change from which there will be no going back, and in this way a new order is established.

When Aristotle discussed ancient theatre in his *Poetics* he observed and set down certain principles and conventions which later came to be known as the Rule of the Three Unities – these being time, place and action. It was thought ideal that the events in a play should unfold in one setting only, over a period of 12 or 24 hours, and should concern themselves with just one plot; hardly your average James Bond movie. Although that said of course the American television drama *24* is predicated almost exactly on the classical unity of time, each episode contrived to give the convincing appearance of running in real time, and each season's programmes intended to span just twenty-four hours in Counter Terrorist Unit operative Jack Bauer's life. This illusion is further supported by the split-screen transitions and the regular appearance of a digital clock on screen counting down the time. And *24*'s intricately plotted stories, in which Bauer and LACTU consistently fight to protect the nation's safety, for the first six seasons also adhered fairly closely to the classical unity of place, being for the most part based in Los Angeles and nearby locations with only occasional forays to Washington DC. Of

Figure 1.1   24 © Fox-TV

course there is a paradoxical quality to the idea of twenty-four hours of, as it were, real-time action being screened over several months, and certainly with its pacey, mobile, action packed content *24* is in many ways far removed from classical Greek or Roman drama. It's difficult to think of many screen dramas which adhere to these ancient story-telling principles, though where they most closely do so, they are often derived from stage plays, such as *Twelve Angry Men* (Reginald Rose) or *Sleuth* (Anthony Shaffer), and, as films they *can* prove to be remarkably absorbing and powerful.

The fundamental principles of classical story-telling have abiding relevance, and form an invaluable core-model for new writers to familiarise themselves with and work around. It can be very useful to take the idea of Unity of Action on board and just try writing a single-strand narrative around a single central character to start off with, whilst allowing yourself the luxury of taking leaps in time, and space: we are all so familiar with screen dramas leaping forward and changing location that it can feel very constraining not to do the same. (That said, with a little ingenuity, it *is* perfectly possible to work out a story which does adhere to all those Classic Unities and the discipline of doing so *can* help you produce remarkable results.) Once you're very comfortable designing stories along the most straightforward of classical lines, it becomes much easier for those who want to deviate from that model with confidence. Naturally this is a generalisation and, of course, there are those who will want to manage more complex, unconventional narrative structures from very early on. My experience of working with a lot of people who are just beginning to learn about screenwriting has taught me that it is a tiny minority who actively resist the classic model and that, for those who do stick with it in their early practice, the benefits are significant.

It can be worthwhile remembering that the word 'drama' comes from the Ancient Greek verb meaning 'to do', and it is worth holding this in mind when you start out dreaming up and shaping stories for the screen. Writing a drama will, of course, spring from playing with ideas, but when we form those into a script we are not going to write the *idea* of the story or even write about the idea: our aim, instead, is for actors to convey what lies at the heart of the matter through what their characters do and say. It is that actual 'doing' of the drama we must aim to write. First and foremost, think in terms of a story unfolding as inter-connected *action*, one part causing another to occur, and so on, until the hero's struggle reaches its natural conclusion. To begin with, forget about making characters speak and think about letting them act.

A good way to start out can be to try writing a few short, self-contained screenplays, say 10 to 15 minutes in duration, and to write them in the classical mould. Here's an example, a short animation script I wrote which pulls together and illustrates some of the main working principles outlined above.

TWO SHARP

FADE IN

INT. CLAYTON'S BEDSITTER. SIX A.M.
It's dark. CLAYTON dozes blissfully as the alarm goes off. He reaches out an arm and pats the bell off. He tosses and turns. Tetchily THE CLOCK reaches up and sets its bell ringing again. CLAYTON starts up glaring, then tries to swipe at THE CLOCK which dodges the blow. CLAYTON swings again and connects, sending it skidding across the chest of drawers before sticking his head under the pillow. THE CLOCK collects itself, strides over and, grabbing CLAYTON by the collar, pulls him up nose-to-clock-face. Pointing towards CLAYTON'S drawing board, it rings extra loud.

A deeply reluctant CLAYTON staggers across to his unfinished cartoon strip.

INT. BATHROOM. 6.05 A.M.
Troubled, CLAYTON showers. We see the as-yet empty cartoon frames which fill his thoughts.

INT. CLAYTON'S BEDSITTER. 9.30 A.M.
CLAYTON paces broodily, still haunted by the empty frames.

He breaks off to plunge the coffee in his cafetiere.

INT. CLAYTON'S FANTASY. CONTINUOUS.
CLAYTON plunges a detonator attached to some wires.

INT. EDITOR'S OFFICE. CONTINUOUS.
The wires link to dynamite under the editor's chair. It explodes.

INT. CLAYTON'S BEDSITTER. CONTINUOUS.
A happy smile fades from CLAYTON'S face as he catches THE CLOCK'S pitying smirk. Turning back to his work, CLAYTON purposefully picks up his dog-eared pencil (its top surmounted by a rubber modelette of him holding the same pencil). CLAYTON perks up. Inspiration has struck. CLAYTON kisses the pencil-top effigy. As the pencil makes contact with the paper there is a loud ping and the pencil-point breaks off. CLAYTON searches the desk-top, to no avail, then opens drawers, rooting first through one, then another, as his irritation mounts.

INT. CLAYTON'S BEDSITTER. A LITTLE LATER.
Surfaces are piled with mess. Drawers have been pulled out and CLAYTON tosses aside unwanted pens, paper and so on in his unsuccessful quest.

INT. CLAYTON'S BEDSITTER. A LITTLE LATER.

The whole room has been turned over. Breathless, CLAYTON sits amidst the chaos clutching his pencil.

THE CLOCK coughs discreetly, tetchily tapping an imaginary wrist watch. CLAYTON wings something at THE CLOCK who neatly side-steps.

INT. KITCHEN. A LITTLE LATER.
CLAYTON tries to sharpen the pencil with a pair of scissors, to no avail. Switching to a kitchen knife, he manages a point.

Triumphantly he holds his pencil aloft and makes for the drawing board.

INT. BEDSITTER. CONTINUOUS.
CLAYTON marches across to the table, lowers the pencil to work and the point drops out. CLAYTON re-inserts the point. It falls out again.

INT. KITCHEN. A LITTLE LATER.
CLAYTON attempts to sharpen the pencil using a cheese-grater. He is taken aback when, in the wink of an eye, his pencil is appreciably shorter . . . and still blunt.

INT. BEDSITTER. A LITTLE LATER.
Perspiring freely, CLAYTON furiously rubs at the pencil point with sand-paper. A big pile of saw-dust, and no point to the pencil. CLAYTON peers sadly down the business-end and shakes his head.

THE CLOCK impatiently drums its fingers. The phone rings. THE CLOCK picks up the receiver and proffers it to CLAYTON who mutters angrily under his breath before putting on an over-sweet smile and taking the call. We hear the muffled rise and fall of an impatient EDITOR, mixed with indistinct yet soothing monosyllables through CLAYTON's gritted teeth. CLAYTON replaces the receiver and taps impatient fingers as he stares, blank with anxiety.

THE CLOCK rolls its eyes in disbelief. CLAYTON's eyes light on the Yellow Pages. A flurry of page turning and hunting down columns, then undisguised relief as he picks up the receiver.

EXT. PARADE OF SHOPS. DAY.
CLAYTON searches for and eventually finds the stationery shop.

The moment he does so the 'Open' sign is switched to read 'Closed'. CLAYTON makes overtures to the shopkeeper; a gentle tapping, rapidly escalating via door handle shaking to banging and kicking.

EXT. ANOTHER SHOP. MINUTES LATER.
CLAYTON rattles at another door, maybe a newsagents. Same story. In great distress and near to exhaustion he slumps down in the doorway grasping his pointless pencil.

A PASSER-BY stops and looks. Plaintively CLAYTON indicates his plight. The PASSER-BY points to a clock. It reads 1.05 p.m. CLAYTON is close to tears. The Good Samaritan helps him to his feet and leads him by the arm.

INT. STREET. MINUTES LATER.
CLAYTON and the GOOD SAMARITAN step off a bus and enter the front of a tall apartment building.

INT. BUILDING. CONTINUOUS.
They climb many flights of stairs. CLAYTON shows the strain but every time the stranger looks round he puts on a smile. Reaching the top, the SAMARITAN fumbles for the key. CLAYTON recovers.

They enter.

INT. GOOD SAMARITAN'S LOUNGE. MINUTES LATER.
CLAYTON sits impatiently fretting about time. The SAMARITAN appears brandishing the kettle enquiringly. A simpering CLAYTON holds up his pencil. The SAMARITAN takes it off CLAYTON. He crosses to a super sharpener attached to a desk. A few turns and the point is restored. An ecstatic CLAYTON kisses the bewildered SAMARITAN and rushes out.

INT. CLAYTON'S BEDSITTER. 1.35 P.M.
Breathless, CLAYTON skids to a halt by his drawing.
THE CLOCK points at its face and shakes its head with a wry smile.

CLAYTON takes a deep breath, flourishes his pencil, sweeps it grandly up to table-top level and catches the edge of the table with the point. It pings off and bounces across the floor. THE CLOCK is amused, CLAYTON is grief-stricken.

The phone rings. THE CLOCK picks it up. CLAYTON is galvanised. He does frantic 'I'm-not-here' dumb-play at THE CLOCK. CLAYTON rushes for the door. He double-takes, rushes back for the drawing and tucks it under his arm. He dithers and picks up the pencil, before hurtling out.

INT. LANDING OUTSIDE SAMARITAN'S FLAT. MINUTES LATER.
CLAYTON knocks. No answer. Desperate he looks around, grabs his chance and breaks in using his credit card.

He sharpens the pencil, scribbles a 'thank you' note and leaves a fiver before tucking the pencil, point uppermost in his breast pocket.

Rushes out straight into burly POLICEMAN. His pencil point pings off once more as he is cuffed and led off, protesting, while busy-body NEIGHBOURS nosily speculate.

INT. INTERVIEW ROOM. POLICE STATION. 1.53 P.M.
Forlorn and solitary, CLAYTON sits awaiting his fate. Several OFFICERS enter. One sits opposite and slaps CLAYTON'S credit card on the table. CLAYTON unfurls his unfinished art-work, holds up his broken pencil and breaks down sobbing. Unimpressed, the OFFICER brandishes a biro and starts to fill out a charge sheet. CLAYTON spies a newspaper in a jacket pocket, grabs it and turns to the cartoons. He finds his own strip and points to the name. Much sceptical laughter. By way of a challenge, CLAYTON's pencil is whisked away and returned to him with a gleaming point. Like lightning he

dashes off a finished frame. A quick comparison with the paper and the terrible truth dawns on Plod and Co.

EXT. STREET. MOMENTS LATER.
A police van speeds along, lights flashing, sirens wailing.

INT. POLICE VAN. CONTINUOUS.
CLAYTON finally gets to finish his cartoon strip. As the POLICE ESCORT admire the finished product, CLAYTON stows the pencil, point uppermost in his breast-pocket. He thinks again, removes it and smugly re-positions it point downwards.

INT. CARTOON EDITOR'S OFFICE. MOMENTS LATER.
The CARTOON EDITOR, in mid-tantrum, breaks off and rushes to the window with his YES MEN at the sound of police sirens and screeching brakes. The sound of feet rushing upstairs.

The door is flung open. Exhausted but triumphant, CLAYTON stands on the threshold, as the town hall clock strikes two. Tantrums turn to oily delight. The CARTOON EDITOR whips the cartoon off CLAYTON, and clasps CLAYTON to his bosom. CLAYTON reels dizzily, it seems.

The CARTOON EDITOR takes the cartoon over to the light. He laughs. His YES MEN laugh. He laughs more strongly. They laugh more strongly. Sticking a cigar in CLAYTON's mouth, the CARTOON EDITOR and his happy entourage sweep him back out with them.

INT. CORRIDOR. CONTINUOUS.
Leaving him there they move on to show the cartoon to the editor-in-chief. Swaying slightly, CLAYTON stands alone. A gale of laughter is heard in the distance topped off by the sound of popping champagne corks, the sound more muted as a door slams. All the while we stay with CLAYTON. It costs him everything to raise his hand and peel back his jacket. He is in time to see the pencil sticking into his heart. CLAYTON shakes his head in silent disbelief and dies.

FADE OUT.

Exercise

Before you do anything else, take a piece of paper and write down in single words or short phrases whatever comes into your head. Don't hesitate; don't censor your reactions (though do feel free to stop short of gratuitous abuse!). Part of the object of this exercise is to get past that internal critic who so many of us have, offering us unwanted advice which can so badly hobble the natural flow of what we want to write. Spend, say, ten minutes assembling a whole range of words and phrases which sum up what you notice about the piece – both its content and its form, as well as feelings or perceptions it may have evoked in you. When you've done that, take a look at what you've got; perhaps share this exercise with some others and see what you've all come up with. *Please do this now.*

SETTINGS AND CONFLICT

The setting for any story, the arenas in which it can unfold, may be usefully seen as a set of concentric circles spreading out from the mind (or even the soul) of the protagonist, and reaching out into the cosmos.

Conflict is the life-blood of all drama, and though screen dramas can be predominantly about inner conflicts (say, the battle against an addiction or illness) or outer conflicts (perhaps, most obviously, wars) handled well, it is a story's potential for conflicts on many levels (inner and outer) which can be most satisfying and effective to explore.

Starting with his own indolence, the antagonistic forces bearing down on Clayton soon mount up. There is his creative block; he hasn't got an idea in his head. Then, as soon as he does get one, the point of his lucky pencil breaks, which brings him into conflict with another inner-demon – superstition. After that, he is challenged by the absence of a pencil-sharpener: he tussles with his immediate environment trying first to find and then to improvise a sharpener. Time is, of course, an ever-present enemy, in the shape of a looming deadline and as embodied in the clock. Added to which, his editor waits with mounting impatience and then anger. Desperate, Clayton breaks the law, and throughout is dogged by the bad luck of depending on a lucky pencil which keeps breaking. And, beyond all this, there are also his countless unseen readers, 'the world', waiting to be satisfied.

In telling an engaging story, it's very important to escalate and intensify the action, to raise the stakes, to place the hero in danger and – in his bid to triumph against the odds – to take your hero to his limit.

So, for example, in the film *Patriot Games* (W. Peter Iliff and Donald Stewart from the novel by Tom Clancy) Jack Ryan is taken on a journey which starts with a chance and instinctive moment of heroism. An innocent bystander, his training as an intelligence operative enables him to foil an assassination attempt; in doing this, he kills one of the terrorists and consequently invites a vendetta from the dead man's brother, another of the terrorists, Sean Miller. Ryan's intervention starts a chain of events which leads him first to tussle with his own resolve to stay away from his old life, the CIA, and once his family is threatened finds him drawn into the vortex. After many ups and downs, and just when order appears to have been restored, the story offers an unexpected surprise, pulling him from the bosom of his family into a place of extreme danger. The postponed, private ceremony to mark an award for saving the minister's life held at Ryan's home is infiltrated by a traitor. Ryan's family is attacked and the house plunged into darkness. During the game of cat and mouse, whilst the attackers search for Ryan, he uncovers the traitor and kills him. The climax of the film is a power boat chase across Chesapeake Bay, in a storm. As Ryan's boat catches fire, he is forced to fight hand-to-hand with a crazed Miller whom he overcomes and impales on the anchor lying on deck, moments before he is forced to dive off the boat which then crashes into rocks and explodes. Good beats evil, order is restored and Ryan is free to lead his new life, which will include the birth of his new child. So from a struggle with his conscience at the beginning of the film (intra-personal), the story takes him into indirect and then direct conflict with the enemy (inter-personal) and, at its climax, introduces the universally elemental – air and water (a raging storm at sea), fire (on deck, culminating in an explosion) and earth (the rocks his boat finally founders on). Ultimately, we see him face-to-face with his arch-enemy, whom he finally vanquishes and who is then blown to smithereens. Our hero has been taken to his limit in extreme danger and triumphed to get what he truly wants, against a background in which right has triumphed over might (transpersonal). He and we are satisfied.

In *Two Sharp*, Clayton, a two-dimensional character (albeit with some three-dimensional anxieties) is at the centre of an altogether more light-hearted escapade; but one which nonetheless still fulfils some of these over-riding principles. The action does escalate, the protagonist's dilemma is intensified (time marches on, the law gets broken, the cartoon is still not drawn), the hero is placed in danger (of prosecution, of dismissal) and a surprise reversal

Figure 1.2   Arenas of Conflict

occurs; just when Clayton has succeeded he dies. The very editor he has worked so hard to satisfy, carelessly and unwittingly kills him. Just when our hero gets what he wants, he does not. Clayton's comically-obsessive quest could certainly have been even more ridiculously intensified, and in any comedy what transpires must always be 'too much'. However, the guiding principle should be to know when you have at least done enough. In *Patriot Games*, that need is clearly satisfied.

SOME MORE ABOUT STORY

You may think there are many kinds of story, and you may also be feeling a need to identify them all accurately before you can try your hand at writing one successfully. In *Hamlet*, with the touring players about to perform at Elsinore, Polonius shows off his extensive grasp of the full range of dramatic possibilities, reminding us plays may be:

> tragedy, comedy, history, pastoral, pastoral–comical, historical–pastoral, tragical–historical, tragical-comical-historical-pastoral; scene indivisible, or poem unlimited.
>
> *Hamlet*, William Shakespeare, Act II, Scene ii, lines 395–8

Shakespeare clearly had his tongue firmly in his cheek when he gave the pompous, interfering courtier this exhaustive survey of genres to run through. The reason I am quoting it here is because with new (and not so new) writers I think there can be a real risk of 'Polonius syndrome' setting in. It can be much more profitable, primarily, to concentrate on satisfying the requirements of simple story telling, than to be worrying over the stylistic demands of one televisual or cinematic genre or sub-genre. In the longer run, it will be very valuable to make a conscious study of the elements used in forming different varieties of stories: at the start of your writing adventures, however, I think it's a good idea not to suffer what can be the fatal distraction of so concentrating on emulating the form of a particular story mould or genre, that you miss your own essential creativity or lose sight of the need to acquire fundamental craft skills. That said, for those who *are* keen to learn more in advance of setting off, there is a comprehensive list of the essential range of archetypal stories to be told in lots of screenwriting books. *The Art and Science of Screenwriting* (Philip Parker) covers this ground in some detail, and there is an even more exhaustive list of cinematic genre and sub-genre in Robert McKee's *Story*.

However, as a newish writer you can easily be too concerned with trying to find and fit into accepted programme or project 'shapes' and attempting to imitate successful models. This potential fascination with the *outer* and, indeed, the concentrated effort required to knock the corners off what you may have come up with so it will fit into a popularly recognisable 'story room', can be a damaging distraction: it may also prove quite stifling to the beginner trying to listen to the *inner* and discover his own voice. When we dream, we don't consciously decide what form the dream is going to take: story telling, in essence, is the process of day-dreaming with conscious intent. It is a mixture of the two, and I think it can be a great loss to let the dream element be damagingly subordinated to the business of conscious shaping. So, whilst remaining intent on telling a straightforward story and getting on with doing that, also give yourself totally free space to operate in at the beginning. Along the way, as much as seems valuable and not too inhibiting, do also pay *some* attention to forms and conventions. It can be valuable to see which sorts of story and which modes of story telling you have a leaning towards.

I recommend reading the section in Robert McKee's book *Story* (McKee 1999: 55–7) in which he advances his model, the story triangle. It is an interesting and useful overview of the arena in which we choose to form our screen dramas, and illustrates some helpful observations on the variety of story forms we employ, ranging from the most conventional classic narrative, via multi-plotted films, through to avant-garde and anti-plot. What he suggests is that, as story tellers, we all have a 'natural address' somewhere on that map. I think that's true, and that to a large degree it's important to let your story tell you, as it were; especially when you're first starting out to write and want to discover a voice. Some writers, when they set out, can be so preoccupied with trying to imitate the saleable and the popular, perhaps trying to ape a blockbusting formula, that they choke off their own voice. Even more damagingly, in pursuit of 'trying to be themselves' (meaning, not like anyone else) others may so cultivate the obscure and the arcane in their writing that they get in their own way, and miss being their true story telling selves. Don't try and dress your writing up in clothes it would not choose to wear. What form and style your story wants to take will emerge along the way if you let your writing come from your immediate and true story telling self. McKee pinpoints the danger of ignoring this:

> The danger is that for reasons ideological rather than personal you may feel compelled to leave home and work in a distant corner, trapping yourself into designing stories you don't in your heart believe.
>
> (1999: 58–9)

I agree. A writer who writes from his head but not from his heart is only half a writer. If you want to give your writing presence and impact, then write it with energy, simplicity and truth; that way you'll give your writing inextinguishable life. And if you think this is whimsical nonsense, that writing is no more than words on a page and its 'life' just a figure of speech, then think again: we write those words on a page, and we *are* alive.

THE DRIVE TO BE ORIGINAL

If they are not consciously forging or smashing moulds, copying voices, or disguising their own, then another way that out-of-touch writers can ham-string themselves is by being intent on producing material which is completely original. To such individuals, their disappointment can feel boundless; this idea seems a bit clichéd, that idea a bit too low-key. Nothing seems to hit the mark, and they set about the writing of those ideas, if they get round to setting about them at all, with little active enthusiasm or commitment. This dispassionate, judgemental stance, an arm's length approach to the creative process, simply messes around with ideas without ever getting fired-up and, above all, involved. It is necessary to climb inside your story and start being in its moments, rather than subjecting the whole to a cold appraisal. Of course you're bound to look at what you're writing from the outside as well, but not before you've started living it and finding out the way it wants to take you. Once you have done that, you're unlikely to feel so detached and, if there is still disappointment, that may be par for the course; what if your story does seem a bit like an old one? If its essential life is intact, it can be nothing else. What can be new will be the blend of story elements you have chosen and the proportions in which you chose to mix them, the characters you populated the story with, the particular setting you give it, and the voice you tell it with. Pay proper attention to tangling with these aspects and you cannot help but give it the fresh stamp of your individual, creative expression. An interesting example of what I mean is the film *Shallow Grave* (John Hodge): compare the modern day story of three young friends falling out, fighting, and in the end two of them killing each other whilst betraying the third, all over money which drops into their laps through the death of a dodgy lodger, with the essentially identical core story in Chaucer's 'Pardoner's Tale' from *The Canterbury Tales* written way back in the fourteenth century. Both stories are based on the scriptural pretext cited in Chaucer: 'radix malorum est cupiditas' (desire for money is the root of all evil). Two stories, 600 years apart, powered by an identical premise, and enshrining the same core story. *The Fisher King* (Richard LaGravenese) consciously plays with the myth of the Holy Grail, both making explicit reference to it through Perry's retelling of it to Jack in the park, and also constructing a modern day counterpart adventure which echoes the essential elements of the legend. Noticing such comparisons and similarities can be very helpful as you go on to develop your story-making skills: to begin with, as I've already suggested, don't be distracted by consciously trying to study outer story form too closely. At the same time, don't fret about achieving originality.

WHAT MAKES A STORY?

What I'd like to suggest is that, no matter what the type of story and the particular constraints of its style or form, essentially writing drama for the screen rests on some universal and clearly recognisable principles which do need mastering. And it's in this context that the broad and simple definition of story offered above will hopefully form a useful starting point for you to refer back to and use as a basic reference and reminder of the vital ingredients you will need to include and manage.

After you read *Two Sharp*, I urged you to make a list. I'm sure it will have covered a range of reactions, and observations; amongst these you are bound to have touched on aspects of story telling common to much if not all screen dramatisation in general, as well as some aspects and features quite specific to this story in particular. What follows is a glossary and brief discussion of the essential ingredients needed for the spinning of any tale, and some discussion on how these and one or two other frequently-used devices relate to *Two Sharp* and story telling in general.

The plot

The plot is the essential series of events which immediately involves the protagonist and which unfolds around him to advance the story. In classic narrative, these events are going to involve setting the scene and offering us the extraordinary or disordering event in that central character's life which will force him into activity. This phase of the plot is all about *exposition*. The next phase deals with the obstacles that have to be faced in pursuit of the goal and is all about *complication*. Finally, there will come a climactic point of crisis which will lead on to the hero getting or not getting what he or she wants, and offering us *resolution*. This resolution may be total, all the ends being tied up and the audience's emotional journey complete; or it may be partial, leaving the audience to speculate on aspects of the plot or sub-plots. A vivid example of a plot left dangling in a literal cliff-hanger is the end of the film *The Italian Job* (1969, Troy Kennedy Martin). A massive heist successfully completed, the get-away coach carrying the gang and the gold bullion swerves off the road, coming to rest balancing on the edge of a precipice, the gold slipping slowly closer to the back of the bus, dangling in mid-air. Charlie Croker and his accomplices hardly dare breathe; the film ends on Croker's memorably famous line – 'Hang on a minute lads. I've got a great idea' – leaving us to wonder whether the protagonists get away or even survive.

Interestingly, the original screenplay ended with a different kind of open ending. The gold is safely deposited in a Swiss bank account, but the only two people who know the account number are killed by the Mafia, leaving another character to stick a pin into a list of account numbers in the hope of finding the right one. There have also been several proposals for sequels to the original film, all of which have had to find ways of getting the gang safely off that coach.

Sub-plots

In a longer drama the main plot will be surrounded and supported by sub-plots. The fortunes of those involved in sub-plots may contrast with, parallel, or help to point up the progress made by the central character in the main story. Domino-like, they may spring directly from the major plot line, or they may have come about through no consequence of the main plot whatsoever. Whichever, they should still relate to the main plot in some interesting way. Sub-plots are there to provide additional interest and enhance the effect of the main plot, often illuminating meaning by offering us an interesting comparison. They may intensify the narrative tension or offer some welcome relief from the roller-coaster the writer has chosen for his protagonist to ride.

Suspense or narrative tension

Suspense is a vital ingredient in the telling of a classic narrative. It is the elastic in its underpants, as it were. First we upset a character's life and, having invited the audience to identify with them, we place a question mark over whether the protagonist will attain his goal or not. The business of alternately stimulating the audience's hopes and their fears provides the vital narrative tension which keeps us emotionally invested. In continuing drama, the use of key points in a story's narrative tension is particularly important: the audience tunes in next time on the strength of a good cliff-hanger.

Intensifying and relaxing narrative tension is an essential part of the writer's craft. Overall, the tension should be screwed up to an ever-greater pitch, and along the way there should be opportunities for respite. Lulling the audience into a false sense of relaxed resolution before hitting them with a shock is, of course, a staple of many thrillers. The ending of *Fatal Attraction* (James Dearden) springs to mind, with its echoes of *Psycho* (Joseph Stefano); obviously vulnerable, still smarting from her physical and emotional wounds, and her relationship with errant husband Dan only just on the mend, nevertheless Beth Gallagher finally believes herself to be safe. She goes to take a bath: much to her surprise (and ours), who should be hiding behind that bathroom door? None other than the terribly disturbed Alex Forrest, object of her husband's recent attentions. There is a tremendous struggle, Dan intervenes and finally drowns Alex in the bath. We heave a sigh of relief. At last it's all over – except, of course, just as they and therefore we are feeling *really* safe, suddenly the dead are undead, as it were, and Alex resurfaces lunging towards us with the knife. A great example of keeping the audience on edge until the very last moment, having lulled them into a sense of false security.

The protagonist

Though your story may involve a range of characters, in a conventional, classical narrative, the main interest centres on the hero, or protagonist. Though it may have become totally clear to you by now, for the record the protagonist is that chosen character whose life is upset by the extraordinary event (inciting incident, or disordering event as it is sometimes called) and, as a consequence of that event, pursues a goal to restore a new order. Put simply, he wants something and will keep going until he does or does not get it; we will keep him company throughout, seeing events from his point of view. I mention this since new writers of drama can often get confused about whose story they're actually writing. Keep the story definition offered above in mind – particularly the fact that the protagonist *always wants something* – as you get involved in formulating your stories.

Shared protagonism
Sometimes stories centre on groups of people, say for example expeditions, criminal gangs, survivors, militia, sports teams, whose members all share the role of protagonist. As long as their goal is a common one, and they face the obstacles together, this is a perfectly valid device, and we will still identify with what the group is striving for.

Transferred protagonism
Like a baton in a relay race, protagonism can be handed on in a drama. It can happen that what starts out as character A's goal gets handed on to another character who then becomes the protagonist. For example, a man is being forced to collude in a robbery. He starts out by playing along, but as the day of the planned crime approaches he meets a friend with the aim of confiding in her. As they meet our hero is shot dead. Unseen by the killer, the dying hero slips a cassette into his friend's pocket. She finds this later, listens to it, and decides she will get involved in trapping the thieves. What was his story now gets handed over to become hers.

Whether or not we find the central character(s) of a story likeable, it's important that we can identify enough with their plight to empathise, and thus, go along with them. If we don't care about them, we won't care what happens to them, and an indifferent, emotionally detached audience is the last thing you want.

In fact, the reason classical narrative in its purest form centres on a single protagonist is to ensure an intensely focussed level of emotional identification by the audience.

The wounded hero

A common device in making the hero more accessible to the audience and binding the two together is to render the protagonist vulnerable in some way, even to the extent of giving them a wound. Handicapped individuals drawn from reality, like writer and artist Christy Brown, who suffered from cerebral palsy and whose life was dramatised in *My Left Foot* (Jim Sheridan), can lend themselves to the makings of a particularly engaging story because their struggle has been made all the greater by the handicaps, physical, mental, emotional or spiritual, which they suffer. *The Miracle Worker*, another bio-graphical film, written by William Gibson, tells the story of Helen Keller. Struck down by severe illness in early infancy, she triumphed over her loss of speech, hearing and sight to become a celebrated teacher and campaigner on behalf of the visually handicapped. Purely fictional pieces such as *The Man Without A Face* (Malcolm MacRury), *Forrest Gump* (Winston Groom), *Rain Man* (Ronald Bass, Barry Morrow) are all examples of 'the wound' at work. The story of the wounded hero who triumphs against the odds, often making the journey from exclusion or stigmatisation, to acknowledged and beloved insider, in one sense or another is a popular one with screenwriters, and can indeed prove to be very affecting and inspirational.

Antagonism

Having settled on a protagonist for your story, there needs to be someone for him to strive against; remember – *no conflict, no drama*. The arch-villain *is* that antagonist. In many stories a face-to-face confrontation between protagonist and antagonist is an essential part of the telling.

All of those people and forces ranged directly against the hero are antagonis-tic: this includes those inner obstacles a character may have to face – cow-ardice, despair, cynical indifference, and so on; they form no less of a barrier in their own way, and can be fascinating for writers to exploit.

Irony

An ironic moment, such as that which befalls Clayton – his boss embraces him in gratitude and kills him – can be very satisfying for an audience, who can empathise with the idea of goals attained at enormous personal cost. They recognise their own lives in such a moment and identify all the more. Irony of this sort acknowledges the fact that life as lived is a far from ideal business, combining pain and pleasure in equal measure. William Blake's poem *Auguries of Innocence* contains the following fragment which expresses it beautifully:

> Joy and woe are woven fine,
> A Clothing for the Soul divine;
> Under every grief and pine
> Runs a joy with silken twine.

Dramatic ironies

Clayton realises what has happened to him – that he has both won and lost – and we (hopefully) didn't see it coming. However, those moments when we are given the important advantage of knowing more than the characters in a drama, and can 'see it coming' when they can't, not only excite our fears for the character, but also intensify how sorry we can feel for them when the inevitable actually does happen.

As you will see from some of the examples of film and television writing quoted in this book, irony is a major weapon in the dramatist's armoury, and there can be great value in learning how to recognise the potential irony of a moment or a situation and to exploit its power to bind an audience to your story.

Turning points and reversals: the need for surprise

In telling a story, there is a need to stimulate the hopes and fears of the viewer. We identify with what the hero wants and hopes for: we hope for it too, and we fear he may not get it. The more skilfully one can play with these feelings, the more satisfying the story experience may become. So, in *Patriot Games*, just when Ryan thinks the whole nightmare's done and dusted and it's safe to go back to his life, he suffers the most surprising and intense onslaught to date. Likewise, the very moment Clayton meets his deadline, satisfies his masters and can rest, he dies. *Man has deadline, man meets deadline, man dies* – thereby proving, ironically, that he who laughs last, laughs longest. Both examples have been designed to sneak up on the viewer and (in different ways) to intensify both our emotional engagement with the protagonist and our curiosity about his fate.

Surprise and predictability

Keeping your audience interested is perhaps the most important part of the dramatist's work; surprising the audience by making them expect one thing and then delivering another is an effective way of intensifying your audience's engagement with the piece. An excellent example of this occurs at the end of *American Beauty* (Alan Ball) when we are led to believe that Lester Burnham's wife Carolyn is going to shoot him now he's discovered her affair with Buddy Kane. We see her psyching herself up with her gun in her car and we are clearly encouraged to believe she's about to kill him. In fact Frank Fitts, the ex-Marine officer next door, is the one who will kill him, unbearably shamed by having revealed his repressed homosexuality to Lester. In itself this comes as no surprise, ringing true to Fitts' character, but the writer sells us a wonderful dummy by concentrating our attention so powerfully on Lester's wife, who is also in the throes of disappointment and deep humiliation. While the fact that Fitts did it is totally credible, it is not at all predictable, and it is the knack of keeping an audience on its toes, leading them to expect one thing and then subverting that expectation, which can be a real asset in building an interesting plot.

One of the worst things people can say about your plot is that they could see it all coming. That said, when you're starting out and simply gaining confidence in screenwriting, it's most important not to be too hard on yourself. Tell the story you think of for the sake of getting it down, even if it does seem to lack quite the inventiveness or originality you hoped to achieve. As you progress you'll naturally be able to place greater demands on your powers to invent, surprise and intrigue. Striving too hard for originality or complexity of plot can be very counter-productive when you're first starting out. Also, it's worth remembering that often simplicity will produce perfectly satisfactory results.

Maintaining probability. Safe-guarding story-logic

Although it can be powerful to install surprises in your plot, you do need to stay within the realms of the probable and not offend against the logic peculiar to the story you've devised. Conventionally-told stories concern themselves with cause and effect and they need to unfold in line with this principle.

Characters need to act consistently in character, and in line with the rules of whatever level of reality you set up in your story. In a strictly naturalistic piece, this means following the realities of the everyday world – even though the reality of any story is carefully selected, compressed and highlighted so as to offer itself as a metaphor for real life. In other types of story telling – such as surrealism for example – it becomes appropriate to follow other levels of reality. So in the short film *Two Men and a Wardrobe* (Roman Polanski), it is quite consistent with the overall tone and reality of the piece for the eponymous heroes of the piece to make their entrance walking out of the sea fully clothed carrying said wardrobe onto the beach!

Similarly in the surrealistic satire *The Discreet Charm of The Bourgeoisie* (Luis Buñuel and Jean-Claude Carrière), we see a naturalistic setting in which the normal rules of cause and effect are put totally to one side. The slimmest of narrative threads – that a group of upper-crust friends are trying to have dinner together but cannot seem to do so without things going drastically wrong – is used to support an outlandish and ever more dream-like procession of surrealistic and satirical set-pieces, in which what is the characters' reality and what is their fantasy becomes, at points, inextricably bound up.

The film's 'story' follows the surface illogicality of a dream, and juxtaposes the unlikeliest of characters and events to poke fun at the establishment's so-called respectability. Within the logic of the film itself the unpredictable and the random become the film's own predictable norm rather than extraneous aberrations: we can expect the unexpected and must unravel the film's meaning in a more approximate and subjective manner than we could with a straightforward classic narrative.

When screenwriting combines predominantly naturalistic reality with elements of fantasy, different rules are going to apply to the different components of your drama: but it is still necessary to be consistent to the internal realities governing those separate worlds; you can't suddenly change the rules within either of those different levels without throwing the audience's understanding of how those different worlds operate within the overall story.

So, in *Ally McBeal* (David E. Kelley), the sudden replacement of a sober-looking judge sitting in a court-room by an all-singing, all-dancing Al Green as Ally slips into a daydream, allows for a vivid illustration of her fantasy. Each level of story reality is clearly marked off, one from the other, and is logically consistent within itself: so when Ally snaps out of her reverie, there's no more music outside of her head. Likewise, in the same series, John Cage's alter ego, Barry White, makes his presence felt as a song in John's head until that comforting fantasy mentor he is carrying round with him for support leaks out and takes the place of Nell just as they are about to make love. It's a brilliant moment, externalising and ridiculing John's self-absorption. Almost as quickly as the moment is presented, it has gone back inside John's head where it belongs. The logic of the piece remains perfectly intact: these fantasies can assume overwhelming proportions at times for the characters in question. These intrusions of fantasy on reality are also prompted by the moments in reality immediately preceding them: there is a reason for Ally and John to float off, just as in *The Fall and*

Rise of Reginald Perrin (David Nobbs), the reason Reginald (and we) would see a lumbering hippopotamus at the mere mention of his mother-in-law's name is, by implication, clear enough. So, once again, a causal logic is being respected.

I advocate trying your hand at predominantly straightforward naturalism (recognisably 'real' characters operating in a 'real' world to begin with). It can be a temptation to get lost in the realms of the whimsically fantastic or the absurd, and in so doing lose sight of the simple but exacting challenge of delivering a conventional story. As I suggested earlier, I think that practice with the conventional will allow you to know when deviation from it is going to be more honestly rooted in where the story may be telling you to go, than where you just think you might want to take it. It will also most probably equip you to take those leaps into the unconventional with greater success than if you plunged straight in.

Time

I mentioned the Classic Unities before, one of those being the Unity of Time which dictated a drama should unfold within the course of one day. Naturally dramas have always highlighted significant events and compressed the time in which those events are related to the audience. Judging how much to move on and when to join the action again and play the next significant event so that it feels like enough real time (as well as screen time has elapsed) is all part of the challenge for a screenwriter. Several factors are going to influence decisions around this. The general pace of the entire piece and the pace of a particular sequence will determine what fits appropriately. In longer-form drama, it's often possible to postpone picking up a storyline again for much longer than in a busy short piece. A multi-plotted drama can also allow more scope for spreading stories.

There is often a need to avoid melodrama by smashing from one major point of development to another in any given story, missing out essential intermediate scenes, which are appropriately spaced to simulate the feeling of characters taking their time to work things out. Then again, there may be a real need to go out of your way *to* install melodrama in a piece, say for comic effect. Or take the leap forward in time at the end of *2001* (Stanley Kubrick and Arthur C. Clarke), in which the sole surviving astronaut Dave Bowman, seen minutes earlier as a young man, is now at the end of his days and discovered in surreal Empire grandeur, perfectly fits with the fact that his space pod has just time-travelled in real time taking us as the audience along for the ride.

The placement of scenes in the overall time structure is also a matter of feel and instinct, and it is definitely an aspect of screenwriting which gets better the more you have seen how material sits in the overall feel of the actual playing. It's sometimes harder to judge when a scene has been rushed or delayed for too long just by looking at it on the page; however that, too, gets easier with the experience of reading more and more scripts.

A conventionally-told drama unfolds sequentially in chronological order, or linear time as it's often referred to. Screen drama being a highly mobile medium, it can be very tempting and effective to disrupt that linear progression. Perhaps the most commonly used disruptive device in film and television drama is the flash-back.

Flash-backs
This can be used to depict general relevant back-story or background, as well as particular characters' memories which we may see them summoning up, or which may seem to intrude on them. So, for example, in My *Life As A Dog* (Lasse Hallström), young Ingemar summons up memories of happy holidays spent with his mother, as comfort to him now they are separated and she is dying. In sharp contrast Sol Nazerman in *The Pawnbroker* (David Friedkin, Morton Fine from the novel by Edward Wallant) finds himself plagued by the intrusion of unwanted memories from his time held in the Nazi death camps. In the latter film, the fact that the memories are suppressed and unwelcome is signalled by the fact that we see just a glimpse leaking into Sol's present day thoughts, followed by another and another until finally he cannot suppress the memory any more and it intrudes as a steady stream of thought.

When moving into a flash-back, it is more often than not the case that it will need rooting in the present. Something in the character's here and now should cue the memory. It may be an image, an event, something someone says; in that sequence from *The Pawnbroker* referred to above, it's the combination of a gang picking on a young man in a fenced-off derelict site, and an Alsatian dog barking nearby which cues similar images from the camp for Sol as he passes the beating on his way to his parked car.

On a grander scale, time-shifts into and out of the past are sometimes used as a narrative framing device. *Titanic* (James Cameron) is a good example of this. The now-old Rose De Witt is invited to help the present day salvage team in their quest for a valuable pendant. The pretext of her being there to help them is all the excuse the film needs for her to summon up her memories of the journey, her ill-fated, whirlwind romance with Jack, and so take us into her story, which forms the main body of the narrative. At the end of the film we see her real agenda in being there – to exorcise her past – as, unseen by the salvage team, she takes the pendant which had been given to her by the rich fiancé she did not love, and slips it back into the seas above the wreck.

Narrative framing encloses the main narrative: sometimes it is referred to only at the beginning and ending of the story; sometimes it will be referred to at key points throughout the drama.

Flash-forward

It's also possible to flash-forward in time, foreshadowing events yet to come. Sometimes there may be narratively logical pretext for this, as in *Don't Look Now* (Allen Scott, Chris Bryant from the story by Daphne du Maurier). Here we are offered a character, John Baxter, who is unwittingly psychic, and as a consequence is 'gifted' with a moment of precognition in which he thinks he sees his wife Laura actually pass directly by on the other side of a Venice canal: in fact what he is seeing is a flash-forward glimpse of his own funeral procession. Sometimes there may be no particular, individualised pretext for a flash-forward in time, and flashes forward may just be a choice made by the author to disrupt conventional narrative time, underlining the artifice of screen drama and making a virtue of that potential to be totally mobile.

Popular screen dramas which markedly disrupt linear time are relatively few and far between. The danger of stalling narrative drive can more often than not outweigh any advantages to be gained by flitting to and fro in time. However, it can be worthwhile to have a look at examples of where this is done well if only to caution yourself against too readily trying the same thing. If not rooted appropriately and crafted with care, then disrupted time can just come over as a distancing stylistic affectation – being clever for its own sake.

A fascinating and most effective example of disrupted time is to be found in *Toto The Hero* (Jaco van Dormael, Laurette Vankeerberghen, Pascal Lonhey, Didier DeNeck) in which the central character, Thomas, nears the end of his days in an old folk's home. The movement between Thomas' present-day story, his plan to kill lifelong rival Alfred Kant, and the flashes backwards and forwards between three eras of Thomas' life, are all handled with tremendous sleight of hand. Internal cues are used for this criss-crossing of time-frames in which effects of actions end up being placed before their causes, with extraordinary results. The overall feel of these forward somersaults and backward flips in time fits the film well and, in part, this is because the drama depicts the drifting consciousness of an old man's seemingly haphazard memories, mixed in with his here and now fantasies.

However well such time-travelling is executed, and though the unconventional narrative *may* end up spellbinding an audience, it will not promote the same level of audience identification with the protagonist. It will most often feel like the contraflow contrivance it actually is, and will end up holding the audience emotionally at arm's length. To repeat my cautionary note, avoid trying to disrupt linear time for the sake of being clever or interesting. At the outset of your writing, it's well worth getting comfortable with pacing and managing conventional, linear time-frames, perhaps with the occasional appropriately motivated departure, before experimenting too wildly. By all means watch and read widely, and appreciate what is going on in pieces which do play with time.

Flashes out of time

An example of this is the sequence of psychotic episodes Perry is prone to in *The Fisher King*, in which the Red Knight appears on horseback to hunt him down. They are happening now and yet do not exist. Fantasies or delusions are frequent interpolations in screen dramas, and their timelessness can prove a powerful counterpoint to the onward drive of the main narrative. They may still benefit from us seeing their logical prompting in the here and now, for us better to understand what their inclusion in the drama is all about. In *The Fisher King*, it is Perry's present day fears which trigger his suppressed horror about the death of his wife, in the form of the stalking apocalyptic horseman.

Speeding up, slowing down

Finally, the device of speeding action up to encapsulate long periods of time in a much shorter period of screen time can produce striking comic effect. It can caricature superhuman powers, or then again the magic of time-lapsed sequences can capture the growth of a flower or the transition of whole seasons in a few seconds. Step-editing (jumping between key-points in a sequence of action) can also install comic effect or simply transform the otherwise mundane into an engaging few moments.

Conversely, slow-motion can form a lyrically emphatic counterpoint to the action depicted. If we see soldiers charging into battle, for example, suddenly slowed down, perhaps with the loss of the actual sound, the action is lent that timelessness we can experience in heightened moments, and made all the more extraordinary – the violence suddenly appearing graceful and, thus, at odds with the event. Moments of great realisation, of the penny finally dropping as it were, can also benefit from this effect: the dropped cup near the end of *The Usual Suspects* (Christopher McQuarrie) is a good example. And, yes, such moments *are* to be written, not just directed, as long as they demonstrably serve the content of your story well.

Coincidences

Love them or loathe them, coincidences are a thorny issue and, in my experience, the world does divide into those who object to them and those who seem to revel in them, claiming, 'Well that's like life. That kind of thing *does* happen'. Maybe so, but it is worth remembering that well-worn maxim,

'Fact is much stranger than fiction', and this certainly tends to be the case in relation to naturalistic drama. As story tellers, we're in the business of generating engagement in our hero's adventure through creating what the poet and critic Coleridge matchlessly called, 'a willing suspension of disbelief'. Traditionally, a story is told so that our audience may go along with it without so questioning the probability of a moment that they fall out of this crucial level of identified engagement. In story telling terms, coincidences can become really problematic when they are used as a way of contriving the plot. Again, that certainly applies to their inclusion in straightforward, naturalistic drama. Obviously, where certain types of story are concerned, it may be a very different matter. Farce or slapstick-comedy, for example, often depend heavily and most effectively on coincidental contrivances. The romantic comedy *Return To Me* (Bonnie Hunt and Don Lake) hinges on a whopping coincidence. Architect Bob Rueland is devastated when his wife Elizabeth is killed in a car accident. As he finally starts to pull out of his grief, he is fixed up with a blind dinner date. At the restaurant he meets and instantly falls for waitress Grace Biggs who (of course!) turns out to be the recipient of poor, dead Elizabeth's transplanted heart. Such resoundingly massive coincidences are more acceptable to an audience in a film like this because of the level of wish-fulfilment being addressed. The whole narrative drive is to get the lovers fixed up and happy – so whatever it takes is okay.

The Fisher King is another case in point. Jack Lucas, a radio DJ, incites a desperate caller to go out and rid society of yuppies. In doing so he is indirectly responsible for the death of innocent diners. His career in pieces and wracked with guilt, he is himself saved from death at the hands of well-heeled young New Yorkers who are on a mission to purge the streets of down and outs. Perry, the man who intervenes to save him, was married to a woman wiped out in Jack's caller's killing spree. *The Fisher King* is deliberately fantastical in its construction, aiming to parallel the legendary and the mythic. In the realms of fable, we accept the totally extraordinary and highly coincidental, and in *The Fisher King* the story has a deliberately symbolic, magical posture which makes such devices self-justifying.

In such cases, because the absurdity of an outrageous coincidence fits the tone of the piece, the wholly different kind of 'suspension of disbelief' at work is not interrupted. If, however, you're writing a serious, naturalistic piece and its plot is reliant on a coincidence, do check whether its being introduced to the story so as to help you 'cheat' your way to a plot point further down the track you really want to write but can see no other way of reaching. This is a terrible temptation for some writers when they're first setting out. All of that said, if you're going to go for a coincidence and it seems to fit with the levels of belief at work in your drama, then it can be a very good idea to make the coincidence massive.

Repetition

Another mistake new writers can make is needlessly to repeat elements of their script. The essential aim of writing a conventional drama is to get on with telling the story, to maintain the narrative drive of the piece, by assembling a large number of moments which, taken all together, will add up to the whole piece. Unless you can think of a very good reason for it, don't repeat any of the moments. Repetition can be most effective in building comic effect. A case in point is *Groundhog Day* (Danny Robin, Harold Ramis) in which weather man Phil Connors is stranded in a small Pennsylvanian town, by a snow storm he failed to predict, and is destined to repeat the present until he becomes a better person. Repetition can also be very effective in building suspenseful intrigue through the gradual revelation of an important moment: a good example of this occurs in *Catch 22* (Buck Henry from the novel by Joseph Heller) where we are offered tantalising and cryptic glimpses of what, it becomes clear, as those flash-backs lengthen and we hear him gasping and mumbling how cold he turns out to be, is a dreadfully wounded crew member on a shot-up bomber. The sequence culminates shockingly with a brief scene in which, while trying to help him, Yossarian turns Snowden and sends his guts spilling out onto the floor of the plane. It's a moment whose impact is tremendously enhanced by the previous repetitive build up. Repetition can also help in building emphasis. *Repetition can also help in building emphasis.* But if a repetition is not serving a specific purpose, and since a repeated moment is not progressing the plot, you could be writing something else. So why not do it?

Clarity

This is of paramount importance. Firstly it's most important to make sure that the details of every scene are clear; a script is a blueprint from which programme or film makers are going to work. So there is nothing to be gained by shrouding a moment as written in your script in ambiguity or mystery. There is a vital distinction to be drawn between gradually and subtly revealing something to the audience – for example that a scene they thought real is in fact a fantasy – and not letting the production team in on the secret either. Sometimes beginners think if they make it clear on the page for those who are going to realise the script, then they've also blown the surprise for the viewer; this is not so.

Ambiguity

A not infrequent aim of the budding dramatist is to be deliberately ambiguous. They want to leave it up to the viewers to make what they will of one or many moments, and often, in particular, their stories' endings. There is one inescapable fact about setting out to be ambiguous and that is you will be. When challenged on this matter, newish writers will often admit that actually their ambiguity is not so much about wanting to allow their audience freedom to react, but far more to do with their own reluctance or inability to make a clear choice for their drama. They fudge a moment and pretend it's cleverness, or originality – or even worse that anything the audience comes up with as interpretation is right; they meant all of them. I'm not for one moment decrying all ambiguities or choices made not to resolve every story strand. The power of moments left open to query by the audience can be great and feel quite appropriate. What I'm talking about here is a lack of rigour in the endless process of self-interrogation – the endless 'what-if'-ness – which is the process of necessary decision making in good story telling. It really is important early on to recognise when you're copping out on that hard but vital work. An acid test of whether you have conveyed the meaning you intended is to give it to someone else to read and see what they make of it. At the end of the day, an audience may indeed not know what to make of something you have written. You, however, must know what it was you intended. As a writer, that is a sacred responsibility. It also makes sense that, once you're clear, you would want your audience to be equally clear about the matter.

Theme and meaning

There is a school of thought that believes a writer should know what a story is about right from the word go, and that it should, in any case, enshrine some proverbial or mythic truth. Such wisdom holds that, without a premise there can be no story. With an individually authored, totally original piece, knowing what a story is about before you start writing it can actually get in your way. Meditating on broad themes – environmental consciousness, world peace, the power of self-awareness – are of very little help in the framing of a specific story. Not only may you try to model too consciously on existing programmes or films, in a bid to get in line with the sort of thing you think you want your story to say, but you may also stifle the very life out of what could have emerged from your imagination organically, by being intent on checking that every bit of what you put down conforms to the line of argument in your premise.

Having said that, it is inevitable that a well-told story will deal with themes and will have a meaning (several layers of meaning, perhaps), and may well rest on a proverbial or mythic truth. By the time you have unfolded how your story will flow, you will almost certainly have discovered more than you knew about it at the outset. But to start off with, it's far more important to find out the way a story is going to go rather than worry too much about what it means. In other words, concentrate on working out how it *actually* goes rather than trying to write the *idea* of how it goes.

To say a little more about this, let's just return to the question of how many stories there are. It has been argued these number as few as eight, these being:

- *Cinderella* – unrecognised virtue recognised at last; the dream come true.

- *Achilles* – the fatal flaw which leads to the destruction of a character previously thought flawless.

- *Faust* – selling your soul to the devil in return for instant power and riches has a price which must inevitably be paid.

- *Circe* – the spider and the fly; the chase and final ensnarement of the hapless hero.

- *Candide* – the hero who cannot be kept down; the triumph of naïve optimism.

- *Tristan* – love triangles. The trouble which follows falling in love with an unavailable other.

- *Orpheus* – the gift taken away and the consequences of that loss.

- *Romeo and Juliet* – boy meets girl. Boy loses girl. They do or do not end up together again.

Now what you *could* do is take the germ of your story and then write it in accordance with how stories of this type have to go. In other words, you could take the germ of your story, mould it to fit the conventional demands of this sort of tale, imposing those characteristics onto your tale to make it a recognisable kind of story.

You could consciously model your storymaking on that shortlist above, or really go to town and immerse yourself in Christopher Booker's admittedly fascinating encyclopaedic survey of what he calls 'the seven basic plots' (rebirth, tragedy, comedy, voyage and return, the quest, rags to riches, overcoming the monster), or move on to elaborated and modified definitions (for example, Philip Parker's list of ten story types, or Robert McKee's list of 25 genres and sub-genres). The danger is that, whilst enjoying the security of 'recognising' where your story fits into one or more of these categories, you miss the opportunity of letting your story tell you. What I mean is that we all know about stories and we all know more about their nature than we perhaps consciously recognise, and it is this unconscious level of narrative skill which I believe can power the process. Certainly when you're starting out to write, I believe it is better to learn to trust this unconscious story teller in you, rather than put what could well be the dead-hand of story classification on your shoulder whilst you are trying to bring your story to life. By all means recognise which shelf it's going to belong on after the event, but don't let that determine how you want your story to unfold at the beginning.

So what I did *not* do with *Two Sharp* is sit and think I was going to write a particular kind of tale. At the start I did not have much of a clue what I was going to write; but I did have an imaginative impulse . . .

Exercises

1   For a few days keep a diary, writing in present tense, and in the third person, as if you were being observed by someone else. Leave out all thought and feelings, but do describe your actions vividly and accurately. You are simply using your own activities as the raw material for some practice screenwriting.

2   Collect about a dozen photographs, postcards or a mixture of both, with a range of images: people, places and objects. If you use personal photos try to go for those which conjure no particularly strong pre-existing associations or feelings. Spreading these out before you, arrange them into an order which suggests and supports a narrative. Now try writing some brief working notes for a short screenplay with a single protagonist and a single narrative strand designed to unfold with no dialogue – action only.

Do make sure you think about imagining what can be seen. If you do this in a group, mix all the images up and make sure you use some images that other people have brought. After the writing, read out and discuss your work, with reference to those images. Get other people's reactions, both to your work in progress and to the images on which you based your work.

2
Ideas into action

FORMING IDEAS INTO STORY

Ideas are by their nature *nuclear*. One of the dictionary definitions of a nucleus says it is 'an initial part meant to receive additions'. What is also true about ideas is that, at the beginning, they rarely if ever come fully formed; they are not only nuclear they are *unclear*. Part of the story inventor's job is to learn to sit peacefully with that lack of clarity and let those 'additions' come up for proper consideration.

So how does one clarify the components and direction of an unfolding story? Here are a couple of techniques which may be helpful.

Mind-mapping

The impetus for *Two Sharp* was no more than a blunt pencil and the very tough time I then had tracking down a sharpener. So the image of a blunt pencil began the process and went down as a boxed note in the middle of an empty page. This rapidly changed to the idea of a broken pencil. The next idea was, naturally enough, a sharpener and so I noted that down. The next was a cartoonist and so that went down, swiftly followed by an alarm clock and an editor. As each successive thought came, I mapped it out, constellating those which belonged together and drawing in connections where I could see them. I was left with a kit from which the story could take shape, and in the shaping of this story, other parts suggested themselves and were happily incorporated. Looking at a page drawn out like this can help you decide which thoughts really do or do not belong to the story you have to tell. It can also give you a strong sense of where the core action is going to be, what is incidental to the core and what lies at the margins but strongly informs the core. Whatever you can do to get thoughts out of your head and into some useful visible form will help you make decisions, and feed-back into your story development process.

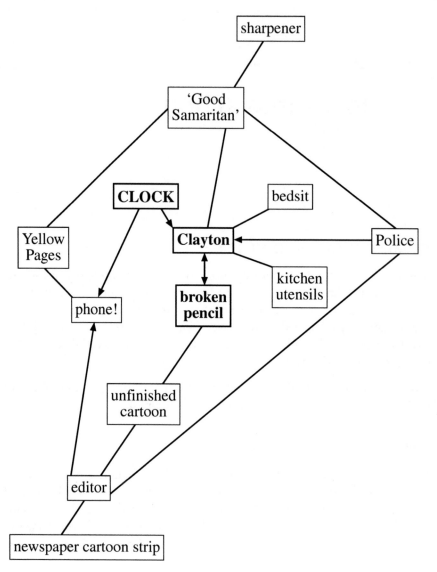

Figure 2.1   A 'mind-map'

Image banking

In thinking up stories, you may well conjure up images. They may be objects, landscapes, settings, characters, moments of action. It is important to make a habit of noting these; put them in the bank. It may not be at all clear where or indeed whether they will figure in your story, but it's most important not to lose track of them. When you dream, unless you make a note of what occurred in the dream soon after waking up, most often the memory of it will fade away, first to major moments and events and finally to key images and words, before even they disappear into total obscurity. It can be useful to think of the process of getting hold of your story as recovering an all-but-lost dream, starting with one or two fragments, which are gradually filled out into pieces and brought into sharper focus until there is a solid procession of sound and pictures. We even use the phrase 'to dream up a story' and I think that is far from accidental: however insignificant or arbitrary those first images which surface might seem, in retrospect they will often be seen to have formed the cornerstones of your drama.

So with *Two Sharp* the coffee-maker was there from early on, as was the pile of saw-dust, as was the opening picture of a happily snoozing cartoonist and an irascible alarm clock. In noting these images they can help provide beacons which help you steer your story's course. They will form a part of the vital business of visualising you'll need to do to tell any story well for the screen. Some people are strongly visual and get their inspiration mainly in the form of pictures, others may get snatches of dialogue or music; whatever form those story fragments come in, make a habit of noting them down and storing them away. Any film or video editor will tell you, when faced with a shortage of material to choose from, you can't include what you didn't bother to record. So collect your imaginings: you can always choose to leave material out. You may well decide material has no place in the story you are forming, but that it will and does have a place in another story on another day.

THE POWER OF 'WHAT IF ...?'

Alongside the unfolding characters and settings some plot possibilities were unfolding in my head. I noted these and thought about which appealed and which held the maximum potential for conflict:

What if ... a cartoonist is up against his deadline, has an entire comic strip to draw, is blocked and at the very moment he gets inspired, has the misfortune to break his favourite lucky pencil ...? Misfortune, because he has no sharpener and relies totally on this pencil for the completion of his work? What then?

At this stage it is also most important to play with alternatives. For example:

What if ... a cartoonist needs to sharpen his pencil, finds he has no sharpener, decides on using a new pencil and cavalierly snaps the old one in two and then throws it away ... only to find he is then totally blocked and is finally driven to track down his broken old pencil by now on its way to the dump?

What if ... a traffic warden needs to sharpen his pencil and finds no one will help him. He is driven to disguise, gets help, is then unmasked and suddenly faces numerous obstacles to doing his job ... and then ...?

What if ... a woodwork teacher who is obsessive about keeping the sharpest point on his pencil finds it broken and his sharpener missing? ... Control of the class, if not his very life is thrown into the balance.

How do you know which of these ideas is right to go with? Well the process of mind-mapping will already have thrown up some immediate choices for you. At that stage I wrote down a cartoonist, for instance, and not a traffic warden or a woodwork teacher. Clearly it's entirely a matter of choice whether to go with these choices or to revise them, bearing in mind the need to provide an appropriate sort of hero, generate lots of complication and maximise conflict.

Heretical though this may seem to some, I suggest you do *not* agonise over this process, or even if you do, then settle on the choices which simply feel right for you. In just the same way that a blunt pencil woke up the story telling instinct in me, and gave me the feeling that there was potential in playing with this image, so the ideas which followed also felt right.

You will notice that none of the alternatives outlined above are complete. In fact, all you need to write a story is a promising start. You need a situation in which something extraordinary can happen to your protagonist which will throw his life into turmoil and present him with an extreme challenge. After that, you're off and in the writing of the story.

THE IMPORTANCE OF LISTS

The business of accumulating lists is a constant in the formulation of a script for the screen. From the very first jotted notes to the final draft, what you are dealing with is an ever-more elaborate process of listing character traits, settings, large story events, smaller story events and small parts of those smaller story events. A simple thought or an unexplored moment of recognition will inevitably lead on to a process of teasing out the content and its dynamic, pace, rhythm and structure. It is a process in which you are setting these details down on paper to be reflected on and revised, with the constant aim of clarifying them to yourself, before communicating them to others. It is also an ongoing opportunity to see the structural relationship of each of the parts to the whole drama, and of the whole to each of its parts. This essential process gets harder to mobilise once you're embroiled in the cut and thrust of getting your characters on their feet and giving them lives. What's more, once you have committed to specific ways of writing scenes in detail, it's all the more difficult to detach, give them up, and try something completely different.

In his highly entertaining account of scriptwriting for Hollywood, *Adventures In The Screen Trade*, William Goldman declares as one of his guiding tenets the resounding conviction that 'SCREENPLAYS ARE STRUCTURE':

> Yes, nifty dialog helps a lot; sure, it's nice if you can bring your characters to life. But you can have terrific characters spouting just swell talk to each other, and if the structure is unsound, forget it.

As someone who was a relatively late convert to the idea of detailed planning – choosing instead to believe that writing was such a magical process that detailed planning was a gross, mechanical interference – I have to say I am now a staunch advocate. Getting material out of my head and on to paper or a screen has proved enormously beneficial in organising and clarifying my thoughts and feelings as well as stimulating further imaginative flow. I have also seen how much it has helped others – especially complete newcomers to scripting. As I've already suggested, there are writers who resist this process or who do not seem to need it. Here is Richard LaGravenese, talking about writing *The Fisher King*:

> I just followed the natural progression – I let each scene tell me where to go next. I tried writing outlines and index cards. But nothing worked as well as getting in there and getting my hands dirty.
>
> *The Search For The Holy Reel*
> (Screenplay of *The Fisher King*)

Whilst I think there is much to be said for following instinct and not being over-formulaic, it is worth noting that in LaGravenese's we have a practised writer who has already internalised strategies for shaping screenwriting structure. (What's more, it's worth noting, he *was* also trying to shape and list material – a process which will have informed the work.) When you start out, you have still to learn and internalise the organisational process. Whether you feel drawn to this approach or not, it is most important to recognise that if you have aspirations to write professionally, the industry depends on and believes in various stages of listing ever more detailed versions of your work on paper whilst in development. These are: synopsis, treatment, step-outline, scene-by-scene breakdown.

Synopsis

The least list-like of the lot, a synopsis is a short summary, usually no more than a page aimed at summing up and selling your drama. It will have the main plot points, mention the principal characters, cover the story and may indicate the main themes dealt with. In the spirit of a promotional campaign, it may also tease the reader by omitting the resolution of the plot, and so inciting the reader to open that script and find out for themselves. Though Lajos Egri may pronounce with such ringing certainty:

> If you have a clear-cut premise, almost automatically a synopsis unrolls itself.
>
> *The Art of Dramatic Writing*

I'm a believer in writing what it's all about once you really know – and that may be when you've finished writing the script. In my view, a synopsis is a good accompaniment to a script, a brief taster which covers the ground and whets the reader's appetite.

Treatment

If you are developing an idea from scratch, and writing to commission, you will undoubtedly have to produce a treatment. Depending on the length of the finished piece this will be up to, but no more than, four or five pages, which offers a detailed summary of the plot, mentions all the major characters, giving a feel for what they are like, and also touches on other significant players. Major scenes and moments will be described in some detail, but otherwise the treatment will accurately cover the broad sweep of the story. The structure and dramatic integrity of the piece need to be clearly visible; in other words the reader/potential buyer needs to be able to see that the idea is workable. A good treatment should also form a sound working basis from which to develop the script. What I mean is that it may be a temptation to blithely busk a story from the top of your head, believing you will be able to go back to move things around and fill in the gaps later. To an extent this *will* always be the case, but only to a limited extent. The basics – the planks on which a script can be constructed – do need to be firmly in place.

Step-outline or scene-by-scene breakdown

These are very often, but not always, the same thing. Sometimes the step-outline is a half-way house towards a scene-by-scene breakdown. In such cases, more scenes are detailed than in a treatment, but there are still sections of the story dealt with in generalised terms. The final stage script development can progress to before it actually reaches a draft is the scene-by-scene breakdown; every scene is reduced to a maximum of a three or four sentence description which covers characters, their emotional attitude, and also details the plot development. When writers submit an idea for a series of dramas, it is not uncommon to put together a package which comprises a synopsis, a full episode, a scene-by-scene breakdown for, say, three further episodes, and a treatment projecting further development.

In the quote above from LaGravenese, he makes reference to index cards. If you haven't come across the idea yet, it can be very useful to put brief individual scene descriptions on index cards. This means you can play with setting scenes out in different orders, and assess the overall structural feel and effect. Somehow doing this in the flesh, as it were, rather than just cutting and pasting on the screen, can be a more involving and satisfactory process, helping you to absorb the emergent and shifting bigger picture. Using a wall-mounted board and felt-tip markers can also be a great asset.

In the preface to this book, I said its intent was not to offer tips on pitching or selling. This process of graduated listing and refining of lists is one which is of benefit to you before it is useful to anyone else or an invitation for them to interfere with the content and structure of your idea. Learning and practising with these planning and summarising processes will help you clarify intent and will also sharpen your own critical faculty. Part of developing as a writer is stretching your ability to read with insight and sensitivity: the more you learn to plan, to reflect on and analyse that planning, the better your writing will be.

This book details strategies for informally listing opening ideas, and also takes a close look at some scene-by-scene listing in the later chapter, *Making a Scene, Building a Sequence*. My recommendation is that you do give both of these processes a lot of thought and practice, using both as a support, and for the moment put to one side the aspects of summing up and selling which are useful later adjuncts once you have written something worth selling, and which in any case there is no shortage of advice on elsewhere.

ENDINGS

Some people find forming endings a difficult matter, perhaps even being reluctant to set out on the story telling journey at all until they feel sure they know how their tale will resolve. Often, if you follow the energy of a piece, happily complicating your protagonist's life and driving them ever onwards against the odds in pursuit of their goal, then the natural conclusion to the drama will probably suggest itself. If you do find yourself wrestling with how the story should resolve, it is always important to play with different possibilities:

What if ... Clayton delivers his cartoon, relaxes in the editor's chair with a celebratory cigar. Moments later a blank set of frames for the following week's strip is gently placed in front of him ...?

What if ... Clayton takes a walk. He goes into a favourite café and buys himself an ice-cream. Sitting nearby is someone who is reading a paper. On its back page is one of his cartoons. The stranger leafs impatiently through the paper, turns to the back page and scans down its contents. Clayton studies the stranger's face with eager anticipation. However, she remains impassive. A second or two and then she folds the paper, strides off, tossing it in an adjacent waste bin.

Try out several different kinds of moment and try turning them on their head. *What if ...* it all happened exactly the opposite way round? What then?

As with other aspects of your narrative, which ending you settle on can be largely a matter of intuition. As a broad generalisation, try to avoid artificially tacked on flourishes which are there to announce 'that's all, folks'; ideally, the ending of your drama should be seen to have grown out of everything which has come before. Narratives often have a deliberate circularity, ending up to all appearances with an identical moment to the one which started the piece. Sometimes the character(s) in question are discovered back where they were first introduced, but having undergone a major life-change. Sometimes, as in that framing device in *Titanic* we discussed in Chapter 1, we are taken back to the same character(s) in the same setting as at the start, but now knowing much more about them. (In *Titanic*, one more significant action is going to unfold which will resolve matters for Rose and for the audience.) Sometimes this circularity comes in the form of an echo. Where we may have seen one character in a particular setting, we now see another in the same situation.

Whatever you choose, if the ending is a closed one, fully resolving the narrative tension and completing the protagonist's journey, then it should bring what Andrew Horton (*Writing The Character Centred Screenplay*) neatly sums up as 'relief and release'.

In his excellent summary of endings, he also observes how endings can fall broadly into one of two camps leaving the central character(s) isolated or embraced (actually or metaphorically). He goes on to list several more kinds of ending including:

- the fantasy triumph ending – it all turns out well, but only in the hero's mind;

- the blessing – of love, friendship, or the discovery of a common bond;

- solitude – characters walking off into the sunset;

- long shot – a retreat from the setting and the action allowing for us to put everything into perspective.

'Embrace versus solitude' seem to me to be particularly useful ideas to bear in mind, and I would recommend reading the whole section (Horton 1994: 172–5).

If you can, avoid falling back on simply copying others; though, of course, we are all endlessly influenced by others. Try to follow your instinct and see what you can create, partly to experience the empowering feeling that you told this tale all on your own, and partly because in that very process you may plumb greater depths and tell a better tale. Tell it from the inside first, and shape it from the outside as a secondary process. When you're balancing out the inner and outer processes – reflecting on which choices you would be best advised to make – a rule of thumb is that your story will gain most from those alternatives which offer most complication and generate most conflict for your central character to deal with. It can also be a very good idea to generate contradictions in your story and in your characters, with the aim of adding ironic edge and so producing a universal recognisability to your piece.

A WORD OR TWO MORE ABOUT MEANING

The title of *Two Sharp* came last. Obviously it ties together the idea of the deadline, the means to meeting that deadline and the protagonist's nemesis. The pointless pencil leads us to question the point of Clayton's pursuit. It is an ironic tale in which success and failure are closely entwined. In winning he loses and so finally gets the point – both literally and metaphorically. That first image which kicked off the telling of the story was indeed a potent little metaphor. I didn't know where it would lead but I did have the good sense to follow. Until I was done I did not sit back to scrutinise what it might mean, and when I did I was pleased to see it had both meaning and irony – the potential to be recognised as a transferable truth in others' lives. Sitting with that first idea threw up more and stimulated plotting possibilities. A story picture started to clarify and, in following that, I arrived at a story which goes:

Man has deadline,
Man meets deadline,
Man dies.

THE DEEPER MEANING

Beyond the literal level of the unfolding story, there is very often a deeper level of meaning. In this story, at the literal level Clayton fights to get his cartoon finished and meet the deadline. Why? So it will go in the paper. Why? So that his work will be included in the next edition. Why? So lots of people will read it. Why? So he will get recognition, even admiration for his work. So, tracked to its source, the need for acknowledgement is what may ultimately be driving him.

It's a story which is surrounded by proverbial resonances and everyday sayings:

> 'He who laughs last laughs longest'. (So make sure it's you!)
> 'The pen(cil) is mightier than the sword'. (Make sure you don't fall on yours.)
> 'This job is killing me'.
> 'He finally got the point'.
> 'Cartoon fun'. (Not.)

And yet – to emphasise the point – this little film script started with just a feeling that a pencil which needed sharpening had the makings of a story. I recognised something in the moment, and I do suggest that from now on each and every time you have that kind of intuition you make a note of the image, the sensation, the snatches of dialogue – any or all of these – to reflect on and work with at your leisure.

FORMAT AND WRITING STYLE

Having attended to the inner, it's now time to look at some of the outer (though no less important) aspects of screenwriting. Some of the mechanics and superficial characteristics of screenwriting often present needless problem areas for new writers, so I'll spend just a little while looking at some of the areas where there are specialised demands and not infrequent pitfalls.

There are set industry formats for screenplay writing which constitute good practice. Having said that, you will come across variations on these and different house-styles, as well as different schools of thought on their merits or otherwise. That there is no one definitive way to set down a screenplay is reflected in the differences you'll find amongst the excerpts quoted in this book: and for those who might be thinking some of these variations simply reflect bad practice, well, firstly – all of the writers quoted here will have had different models and influences acting on them; secondly, some of the films and TV dramas quoted here have quite clearly gone into production in this form and gone on to win awards at the highest level.

Whilst I'd discourage too great a preoccupation with getting layout absolutely 'right', whatever that means, there is broad consensus on the difference between laying out drama for film (which may actually mean video as well), that's to say single-camera shooting on location, and laying it out for multi-camera studio recording. That said, drama written for television which is destined to be shot single camera on location will very often be set out as if for studio recording: the excerpt from *Our Friends in the North* (see p. 200) is a good example of what I mean. Both this extract and the extract from Patrea Smallacombe's *Coronation Street* script (see p. 111) demonstrate the split-page television drama format. That characters' names are centred in one and not in the other illustrates unimportant quirks of differing house-styles. Patrea's script is laid out in Granada's house-style, though for the publishing purposes of this book it has been compressed from the double spacing it would actually have been given in the original. The other important point to note about TV format is that each new scene is given a new page. Screenplays for film do not follow this convention. The point of laying out a TV script with text on half the page is to allow appropriate space alongside the action and dialogue for the inclusion of camera shots and other technical requirements. If you want to know more about this, Harris Watts' book, *On Camera*, offers a clear and full explanation. I would encourage you to learn at least the basics of the media you are learning to write for since this will enable you to exploit their potential more fully.

Two Sharp, The Green House Effect, The Odd Couple, and the extracts from *Some Mother's Son, My Left Foot, The English Patient, The Fisher King, Network* and *Shallow Grave* are all in feature film format, which by convention is spread right across the page. In addition to these formats there is also an alternative convention used for scripting documentary, as well as some corporate training productions. Examples of these can be found in Richard A. Blum's *Television and Screen Writing* and Dwight V. Swain and Joye R. Swain's *Scripting for the New AV Technologies*. Whilst your business is scripting drama, you need not concern yourself with these at all.

Scenes

Common to both TV and film scripting is the need to clearly define each scene. Newcomers to drama writing are often confused as to what a new scene is. Very simply:

a new scene is a change of time or place or both.

Whilst some might take issue with this definition, (claiming that where there is continuous action it is basically all the same scene), it is a recognised convention to mark every change of time or place with a new heading. This does *not* mean that every new angle your mind's eye conjures constitutes a new scene.

Each and every scene has a scene heading. This is not merely some stylistic affectation. Important information is included in this line. 'Int.' and 'Ext.' are

short for 'Interior' and 'Exterior'. These are followed by the exact location of
the scene. This is followed by the time the scene happens. In some scripts this
is expressed simply as 'Day' or 'Night'. In some, you may find the exact time
of day or night specified. All of this information is directly relevant to the
lighting of any scene. The fact that we include all of this information in a
script is also a reminder that it is, in one sense, never a finished piece of work,
but only a blueprint yet to be realised in production.

Typographical conventions

In TV drama scripts, all the action, as well as the characters' names, are written
in upper case. They may or may not be centred and may or may not be followed
by a colon – take your pick. If a character's speech is happening out of shot, the
character's name will be followed by (OOV) or (OOS) – short for 'out of
vision' or 'out of shot': I've also seen (OS) used for this. Similarly, you may see
(V.O.) by a character, indicating that the lines are voice-over as opposed to
synchronised dialogue. Any directions relating to a character's line are in upper
case and may be found directly under the centred name, or at the start of the
actual line, depending on which convention you choose to follow; either way
the directions should be enclosed in brackets. A character's dialogue itself is
written in lower case. If a character has two (or more) speeches interrupted by a
chunk of action, where the character resumes speaking it can be very useful to
insert the character's name again to make it clear who is speaking. The major
point to remember about scripts is that *they are working documents*: the clearer
you make any division between character and character, speech and action,
scene and any other scene, the easier you are making life for everyone who is
going to be part of any revision, rehearsal or production process.

As I said above, scripts for TV dedicate a fresh page to each fresh scene.
Some TV writers are used to putting a generic CUT TO in the bottom right-
hand corner on the last page of a scene to underline the scene change.

When writing action for TV drama, some scripts follow the convention of
allowing a fresh paragraph for each shot; others I have seen simply lump all
the action together, making no distinction between what the writer has con-
ceived as separate shots.

Montage, a rapid accumulation of images, is expressed (as with film scripting)
by single lines of action or image, one following another.

When there is rapid inter-cutting between scenes, some layouts choose not to
go to the bother of inserting the separate scene headings for the separate
scenes simply combining both in one scene heading, and perhaps assisting the
transitions from one scene to another with the word 'RESUME' or 'CON-

TINUE'. This is more frequently found in film scripting: in any case, I recommend you use a fresh scene heading for every scene, however brief that scene.

Where a scene is happening both interior and exterior, say two characters chatting at a front door, one in the house and one outside, the scene needs to be headed 'INT/EXT'.

Now that I have set out some conventions, you may well come across deviations from, and variations upon these. This is particularly true of the film screenplay format, though what differences there are tend to be relatively unimportant. A major difference, however, between TV and film formats is that, on the whole, use of upper case lettering is reserved for characters' names, which again may be centred or ranged left before a character speaks. Every time a character's name appears, it should be written in upper case. According to which convention you follow, other key words may also be found in upper case; these usually refer directly to anything which is going to find its way onto the sound track. However, I have also seen characters' actions, certain props and specified camera shots and shot transitions marked out in capital letters. Personally I favour sticking to just using upper case for characters' names and for scene headings as well as the obligatory FADE IN and FADE OUT, also found as FADE UP FROM BLACK, and FADE TO BLACK. Or even FIB, FTB. Take your pick!

Whether sections of dialogue or sections of action are centred, how far either are indented, and whether or not italics are used to distinguish one from another can and do all vary slightly in screenplay format. The basic layout of screenplay excerpts included here adhere, for the most part, closely to studio norms. Screenwriting software and internet downloads also offer industry standard templates.

You may have guessed I don't have too reverential an attitude to the minutiae of all these conventions, but I do have one or two pieces of advice. Firstly, read plenty of scripts for film and TV and, as you do, observe the differing styles and conventions. If you end up writing for a specific producer or company who you know favours or requires certain conventions, then it makes sense to comply. Attend to the content of your scenes first and foremost. Make sure scenes are explicit and clearly headed; make sure action and dialogue are distinguishable one from another; make sure it's easy to see who is speaking. After that, as with TV scripting, individual foibles and leanings are relatively unimportant. No-one is going to want to make your script just because it's perfectly laid out in accord with one convention or another: they may, however, never get as far as picking it up to give it consideration if it's not clearly laid out and easy to read.

Numbering scenes

Between first draft and shooting script most scripts go through several if not many changes. For this reason alone, whilst it is essential to number pages (try having a phone conversation about your script without page numbers to refer to) it can be quite counter-productive to number scenes before you reach a final draft.

Logistics

I've mentioned that scene headings have vital information with reference to lighting. It can also be useful to scan scene headings in a storyline to check for logistical viability; are all the sets available to shoot in, and are all the exteriors feasible? These are considerations a writer is not immune from being party to. Checking through scene headings can also be a good way of noticing whether you've achieved an appropriate variety of settings, or indeed been too lavish or needlessly exotic. One of the joys of drawn animation is that it costs no more to take your action to Honolulu than it does to keep it in the frontroom at Acacia Avenue. In live action, sadly, such is not the case. However, that should not constrain you unduly. Within reason write your piece to be played where it seems truly appropriate. Let your imagination roam free and worry about changing locations later should you get to that stage with a script. Naturally the advice I've just given does not apply if you find yourself writing for an established project or programme, when paying attention to logistical possibilities is an all-important part of the job.

Staying present

Another crucial characteristic of screenwriting is that it is *always* in the present tense. Although you are, of course, recording on paper what you have already imagined, a screenplay describes *no more nor less than what we can see (and hear) happening in the moment.* I emphasise this point since it's not uncommon for new writers to lapse into past tense, either seduced by the sensation of what they've imagined having already happened, or because what they want to write is happening in the past relative to another time-frame. Nevertheless, past, present or future, it's all unfolding before your eyes and ears *now*, and so must all be written in the present tense.

Watch out for the limits

Since a screenplay is only what you can see and hear happening, it's important to realise that screenwriting also has some severe limitations. You may find yourself so wrapped up in your character that you write:

INT. CLAYTON'S BATHROOM. 6.05 A.M.

Looking in the mirror CLAYTON sees his ravaged face and senses the deep dried-out well which is his imagination. He remembers the tortured nightmare which was yesterday and can almost taste the dread he had been so close to drowning in.

Good stuff, huh? But before I put the kettle on and we crack open the biscuits, can you tell me just how you are going to see this scene I've lavished such care on?

Basically, interior process – that is, *thought described as if it's action*– is a no-no in screenwriting. A character's interior process is either going to have to find its place (if it really needs to have one) dramatised as part of a dialogue scene or will have to be incorporated as voice-over narration. (The films of Woody Allen, as well as *Stand By Me* (Raynold Gideon, Bruce A. Evans from a story by Stephen King), *Days of Heaven* (Terence Malick), *The Great Gatsby* (Francis Ford Coppola from the novel by F. Scott Fitzgerald) or the TV adaptation of *Brideshead Revisited* (John Mortimer from the novel by Evelyn Waugh), have all offered interesting and very engaging ways of using voice-over to express interior process.)

So that scene now becomes:

INT. CLAYTON'S BATHROOM. 6.05 A.M.

CLAYTON looks anxiously at his ravaged face in the mirror.

AVOID NOVELISATION

When setting out with screenwriting some people can have a tendency to let their writing drift away into a novelistic form. Here's an example of what I mean:

Int. Bar. Night.

Paul is standing in front of the café. He opens the door and enters. Now the real nightmare begins. From every corner the sound of people talking presses in on him. He wonders how he will be able to spot **Judith**. He stands where he is, looking around. He 'looks' for her: she saw him coming in and now moves towards him. She reaches him and stands opposite. She realises he is blind. **Paul** asks: 'Are you **Judith**?' **Judith** is surprised and replies with a Yes. She is just about to ask him how he could have known that she was standing there. **Paul** interrupts her, knowing what she wants to ask: 'I could smell you . . . in a nice way of course.'

The passage looks like a chunk out of a prose work, and is actually uncomfortably poised between prose and drama. It has interior process (thoughts and realisations) which we cannot see, reported action and speech where there should be just action or speech, and also novelistic preamble to character's speech. It is cumbersome, redundantly reflective, slips tense, and is, in any case, partially unrealisable as a screenplay. Those last three lines could become:

JUDITH

(surprised)

Yes! How did you – ?

PAUL

I smelled you.

JUDITH

Oh . . .

PAUL

(charmingly)

You smell very nice.

This trap of writing half prose, half drama is easy for some to fall into at first. Watch out for writing material you don't need to include (for example, 'he said' or 'she interrupted him') between lines of dialogue, or expressing material which could easily be dramatised as description or characters' reported thoughts and feelings, which in any case cannot be seen.

DETAIL AND DESCRIPTION: GETTING THE BALANCE RIGHT

I have come across scripts full of the most intricate details of setting and design. One such not only specified the colour of a lizard, but actually specified the colour inside its mouth. Unless details such as these are vitally relevant to plot or character, you can forget them. This is a lucky break for prose fiction writers used to toiling away and generating every bit of costume and scenery in their stories, and terrible news for control freaks. Joking apart, debate often rages about how much or how little description to put in the action. The fact is, a lot of the time you do only need the bare bones. But then again part of your job as a writer is to evoke mood and atmosphere, and with that in mind you may want to offer more than a totally uninflected, functional description. A script should be a good read. It has to fight its way out from under a pile of others, grab the reader's attention and keep them happily absorbed. Choose your adjectives with care so that they work hard for you and suggest a great deal, whilst spelling out very little. What you don't want to do is to get so specific that you tie everyone's hands and feet. It's important to remember that a script *is* and *is not* a finished product. It should be as finished as you can make it – a tightly constructed, engagingly written piece of work. It should be as pacey, vivid and energised as you can make it, so that it comes to life off the page. It should not be over descriptive but then again, it needs to evoke enough atmosphere to keep the reader hooked. Scripts are intended for interpretation: what you are after is establishing and conveying the right kind of territory for those interpretations to inhabit. If your script goes into production, it will be serviced and interpreted by a whole team of people, including the director and designers. You may well feel you know exactly how it should look and sound and, whilst that may have been invaluable in the process of imagining the action, unless you are going to be the producer and/or director of the piece, learn to let go.

TECHNICAL SPECIFICS: WHO CALLS THE SHOTS?

We now come to the highly charged and undeniably political question of how much or little the writer should specify camera angles and shots; or even how much he or she should try to *manipulate* the director into a way of shooting. Even the convention of writing each shot as a separate paragraph of action might not find favour with some unbridled egos, who may object to the writer expressing any of the action in a way which suggests implicitly where shot changes should happen, let alone how or what those shots should be.

Opinions on this tricky question do change, and there are a number of different schools of thought on the subject. I recommend you stay your side of the fence and simply write the action and dialogue without trying to specify shots or the nature of transitions between them. Whilst no-one's going to object wildly to an odd suggestion here and there, on the whole it's far better to work by stealth. If, for example, it seems crucial to you to specify a close-up of a character, think hard why this is so and if still convinced write the action or dialogue in such a way that a close-up is going to be irresistible.

Try to avoid

INT. CLAYTON'S BEDROOM. 9.15 A.M.

A big close-up on Clayton as, heartbroken, he examines the broken pencil point.

Instead try something like:

INT. CLAYTON'S BEDROOM. 9.15 A.M.

CLAYTON lifts the broken lead; he rolls it between thumb and forefinger, fighting hard to hold back his tears.

Of course, there's nothing to stop a director shooting that as a very wide shot. But at least you've done your best, and often there will be an opportunity to comment and negotiate if you stay alert, know what you want and are sure of your ground. The danger with specifying shots is that you may very well not be able to do it as well as the director. It's not your job anyway; it's theirs. The crucial question is whether or not you have radically different visions, and even more crucially, whether the director's vision negates or markedly distorts yours.

A compromise some writers make towards getting out of the director's chair (whilst leaving their jacket draped over the seat-back) is to specify 'another angle', as a way of nudging the director into seeing it their way. Don't do it. Which other angle did you have in mind? Same as the director? This kind of back-seat directing can really end up alienating the person you most need on your side.

PRECISION AND VIGOUR

In *On Directing Film* (a book I thoroughly recommend you read), leaning on theory of montage, David Mamet argues that, just as an assembly of unin-flected shots – (that is a procession of plainly-related images) will excite an inevitable sense of understanding in an audience's mind, so actions too should be as uninflected as possible. That's to say an actor will very often be able to simply give a look, rather than give a particular kind of look, and the unelaborated action will more than suffice. He takes actors to task for being over-preoccupied with the 'arc of the performance':

> This commitment to the arc of the film – it's ignorance on the part of the actor, ignorance of the essential nature of acting in film, which is that performance will be created by the juxtaposition of simple, for the most part uninflected shots, and simple uninflected physical actions.
>
> *On Directing Film* 1992

While I think *On Directing Film* is, in so many respects, essential reading for those interested in the process of putting screen story telling together, I also think that too dogmatic an adherence to stripping away all expression can be counter-productive. There is a danger that if you write a completely unin-flected script, in which characters simply 'enter', 'sit', 'look', and so on, it will, at the very least, be far less arresting on the page than it might be. If you know the moment you're depicting and are certain that a character 'cau-tiously slides into a room', or that 'she slumps wearily' onto a chair, by all means write this in. Be open to having your mind changed by anyone who might interpret your script, and then again be prepared to stand your ground and argue for the moments you have written. On the other hand, as Mamet argues, there is also great strength in not defining *every* moment too descrip-tively, or investing *every* action with emotional background. As you will see,

later in the book, the whole business of sharply and precisely defining emotional attitude and specifying action can be immensely helpful to the process
of writing your script. Without becoming too novelistic, it can be a good
thing that a certain amount of this colour and precision finds its way into
your finished script. It both enlivens your piece and makes it more vivid to
the reader: anything which helps the drama live for them a bit more while
they read is, to my mind, no bad thing.

I've detailed a lot of things here. Don't worry about taking them all in at
once. Writing is an ongoing practice and every script you work on gives you
an opportunity to reflect on what you've achieved, and think about what you
might like to have improved on or done differently. From the beginning, do
try to ensure your screenwriting always happens in the present tense, that it
avoids unnecessary repetition, and above all, that it has energy and impact.
Be yourself, get involved and enjoy the telling, without resorting to any bogus
razzmatazz. Allow your voice to come through, and try to set your story down
with enthusiasm and presence. To write a drama is, in one form or another,
to write a play; and as the name suggests that process offers space to explore
your imagination, to abandon yourself and, despite the demands making plays
places on you, and the discipline you will need to develop, it also offers a real
chance to learn through having fun. Don't forget to keep playing.

Exercises

1   Perhaps taking one of the images you used in the picture exercise at the end of the
    last chapter, or perhaps using an image you left to one side, start dreaming up a
    new story. Make a list of 'What ifs' and mind-map the key images.

2   Write a short screenplay based on this material with no dialogue. (Don't feel this has
    to be an animation, and try to avoid doing too similar a story; feel free to do your
    own thing.)

3   If you have done this as a group, do copies for the other group members and take
    turns at reading them out and discussing them. Try letting other people read your
    script: it can be very useful to hear someone else speaking your words.

3
Just picture it: visualising the action

Television and film are primarily *visual* media. That is to say, wherever possible, the pictures and the action should always come first. It is what we are *watching* which truly engages our interest, over and above what we are hearing, however important that may also be. Clearly, different forms offer different opportunities and emphases, placing different demands on the writer. Nevertheless, the ability always to visualise action, to 'see' your drama through, is a vital one to develop. It's worth remembering that early cinema managed to tell very effective and engaging stories with little or no supporting explanation or captioned dialogue.

Parallels have often been drawn between watching screen dramas (particularly in the cinema) and the experience of dreaming. Certainly the business of writing screen dramas calls for sustained acts of imagination: we need to see the events in our mind's eye, to day-dream but to do so with conscious intent if we're going to shape those imaginings into a drama.

Two Sharp (p. 3) is offered as the first example in this book because I want to encourage you to develop your abilities to visualise your drama from the start. Many writers starting out to write plays or screenplays make the mistake of thinking it's all about making characters talk to each other. Yet, others think screenwriting is about composing beautiful visuals and arranging arresting shots to best effect. Whilst both the verbal and the visual have their vital places in writing effective screenplays, the essential capacity is to be able to imagine how the action of your story unfolds first visually, and then verbally. That is to say, it's about getting to know what every moment in your drama looks like as well as knowing what it sounds like.

A helpful step in building up the visual picture of your story's unfolding action is to understand a little of how separate shots, when put together, carry both their own separate meanings as well as a cumulative meaning which is more than simply the sum of those separate meanings.

INT. OFFICE RECEPTION AREA. START OF OFFICE HOURS.

The lights flash madly on BERNICE's telephone desk-switch. Many calls are there for the taking, none are being taken.

We see the desk-surface in all its glory. Des, a soft toy and BERNICE's mascot sits in pride of place astride a small radio. A magazine lies open. A jacket is draped over the back of the chair. it is a bright and definitely more-fun-than-work type garment.

INT. ERIC'S OFFICE. CONTINUOUS.

ERIC's fingers drum impatiently on his desk-top. In front of him is a stack of letters with his written answers noted on or attached to them.

Long suffering, he hangs on the phone trying to get through.

INT. WOMEN'S TOILETS. CONTINUOUS.

Humming happily away to herself, BERNICE applies blusher, sucks in her cheeks and blows herself a kiss.

INT. ERIC'S OFFICE. CONTINUOUS.

ERIC hangs up and resigns himself to attending to some more writing.

INT. GROUND FLOOR LIFT ENTRANCE. CONTINUOUS.

Bearing briefcase and mobile phone ADRIAN arrives at the lift, presses the button and stands waiting.

INT. BERNICE'S RECEPTION AREA. CONTINUOUS.

The phone lines still flash away as if for Britain. In front of where BERNICE should sit is a magazine, its pages flagrantly spread wide open. To one side is a pile of documents begging for attention. In pride of place, at the front of the desk is a small, fluffy bear. BERNICE appears from round a corner clad distinctively, humming happily. She sits. With blatant disregard she flicks all the lines on her telephone switchboard off, then re-opens one line, rapidly dials a number and leafs through her mag.

As viewers we are always trying to make sense out of what we are shown. Since the one follows the other, we assume a connection between Bernice's deserted desk and Eric's impatient efforts to make a call. The flashing desk-switch is what helps us make that initial link. We connect Bernice to the desk via the jacket and also via her blithe indifference, which in itself connects her back to Eric's long-suffering expression and the pile of correspondence in front of him.

Broken down to essentials we see:

1   An empty desk and unattended desk-switch.
2   A man trying to make a call.
3   A woman happily making her face up in the toilets.
4   Fed up, the same man gives up trying to make his phone call.

The nature of assembling shots in this way gives us a cumulative meaning which none of the shots on their own could carry, and also an overall meaning which would not be available if any of the shots were missing.

The simplest assembly of action can engage our curiosity as viewers, and allow us to engage with the process of making meaning and following the story. This happens quite simply by our being presented with a stream of questions. 'Who is this man trying to ring?' 'Who's *not* at this desk?' 'Is this woman the secretary who works at the unattended desk?' 'Is this who he's trying to ring and is that why he can't get through?' 'What will he do next and will he make contact with her?' 'Will he get what he wants?'

By reading the stream of images we can follow both characters' individual stories in parallel: in Eric's story he is hard at work and wanting some kind of assistance with that process. Bernice is on a toilet break, and from the evidence we are given from the state of her desk, we can safely assume she is not employee of the month. The inter-cutting of both sets of images bring two characters who are *not* in contact into meaningful contact in the viewer's mind, so that the relationship their individual stories have to each other can be understood. He is busy and diligent whilst she, his secretary, is not; therefore they are likely to be at odds with one another, and we eagerly anticipate the moment when they actually do come into contact.

We can see how small but relevant details can enhance this basic dynamic between the two characters. The first bit of action we see in Eric's office is a shot of his fingers drumming impatiently on the desk-top. Bernice's happy humming and carefree kiss to herself in the mirror contrast strongly with this, and are topped off by the cavalier way she ditches all the incoming calls when she returns to her desk.

Cutting between different story strands creates the opportunity to skip forward in time and to leave one dramatic question hanging whilst another is picked up and developed. This leap-frogging of one story by another is the mainspring of many serial dramas, and is common to the progression of all conventionally told narratives containing more than a single plot. Where two (or more) characters' stories are intercut rapidly, the effect can be to intensify the audience's engagement with the unfolding drama by sharpening our curiosity about the consequences of each scene and the connection between them. One of the great advantages of employing this device can be the enhanced level of audience interest the writer can generate by juxtaposing complementary yet contrasting action and imagery. Here is another example, taken from *Some Mother's Son* (Terry George and Jim Sheridan) where cutting between parallel progressions is used most effectively:

EXT. GLENARM. MAIN ROAD. DAY.
A small village dominated by the local police station, which is hidden behind wire and sandbags. Today there's a roadblock outside. British soldiers direct traffic through a roadblock. GERARD pulls up in the car.

                    KATHLEEN
              (anxious)
          God, I don't believe this. And I've got
          concert practice this morning.

EXT. SCHOOL. YARD. DAY.
KATHLEEN and LIAM rush from the car. GERARD drives off.
                    KATHLEEN
          Run, Liam, don't be late.

INT. SCHOOL CLASSROOM. DAY.
A choir sings *Panis Angelicus* as KATHLEEN rushes into the classroom, arms full.

                    KATHLEEN
          Sorry I'm late, Brenda.

                    MUSIC TEACHER
          No problem.

                    KATHLEEN
          Is it going alright?

                    MUSIC TEACHER
          Fine.

                    KATHLEEN
          Good God, the roadblocks this
          morning. Okay. I've got the order here.

EXT. SAFE HOUSE. DAY.
GERARD approaches the side entrance. FRANKIE and IRA MAN #2 leave with a heavy bag.

INT. SCHOOL CLASSROOM. DAY.
KATHLEEN watches the girls practise their dance steps.

EXT. COUNTRY ROAD. DAY.
KATHLEEN's car pulls up in a country lane. FRANK, GERARD and IRA MAN #2 get out.
They go to the back, take out the rocket launcher. FRANK climbs over a gate by a field,
followed by IRA MAN #2. GERARD keeps watch.

INT. SCHOOL CLASSROOM. DAY.
The beat of the dance tune intensifies, the dancers' feet pound the floor as . . .

CUT TO:
EXT. GLENARM BRIDGE. DAY.
FRANK and IRA MAN #2 run toward a hedge.
Frank's P.O.V. through the rocket launcher sight: a bridge, soldiers lay explosives.

INT. SCHOOL CLASSROOM. DAY.
The girls dance now in slow motion as:

EXT. HEDGE. DAY.
FRANK fires the launcher.
A loud bang and a trail of smoke from the hedge.

INT. CLASSROOM. DAY.
KATHLEEN hears the roar of the rocket.

EXT. GLENARM BRIDGE. DAY.
The missile smashes into the jeep, an explosion, followed by a larger explosion which
consumes the jeep.

INT. SCHOOL CLASSROOM. DAY.
Windows shatter, girls cry, duck to the floor. Smoke rises from across the field.

EXT. COUNTRY LANE/EXT. CAR. DAY.
FRANK and IRA MAN #2 run back through the field.
GERARD waits nervously.
FRANK and IRA MAN #2 tumble into the car.

INT. SCHOOL CLASSROOM. DAY.
The girls flee the classroom/a young girl is hysterical. KATHLEEN shelters the girl and
leads her out.

EXT. SCHOOL. DAY.
The girls flee the school as bells sound and in the distance sirens wail.

EXT. COUNTRY LANE. DAY.
The car speeds away.

Both Kathleen's and Gerard's story are intertwined here. Her son drops
her off at school and then goes on, supposedly to buy shoes, but in fact, to
take part in the rocket attack on the British army. Whilst her own child
Gerard fights for the mother country, his mother takes part in imparting Irish

traditions to others' children. Thematically there is an interesting tension being explored. The heart of the sequence contrasts close-up shots of dancing children's legs and feet, with the running of the IRA men. The beat of the music and the pounding of the dancers' feet drive and accelerate the narrative tension to a pitch which reaches its height when the rocket is launched and streaks its way towards the target (preceded by a moment in which the dancing is seen in lyrical slow-motion) and is released by the double explosion and the smashing of glass.

Images of innocence and peaceable tradition are intercut with, and used to build suspensefully towards, an act of violence. As I suggested before, the two strands are held together thematically by the idea of national tradition and identity; we are offered a poignant view of alternative strategies for preserving these – direct military action and the teaching of traditional Irish culture. Finally, the two story strands are united by sheer physical proximity. The explosion which we might have thought was happening some way away, turns out to be near enough to blow-in the school's windows and terrify the children.

The sequence continues, incidentally, with one of the children deliberately obstructing the soldiers' attempts to take a grip on the area – a nice reversal of the road-blocks at the beginning.

Visually the quoted passage is a stimulating, exciting sequence which offers the viewer a startling counter-point; children dancing whilst grown men launch a potentially deadly attack. Notice the two shots of Kathleen and Gerard cut into the stream of the action. She hears the rocket, he waits nervously. As well as their separate involvements in the school and the attack, we are also invited to tie the two together through the inclusion of those shots.

The percussive beat of the music and the dancing feet match up with the militaristic mood of the rocket attack, and yet is, in its own right, entirely innocent. Ironically, the viewer gets to know more about her son than Kathleen who is also innocent of all knowledge of his Republican activities at this stage. And whilst the sequence accelerates, builds tension and resolves in an intense, short period of time, it also manages to encapsulate a longer period of real time both credibly and effectively.

BUILDING MOOD AND SETTING

Central to the idea of day-dreaming with conscious intent in order to weave narrative is the process of conjuring up the essential images of your story. I've already mentioned this briefly in Chapter 1. As you start to build up a picture of your drama, try to establish a sense of setting or place, and a sense of mood, within which character and story can unfold. The following excerpt from

My Left Foot (Jim Sheridan again, this time with Shane Connaughton 1989) powerfully illustrates what I mean.

Earlier in the day, the terribly handicapped Christy Brown, just turned 17, has been very reluctantly press-ganged by younger lads into taking a turn at ogling a local girl's breasts. Immediately afterwards, Rachel sitting nearby, preferring Christy to the others, tells him he has nice eyes and gives him an innocent kiss.

INT. CHILDREN'S BEDROOM. NIGHT.
CHRISTY *is painting. It is in the form of a love letter that he is doing for* RACHEL. *In it* RACHEL *is idealized and* CHRISTY *himself is part of a floating couple, perhaps like Chagall or something. Magic. A moon and a heart with the letters RB and CB with an arrow through them. Kisses and a little poem.* CHRISTY *is painting with the aid of a bicycle lamp. Outside is a full moon. He is concentrating. It is difficult to paint the blue in the eyes.* CHRISTY *takes the brush in his mouth and with a huge effort paints a dot of blue. Off screen we hear the voice of* SHEILA.

> SHEILA
> Ah, don't.
> *(Giggle)*
> Brendan, stop. Not here. If
> me da hears us there will
> be murder.

EXT. STREET. NIGHT.
They move into the shadow as CHRISTY *goes back to his painting.*

INT. CHILDREN'S BEDROOM. NIGHT.
He paints the romantic scene in contrast to the occasional noise from below.

> SHEILA
> Not here, Brendan. Later.

CHRISTY *can't concentrate. One of his brothers snores in his sleep.* CHRISTY *shines the lamp round the room. There seem to be about ten children, boys and girls, all asleep in the room.* CHRISTY *knocks off the lamp and lies down.*

INT. CHILDREN'S BEDROOM. NIGHT.
CHRISTY *is awake. Outside the moon. Downstairs there is a row between* MRS BROWN *and* SHEILA. *We can hear* MRS BROWN *shout, 'Are you a good girl?'* SHEILA *replies 'I am, I am.'*
Close on: CHRISTY *wide awake, listening. We hear the sound of the door open.* SHEILA *comes into the room. She stands in the window looking out. She starts to take off her clothes. When she gets to her slip and her undergarments she starts to rub her hands all over her body.* CHRISTY *watches her. Slowly we hear his breathing getting heavier.* SHEILA *stops and looks at him.*

Figure 3.1   Daniel Day-Lewis in *My Left Foot* © Granada/Miramax/RGA

SHEILA
Are you OK? God, you're sweating, Christy.
Are you sick? Look at the moon, Christy,
isn't it gorgeous? Go to sleep, Christy.

The essential images in this sequence evoke both mood and setting and also underpin the meaning of the scene. Love and lust, romance and reality, innocence and experience are juxtaposed, just as the moon shining down on the lovers (also depicted in Christy's picture) is off-set by a very down-to-earth bicycle lamp which later casts a different light on love and romance when it reveals a room full of sleeping children. Although there is an obvious link between the two, the latter is an image a long way removed from two lovers floating through space and time, oblivious to reality.

A key question about both characters' attitudes is expressed visually in this sequence. What light do these characters see themselves and each other in – the soft romantic silvery moonlight or the far less attractive, functional lamplight? As the sequence concludes we see that Sheila – who is clearly not quite the good girl she claims to be when pressed by her mother – cannot conceive of Christy as sexual, thinking instead he must be sick. For his part, Christy watching Sheila relive her most recent memories standing in the moonlight, can't avoid experiencing his sexuality, and another side of himself, quite at odds with the artistic romancer so caught up in the painting. Moreover we see Christy unable to sleep, and in several ways this sequence is about the idea of awakening: romantic and artistic passion awakened in Christy, sexual passion in Sheila, as well as the sexual stirrings later awakened in Christy by Sheila's sensual delight.

Starting with an idealised picture of how Christy thinks love should be, his Chagall-like painting, and moonlight shining down on the lovers, we move into a sexualised version of the same, in which Christy can no longer immerse himself in innocent fantasy: ironically, where *he's* concerned, Sheila cannot believe in anything other than her brother's innocence.

There is a conscious selectivity at work here, with the writer pulling together images which bounce off each other to produce absorbing and ironic contrasts. The whole sequence pictures a complex, contradictory set of feelings and perceptions, which contrast strongly with the idealised simplicity of Christy's painting, with its very own moon and heart. It is this process of getting just the imagery and action you need to express both mood and meaning, whilst clearly advancing the story, which can be so valuable to pursue. In the quoted sequence nothing has been included accidentally.

When broken down to its essentials, this sequence relies on a simple set of images (all of which naturally belong to the real-life setting being depicted) played off one against the other. In just the same way I'd encourage you to let your idea unfold from its nucleus, so take those images which occur to you automatically and work with them. Rather than artificially 'posing' characters in artificially contrived settings to demonstrate an idea you've had of how the meaning might go, let your day-dreaming take you into likely and natural scenarios. In just the same way dreams present themselves to us, so the essential images of what you want to write will also, given space, do exactly the same. The knack, the craft worth developing, lies in how to spot which of those images can be turned to a story teller's advantage, and in then combining both instinct and intellect to work out how best to achieve your goal.

Description and detail

It's essentials you're after and not needless detail. It's the job of a director or a design team to give a script interpretation and particular visual expression: so there's no need to specify aspects of wardrobe or set design *unless* they have a directly relevant bearing on the story. So, at first glance, the set-up below might seem too detailed.

INT. MAGGIE HAMBLIN'S OFFICE. 9.15 A.M.

The ambience is cool. Pot plants and personal touches abound. Mellow music issues from her CD drive as MAGGIE, typically casually attired, reclines, feet up on edge of desk, jots on a pad. A perfunctory rap on the door and without waiting ADRIAN appears, like Mr Punch, in the doorway. A split-second in which the curl of his lip betrays the distaste he harbours for MAGGIE's holiday-like style. Unruffled she slowly looks up as he puts his snarl back in its kennel.

However, this scene is the start of a training video all about personal presentation, and both dress and demeanour are directly relevant to the plot. If this were not the case there certainly would not be a need to go to town on specifics. A briefer, more general description would have been fine. As I've already said there is some merit in conjuring the mood of a scene or a setting. Done well this can enhance the readability of a script, convey essential elements in the drama of your scene and help intensify engagement with the story. However, try to do this economically, and keep your mind on assembling a series of images which, by their simple progression, tell the story in such a way that it holds the interest.

Shots

It is ironic that to write well the action must unfold vividly in the mind's eye of the writer, and yet at the same time, there is no need to convey the specifics of that vision unless they are of direct and relevant bearing to the story. That said, the screenwriter does need to write setting and action expressing them as shots. As far as the writer is concerned, shots are simply separate episodes on camera. These can be static and momentary in duration, or can develop and cover an expanse of time and action. As I've already suggested, I don't recommend too close an interest in specifying *types* of shot or transitions between them; that is the business of a director. However, there may be moments when you are convinced of the proximity (or distance) of the action and may want to indicate that in the way you write the shot. Then again, you may want to underline where you want the centre of attention to be, and that is perfectly appropriate.

Generally speaking, the convention is that each shot is written as a separate paragraph. In a montage – a rapid accumulation of shots to build a particular mood or meaning – each shot is given a separate line, often without the need for accompanying scene headings.

Visualising dialogue-heavy drama

Aristotle identified the importance of visualising drama as you write it in *The Poetics*:

> When constructing plots and working them out complete with their linguistic expression, one should so far as possible visualize what is happening. By envisaging things very vividly in this way, as if one were actually present at the events themselves, one can find out what is appropriate, and inconsistencies are least likely to be overlooked.

The merits of this process are obvious enough when you're imagining and then writing down action. But what about when you're writing dialogue-intensive drama? This is often the case with television drama, TV being predominantly most effective as a close-up medium, that fact, by and large, still holding true even as domestic screens become grander in scale. Surely all that matters is that you hear what the characters have to say to each other and just leave it at that? Certainly it is vital to be able to hear the characters say what they would say, but in fact visualising the scene can also help with the business of hearing it.

Every interaction is a 'dance', and a valuable way of getting the dynamics in a scene right is to see that 'dance' in your mind's eye; indeed, a useful exercise can be to take a scene and imagine how it would unfold without words. How would the characters dance or mime their intent in a scene? Once you've seen this, you may get some very illuminating clues as to how to write the dialogue, and exactly what significant actions to incorporate.

There is an *overall* 'dance', in other words the business of the significant gestures one character makes to another in a scene, and then there is also the moment-to-moment handling of contact between characters which will also find its physical expression and which can also be usefully visualised by the writer as he builds the scene. I'll look at the second of these 'dances' in more detail in Chapter 6, and offer some close analysis on the way this springs from following the dramatic sense. For now, though, have a look at the following scene and start to see it in terms of a dance of pushing hands. There is an exercise actors do which derives from Tai Chi, in which they hold the tips of two bamboo sticks with their fingertips, one stick for each hand, whilst the other ends are held in just the same way by the character(s) with whom they are interacting. The sticks represent both the contact made between the characters and also the dynamic flow of energy in the scene. That is to say, who is driving or pushing the scene at any given moment, and who is maintaining or breaking that contact. So even within this seemingly static, sedentary scene, there is a physical flow of energy at work, an observable ebb and flow which can help dictate how it should go.

INT. THE TREMBLING TROUT. LUNCH-TIME.

ADRIAN brings a round of drinks back from the bar and puts them on the table.

ADRIAN

I tell you she's a waste of space.

ERIC says nothing, preferring to chew on a peanut. ADRIAN settles himself.

ADRIAN

Well, isn't she?

ERIC

(after a pause)

She's still new. She'll settle down.

ADRIAN

She's been with us six months.
That's not new any more. She's
had more than long enough to
learn the ropes.

ERIC

She has got the *two* of us to
look after.

ADRIAN

And falls woefully short of the
mark. Admit it, she's a downright
liability.

ERIC

I think that's putting it a bit
strongly.

ADRIAN

Is it? Has she done any of
those letters you gave her
two days ago? Or was that
a mirage I saw towering
over her comic?

ERIC

She is still a bit slow getting
things done.

ADRIAN

Slow. I've seen glaciers faster
than that girl.

ERIC

Look, at the end of the day
she *is* a secretary, isn't she?
She does know what she's
there for.

ADRIAN

Does she? I'm beginning to doubt

it. Look at that fiasco this morning.
Poor old Paul didn't know whether
he was coming or going, and
neither did I come to that.

ERIC
Yes – pity I had to dash off, or
I could most likely have sorted
things out.

ADRIAN
But that's my point, Eric. You
shouldn't have to. Neither of
us should. It's not our job to
sort her out. Supposedly quite
the reverse. No, she'll have to go.

ERIC
Let's talk to her, eh? A
friendly word.

ADRIAN
Why bother? It's a waste of breath.

ERIC
No, no. Let me try. I'm rather
good at this sort of thing.
Trust me.

Adrian's first line is clearly a continuation of an offensive he's already mounted. He is driving the scene at this point and is pushing Eric to agree to Bernice's dismissal. Eric yields, buying time, chewing on a nut. Visualised, you can see the bamboos pushing Eric back and then gently returning to neutral. Adrian pushes again. Eric holds his ground. Adrian continues to push. Eric pushes back a little, indicating Bernice's workload and so advancing an argument on Bernice's behalf. Adrian shoves back, dismissing the argument as useless. Eric holds his ground and Adrian brings in more evidence to back his case, pushing Eric back. Eric is pushed, admitting Bernice is a bit slow. Adrian presses home the advantage. Eric musters his energy and tries to hold his ground, appealing to Adrian's sense of reason. Adrian counters with yet more damning evidence drawn from that very morning. Eric is really pushed now and, in trying to push back, is blatant in his defence. Adrian pushes Eric again and is blatant in his offence – as far as he can see, Bernice will have to go. Ever so gently, Eric pushes back. Adrian withdraws energy, almost ready to break contact and let those invisible bamboos drop. Eric pushes gently forward to maintain the contact. That 'Trust me' suggests he has slowed Adrian's pull-out to a stand-still, and they are left at a point where Eric is gently pushing to maintain his newly-won edge. We assume Bernice is going to get a chance.

SEEING THE BIGGER DANCE: SENSING THE OVERALL DYNAMIC

If I have a picture of the dynamic of this scene played out, on a caricatured level, as a dance of melodramatic gesture, then Adrian advances on Eric almost threateningly, almost accusing Eric in place of Bernice. He points to a sheet of indictments perhaps even poking Eric in the chest with these. Eric backs off steadily, doing what he can to halt Adrian's progress. Finally, nearly backed into a corner, Eric tries to slip out to one side of Adrian, but Adrian immediately blocks his way, holds him in the corner, thrusts the indictment into his hand and produces a pen for Eric to sign the charge-sheet with. Eric won't take it, gently folds the charge-sheet. Adrian turns away, folding his arms in exasperation. Eric places a reassuring arm on Adrian's shoulder, and when he has his attention offers him back the charge-sheet. Finally Adrian meets his gaze, then reluctantly takes the paper back. Eric smiles and pats him on the shoulder. Adrian shakes his head. He can't believe he's agreed to this.

These physical pictures of the dance emerge as the scene gets written and match up to the objectives each of the characters has and to the emotional journeys they make. Adrian starts angry and with the objective of pressuring Eric to collude in dismissing Bernice. Eric starts the scene impassive, and beneath that anxious on Bernice's behalf. His objective, as it emerges, is to win a reprieve and make peace. He ends the scene openly happier as he has won the reprieve. Adrian has failed to fulfil his objective, to get Eric on his side, and in his defeat he turns first sulky and then sceptical.

So this 'ballet' takes the envisaged scene to an extreme, a procession of magnified, expressive gesture, as a means to track the true dynamic between the characters.

It's important to remember these exercises in imaginative choreography are only a means to an end. They help you form an internalized movie which you can then set down in words, *but* (and it is an important but) they are not *the* movie you are going to write. They are simply a means to an end. Compare the operatic/balletic quality of the bigger dance above, to the action which actually found its way into the finished scene. There was no thrusting of charge sheets, no backings into corners, no hands on shoulders. Adrian bought the round of drinks, Eric chewed a nut and shortly afterwards paused. That's all the writer ended up specifying. That moment of nut-chewing can be seen as a very scaled-down version of Eric backing into the corner (as described above), and indeed it's the appropriate scaling down (or up) of physical moments which will occur in the final piece you write. The 'dances' are no more than a complementary method to help in conjuring up the flow, and identify key, pivotal moments in the dynamic between your characters. As such, these are imaginative exercises undertaken for the writer's benefit alone. After that, it's going to be down to a director, crew and actors to do what they want to build visual interest in this scene in the acting, shooting and editing, whilst remaining faithful to the dynamic the writer has discovered and embedded in the lines he's written. Keeping eye-contact, and breaking eye-contact, may well take the place of larger gestures and could still be all the action that's needed.

I'm at pains to spell this last point out, since trouble can often flow from one of two directions when new writers set down a scene. The first common error is that there is no sense of a dance at all. There may be very little 'ping' and 'pong', as it were, and one character may get the lion's share of the words and action, whilst the other(s) are relegated to the role of stooge. But when there is to and fro, if the dance hasn't previously been summoned up, the scene will often sound like the characters are simply taking turns at speechifying the thread or the argument of the scene. Alternatively, where the dance – particularly the smaller dance of moment-by-moment contact – has been imagined and then *mistaken* for the movie proper, what can happen is that the writer will then try and transcribe every single moment of this imagined action, treating the characters (and by default, the actors and director) as marionettes. This can be a deadly inheritance for those charged with playing your lines, reducing them to the status of puppets. In a bid to make the process live for them, the actors and director may understandably abandon most if not all of what you've written.

SOME OTHER POINTS

You don't need to have characters storming around for there to be plenty of interest in what's going on between them. Indeed, too much action, too great a preoccupation with props, can be an irritating distraction from the real business of a scene. Also, as I pointed out in an earlier chapter, screenwriting has a hard time depicting detailed thought. That doesn't mean the audience isn't interested in working out what's going on inside characters' heads. On the contrary, in a well-written scene, an audience will be watching every moment to track what's unsaid and undone as well as what is made obvious.

In pieces written for studio recording, with the limitations of multi-camera recording, and the necessary compromises which are imposed by time, setting, lighting and coverage available for sound recording, scenes may often get a relatively static, talking-head sort of treatment. It is all the more important, then, that the inner life of the scene has been well and truly 'danced' in the writer's head so it can function well in a relatively constrained physical environment.

AVOIDING WRITING THE LOOK OF A SCENE

There are ways in which writers can busy themselves trying to write a scene from the outside in, as it were, at the expense of other vital considerations. This may simply show itself up as an irrelevant and ill-founded preoccupation with the visual style a piece is to be rendered in. I've certainly come across new writers with only the vaguest idea of what their piece is to be about, let alone how it actually goes, who confidently announce it should all be shot as wide-screen in black and white. Apart from a fatal confusion over what is the writer's and what is the director's domain, this kind of assertion is very much about the tail wagging the dog. How a piece unfolds is really far more to do with its inner life than any stylistic devices which you may find appealing. Moreover, believing you can usefully predicate the development of how a piece is to be written on what you conceive to be its 'look', is a fundamentally mistaken notion.

Then again, there are writers who have such a strong pull for a moment or an image that they put their story through all kinds of contortions to realise these *coups de cinéma*. Below is a brief outline example of the kind of thing I mean.

> A man sits impatiently in a long queue of traffic on the motorway. As time unfolds it becomes clear there has been an accident way up ahead of him and the emergency services are working hard to attend the scene of the crash. We keep cutting back to see more and more of the man's mounting impatience. (Note we do not see anything else in his car, and he does nothing other than get ever more fretful.) At the crash site, struggle as they might, fire crews cannot release an injured woman. They start to consider options and produce cutting gear. Back with the man in his car, we now realise his pregnant wife is in the backseat, and she chooses this moment to go into labour. The man starts to pay attention to her. Back at the crash site, the fire crews have cut a line down the length of the crushed car's roof. In the other car, its rear near-side door open, the woman is about to give birth, assisted by her husband. Back at the crashed car, the fire crew use a jack to prise open the roof of the car and reveal the trapped woman. In the other car, the woman gives birth. At the crash site, the fire crew pulls an unconscious woman out through the roof. Back at the other car, mother, father and child are full of joy. Back at the crash site, the dead woman's head is covered over with a sheet, the urgency giving way to despondency.

This is a good example of one envisaged big moment so entrancing the author that he forgets to attend to some vital questions such as whose story it is and how the plot might more probably unfold. The writer is so intent on getting the cut between the roof being prised open to release the woman, and the other woman giving birth to her baby, that he loses sight of how best to tell the story. If the man is intent on getting his wife to hospital because she is imminently about to give birth why does he make no attempt to summon emergency help or to let others know what's going on? Even more strikingly, why does he not even so much as look at his wife or ask her how she's doing? Why does no-one else around react when it becomes obvious what's going on for the man and his wife?

I'm not saying that there wouldn't have been a way to tell this story quite credibly, making it clearly the father-to-be's story and building all kinds of mounting urgency. What I'm pointing out is that the writer is so busy contriving matters so as to get to the central ironic contrast that he neglects to name his central characters, motivate them properly, follow their credible actions and reactions moment-by-moment, relate one emergency directly to the other emergency, nor usefully involve any bystanders. In other words the writer's eye is so fixed on the ironic (admittedly eye-catching) visual parallel at its heart, that he doesn't care much about how he gets there. He pays his story as little attention as the man in it pays his pregnant wife.

I suppose this is all by way of saying *do* care about the whole piece you're writing, the inner and the outer, and attend to its telling in an integrous manner. How much *more* effective that big moment would have been if our hero had clearly been concerned with his partner's welfare right from the outset, had borrowed a mobile phone, rung for help, and set off a secondary action by some of those same emergency services, battling to reach his car in time to help. It's when big visual moments are delivered *at the expense* of credible cause and effect story telling (entirely appropriate to this piece), and are also spun around characters we are given no reason to care about, that the writer, beguiled by a moment of visual wit and impact, has neglected his real work and sold us well short.

Keeping the balance between form and content is always important in writing, and never more so than in writing for the screen. There are all kinds of writers: those who are thwarted or wannabe directors, intent on achieving visual impact, never mind how inappropriate that might truly be to the drama; there are writers who have no aspirations to direct but who feel duty bound to make their drama more eye-catching, and busily set about devising the exotic, extraordinary or extraneous just to give the director opportunity; then there are those who are so tied up with what the characters are doing that they lose sight of what we can see them doing. My key pieces of advice would be: write appropriate visuals for the medium you are aiming a script at. Cinema thrives on the large-scale, and the landscape; television favours the close-up and the domestic. Having said that, of course, there is always room for cross-over. Also, hold the balance between form and content –

don't let setting, action or visual incident outstrip or overwhelm the dramatic heart of the moments its there to enhance and support. Finally, and most importantly, *with your mind's eye watch every moment of every scene you are writing, and keep watching closely throughout.*

Exercises

1   Using the techniques you've practised so far, devise two stories which will unfold in parallel, for the most part independent of one another, and yet have one or possibly two scenes in common. For example, the extract from *Some Mother's Son* starts for both main characters on the drive into work. Make sure that your stories cross at some point. Again, try and do this with no (or very little) dialogue.

2   Pick a scene involving two characters from one of the pieces you've already planned. Now write this as a scene with action and dialogue. Before you write the scene, try visualising its 'bigger dance' and writing a description of that.

3   If you have a group, copy and share all the work. With the dialogue scenes, cast the parts and choose someone other than one of your characters to read out the action. Be careful to just give the parts a straightforward read. Funny accents and over-acting can be quite needless and very distracting, and sometimes cover people's nervousness. Don't be led astray! On the other hand do get into your parts. Take time to discuss all of your scripts.

4

Character: the 'Who?' and the 'How?' of characters in action

Screen stories, just like other dramas, flow from both plot and character.

The question of whether character or plot is the more important element to attend to in writing a drama is one which gets a frequent airing. Aristotle was in no doubt that the answer lay with the unfolding action, whilst others have argued the case that, without developed character, you cannot know how your story is going to unfold:

> Every great literary work grew from character, even if the author planned the action first. As soon as his characters were created they took precedence, and the action had to be reshaped to suit them.
>
> (Egri 1960)

So which should you deal with first? I think neither plot nor character develops in complete isolation from the other. They have a symbiotic relationship and one way or another we actually start with both; the one inextricably acts on the other, and both have to be understood to find the best way forward for your drama.

What happens to a character is one matter; circumstances throw up significant events which impact on your protagonist. Your protagonist's reaction will depend, in large part, on what makes him tick. How do you know that? How do you avoid the pitfall of deciding how your story goes and then manipulating your characters like marionettes whichever way you have to in order to deliver your pre-determined plot? Put simply, events don't just happen to people, they also unfold along certain lines because of who those people are, and more crucially when writing drama, because of *how* they are in the world; this, in turn, springs from all the characteristics and experiences which make them who they are. Moreover dramas don't occupy themselves with everyday events; they are about characters facing the extraordinary and characters acting and reacting under pressure –

characters who in a sense are *not* themselves, and by the same token also really are.

So where best to begin – plot, character or both? As I've already suggested, it is inevitable that you will have to tangle with both aspects, and my feeling is that both plot and character are subject to a necessary process of clarification. There are those who favour getting a highly-developed picture of their characters before pitching them into a plot. The work of deviser–directors such as Mike Leigh is of particular interest in this regard. The development of characters is at the centre of the process he guides, and only when his actors have a solid grasp on the characters they have individually developed in considerable depth are these characters brought into relationship with each other. The narrative unfolds from a mixture of the consequent improvisations and Leigh's interventions.

Then there are others who like to have a developed idea of where their story might be going before considering character in greater depth. In fact, whichever seems to be centre stage in your mind as you develop a narrative, there is no avoiding the need to clarify both; consciously or not, your characters and the story events which they are involved in are subject to an ongoing process of clarification as each moment of your drama unfolds. In the end there are no short cuts; if you shirk either job, leaving your characters thin and undeveloped, your story events unsurprising and improbable, or fail to weave the drama from the interaction of both character and plot, then your piece is bound not to engage an audience as well as it might.

CHARTING CHARACTERS' JOURNEYS

Once you have the outline of your story. It can be very useful to begin to chart the emotional progress of your central character(s), breaking shifts of feeling into distinct, successive phases. Later in the book I look in some detail at how scenes build into sequences and how those sequences can usefully be seen as the major building blocks of your drama. In fact this sequence approach was once the traditional approach to constructing feature films, each script being seen as an assembly of eight distinct sequences. Defining and describing between eight and twelve broad-stroke emotional steps for your character (interestingly, perhaps, the universal monomyth or hero's journey mentioned a little later traditionally has twelve stages of action) can provide a spine to your evolving story and ensure that you keep your character's/characters' emotional journey(s) in motion and alive throughout your story.

It so happens that there are some observable, common cycles of emotion and patterns of behaviour psychologists have picked up on which can be a useful reference point when mapping the emotional journeys of characters in

naturalistic dramas told in the classical manner. So if, say, we were to consider a story based on a character who has suffered loss or bereavement then
there are distinct shifts of emotion and behaviour identifiably attached to the
process of anyone going through the normal cycle of grief and mourning.
These are stability, immobility, denial, anger, bargaining, depression, testing
and acceptance. In real life these phases, when neither suppressed nor abnor-
mally amplified, unfold over a period between eighteen months and two
years. In a feature-length drama the journey (or parts of it) will of course be
compressed into between one and a half to two hours. None the less those
eight phases (elaborated from the five stage grief cycle identified by Elizabeth
Kübler-Ross in *On Death and Dying*) can provide very helpful, navigable land-
marks, and a progressive broad framework to fill out with finer detail.

So, for example, if we consider *Truly, Madly, Deeply* (Anthony Minghella), a
story centring on love, loss and grieving, very early on in the proceedings
there is an interchange between Nina and Sandy, her widower boss at the
translation agency, in which he voices his, and others' concern that she isn't
going out at all socially, isn't inviting people round, looks terrible, and checks
whether it's her feelings for her dead partner Jamie which are holding her in
this paralysed place. She acknowledges his encouragement to stop isolating
herself but when he asks her out for a drink says 'Sandy I can't, I can't. I just
can't'. A little later we see her with her therapist, very distressed, sobbing and
describing how most of all she is simply angry with Jamie for not being
around any more. Also, early in the drama she is having the infestation of rats
in her terrible flat dealt with, and the place is full of the actual smell of dead
rats, a fact remarked on by her sister Claire when she comes to visit with
Nina's nephew Harry. During that visit Claire asks if there's any chance of
Harry borrowing Jamie's cello for the lessons he is just starting with. Nina
freaks out incredulous at her sister's insensitivity. 'It's practically all I've got
of him. It is him, it is him. It's like asking me to give you his body'. We can
see the grip this phase of the grieving, denial, still has on her, and it's almost
immediately following the shock of this request and Nina's violent reaction
to it that Jamie's ghost appears for the first time; a graphic depiction of the
level of denial still at work. Faithful to the emotions which would naturally
attend the loss of a deeply loved partner nevertheless Minghella poetically
shuffles and dramatically compresses those feelings round a little, partly to
avoid becalming the protagonist's journey in the deadly passivity of depression, and partly as a response to the need in any story to accelerate the
narrative process. So towards the end of the film when we see Nina's row
with Jamie before she tells him and his ghostly friends to go, it does equate to
a phase of testing out letting go of the grief, which Nina is almost ready to do,
poised as she is to reinvest in life and start a relationship with her new love

Mark. The final moment of Jamie, overcome with his own grief and supported by his ghostly friends, watching Nina go off with Mark underlines both his and her acceptance of both her ability and need to come to terms with his death and move on.

In naturalistic story-telling there will often be a close relationship between a character's actions and their unfolding emotions. So, for example, after that row with sister Claire over the cello and left on her own, Nina sits holding (embracing) the cello, before moving over to the piano to play her part of a much loved Bach duet, shortly after which the ghost of Jamie appears to her. What is noticeable is the organic flow of one action to another, clearly motivated as they are by Nina's haunting love and vivid longing for dead Jamie.

Truly, Madly, Deeply happens to provide a particularly apt example to put alongside the grief cycle mentioned above. But 'the change curve', extrapolated from the same model and applied to a much wider spectrum of events, provides a comparable possible template. The movements in question are shock, depression, anger, resignation, acceptance and understanding. Whether either of these models provides a recognisable resonance with your story or not, it's really important to acknowledge that any dramatic story will involve change and the process of change will have its distinct, particular phases. Those phases of emotional movement will relate to the activity or inactivity of a character as they pursue what they want. Where a story is being told in a strongly naturalistic vein then it's quite appropriate to observe those phases of emotional movement very closely just as they would relate to a unique living individual, and not least because the organic emotional unfolding of your central character(s) will help dictate their actions. On the other hand, where a story inhabits the realms of the mythic and the archetypal, or the comedic and the caricatured, the question of closely observed emotionality becomes more blurred, and may seem to disappear altogether at times or figure as of considerably less importance certainly for some of the characters; that said, it is nearly always possible to chart a character's progress against generalised feelings of hope, fear or their opposites. In any case it can still be really helpful to construct a skeletal core to your story and your central character's journey, perhaps building that progression more upon the unfolding stages of action than on the developing emotional process. With some such stories the observable steps of the hero's journey may provide you with a useful structure. (These are described very clearly in *The Writer's Journey* by Chris Vogler.)

And though there may be a huge gulf between a strongly naturalistic story and one that is firmly in the realms of the archetypal, it is also true that there can be very strong resonance between the naturalistic and the archetypal and hence it can be really interesting at some point in the process to take your 'real' story and measure its development against the stages of the hero's journey.

It can also be really helpful in seeing both the bigger picture of how you are building your central character's journey within a drama – as well as in understanding how the smaller parts of that story relate to the whole – to look at three separate elements side by side – emotion, action and pursuit of objective. When charted in three parallel columns one or two facts become clear at once; you will see very quickly where your character is standing still in any of those departments and know whether that aspect is playing effectively or is quite simply stagnant and in need of further attention. So, whilst it's okay for a two dimensional, tragic-comic cartoon character to obsess continuously over a pencil-point, that level of monomania will not fit with other kinds of character or story, and will simply fail to convince an audience or enlist them in an empathic journey. Use of that chart will also help you see whether you are missing necessary shifts of emotion or have emotional non-sequiturs at play, and raise questions about whether you are building your character's journey inorganically, from the outside in; then you should also be able to tell from this chart whether you are needlessly repeating an emotional step or a building block of action; and finally you should be able to see the relative importance and prominence of those different elements of both storytelling and character development (emotion, action, pursuit of objective), both overall and at different points in your developing script. Working this way, whatever the story you're building, you should be able to identify *something* going on in all of those three departments. I want to stress that I'm not offering the idea of working this way (nor either of the particular models mentioned) as a prescriptive formula, rather as a potentially helpful strategy to assist in paying detailed attention to the business of installing dynamism in your character(s) and their story whilst also allowing you a continuous overview of your unfolding process. Certainly for many writers it is far easier and less time-consuming to attend to gaps and problems when a principal character and their story is still in outline form than it is after they are well into the detailed writing of the script and are much more closely engaged with and attached to what they've already set down.

Incidentally, the chart for character development included in this chapter is based on my analysis of *About Schmidt* (Alexander Payne and Jim Taylor). I do want to stress that it is my take on how I see Schmidt journeying and I can of course have no idea whether these writers, or indeed Anthony Minghella, used any such device in their writing process.

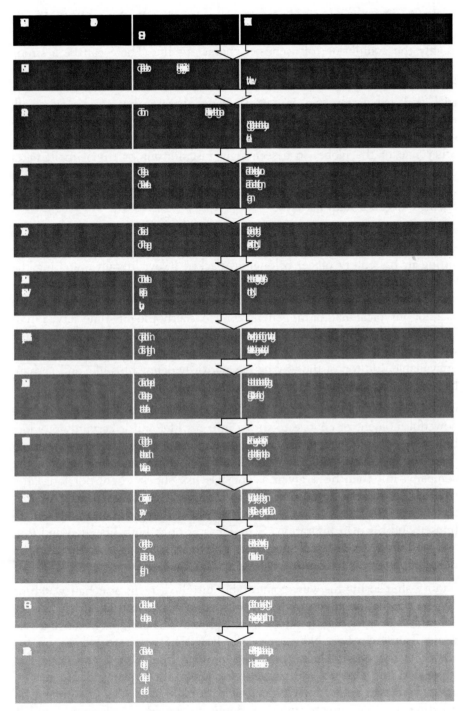

Figure 4.1   Chart of character development

In the definition of what makes up a story, offered earlier in the book, I mentioned the fact that something extraordinary must happen to unsettle thoroughly the equilibrium of a chosen character's life. There can be a strong temptation to deal in huge, unusual events or gestures when thinking about how to unsettle a character's life or indeed resolve their conflict or period of trial and tribulation. So it's worth remembering that *apparently* small, mundane events can have momentous effects. Just as it is proposed in chaos theory that a butterfly fluttering its wings can cause extreme weather on the other side of the globe, so a seemingly insignificant or trivial moment of change can later have huge repercussions. Conversely, sometimes it can be completely appropriate and effective, metaphorically speaking, to subject a character to an instant landslide.

About Schmidt is, just like *Truly, Madly, Deeply*, also a story of coming to terms with loss. The film begins with insurance actuary Warren Schmidt sitting in his empty office, belongings packed away, literally watching the clock on the wall as the last moments of his last working day tick away. At exactly five he gets up and leaves. As the story unfolds we see Schmidt shown as a not untypical man of his generation. He is a thoroughly time-served individual, heavily identified with the company he has spent all his working life with, institutionally married, both to employer and wife, and emotionally unavailable. On top of the way he has narrowly defined his life, and perhaps because of that fact, he is in any case socially awkward.

Given Schmidt's history then, the every day fact of retirement is quite a powerful moment of change to throw into his life, and it certainly provides him with a deep if recognisably common challenge as he struggles to unhitch from his first love and long-term source of status and belonging - the company. But then he is given a landslide-like shock when, not long after retiring, he returns home one day to discover that other beacon of predictability - his wife - has dropped dead whilst doing the cleaning. Left to himself and his own limitations Schmidt is at once both liberated and lost, and we follow his ill-fated, sometimes poignant, sometimes embarrassing or ridiculous attempts to connect, belong and find purpose.

Shortly after losing his wife, comfortably installed in his armchair watching TV, he watches an advert inviting sponsorship of children in Africa. We see Schmidt take stock and then pick up the phone. The child he fosters is a very young Tanzanian boy, Ndugu, and the letters he writes to Ndugu, on the advice of the charitable organisation, provide him with a vital source of expression and also act as a catalyst for important journeying. He sets off across Nebraska bound for Colorado with a half-baked idea of stopping his daughter Jeannie's forthcoming wedding to waterbed salesman Randall, whom Schmidt dislikes and privately rates as 'a nimcompoop'. The trip becomes in part a pilgrimage to his own childhood and youth as Schmidt goes in search of the house he grew up in and visits his college fraternity. As he relates all of this to Ndugu in the letters he writes him, we also see Schmidt start to reconnect with his own younger self.

The stay in Colorado is ill-fated. Jeannie's mother-in-law to be, Roberta, offers Schmidt a fulsome welcome (and more!) as do the wider family. Judgemental and disparaging towards them all, it becomes clear Schmidt cannot begin to cope with intimate warmth and closeness.

Jeannie is unswerving in her resolve to marry Randall, angered by her father's machinations and attempts at manipulation and hurt by the painful, difficult relationship she has with him, which on this occasion culminates in his lacklustre, polite and perfunctory wedding speech. This ends by damning with faint praise both his son-in-law and the match, before Schmidt instantly scoots off to seek refuge in the toilets.

He hightails it back to Omaha, the voiced-over letter to Ndugu relating the fact that he feels a failure as a father and believes he has no purpose left in life. Opening his mail he finds a letter from Ndugu written by one of the nuns who cares for him. Ndugu thanks him and hopes 'you are happy in your life'. As he reads the words and looks at the simple stick-man drawing of himself holding Ndugu's hand, the tears trickle down Schmidt's cheeks, and for the first time in the film (in one of those butterfly rather than landslide moments) we see him really feel his loss and at the same time make a genuine connection both with himself and this little boy in a far off country. It is a muted moment that heralds the possibility of profound change and so its power is huge and undeniable. It is an ending that illustrates very well how misguided it can be, as many new (and not so new!) writers do, to give into the temptation to end a story with a grand, melodramatic gesture, or an obviously extraordinary event. Such a move can be quite extraneous and counterproductive, springing as it often does from a fundamental lack of conviction that seemingly small shifts within a recognisable normality can provide everything a story needs to achieve powerful dramatic impact.

Sometimes, if not always, in a naturalistic story, it is a combination of factors which are going to make for an emotionally powerful story, but always it is to do with the impact of the journey travelled on your chosen character and hence, by proxy, on your audience; and though there can be nothing more commonplace than bereavement, especially for older characters, dealing with loss can, dramatically speaking, be the making of them. Conversely, the arrival of a sudden gift or of a lost or hitherto unknown and significant person into a character's life, can also provide great dramatic potential. *Secrets and Lies* (Mike Leigh) being one such story, where a mother's shock at being discovered by and reunited with the mixed-race daughter she gave up at birth has major repercussions for both that mother and her family. So no need, necessarily, to reach for the unlikely, or the unusual, let alone the esoteric or scarcely credible either by way of presenting a character's circumstances or as means of disrupting them. It is *how* the character deals with the disruption that we are going to travel with and be moved by. But before we can know what that will mean for any given character we do also need to know quite a lot about *who* that character is.

KNOWING THE 'WHO?' AND THE 'HOW?' OF YOUR CHARACTERS

I've already suggested the great value of working with others in developing your writing skills. This can be particularly helpful when you are learning to develop characters. Below is a three-part group exercise aimed at developing and getting to know your characters. Do this exercise in a group of at least three or four.

The 'Who?': building a biography

Over the period of a few days or a week start to spend time individually thinking of a specific character. At this stage you may or may not have the roughest outline of story they belong to rattling around in your head. You certainly don't need one; for now, simply concentrate on the character. When you feel comfortable with the facts you've decided on, write them down in note-form as part of an accumulating profile. These facts should cover anything and everything. I can't emphasise enough the importance of feeling comfortable with your choices. For example, newish writers often find it very difficult to settle on a name which seems to fit their character. Cast around until you've found the name which really does seem to fit naturally, and at the same time don't feel you have to go to extraordinary imaginative lengths to find some special handle for your character. As you work, concentrate on those characteristics or experiences which suggest themselves easily to you, and don't force the process. You may find yourself thinking about people you know or whom you've met and this can be a useful source of inspiration, though I'd suggest you steer clear of lifting a character from life wholesale; this is not only a potential matter of legal sensitivity (should the character ever be published or broadcast) but it can quite simply blinker your creative options. What you want to establish at this stage is everything which could be observable about a character: ethnic background, age, gender, height, how they dress, where they live, where they work, where they shop, where they holiday, hobbies, family, relationships, children, friends; then you're after the character's significant life experiences: background, family history, education, friends, relationships, past illnesses, accidents, beliefs, hopes and ambitions, triumphs and disasters, likes and dislikes.

Don't worry about covering everything under the sun in minute detail, but do get to the stage of feeling you've covered the ground fairly well. Between times, sit and refer to your notes and make sure that you do feel what you've put down is right for your character. Don't be afraid of rethinking and making changes.

Just a cautionary note here. When some new writers set out they feel a need to install a dark secret into their character's life to make it more dramatic: it is as though they don't trust their character to be interesting enough unless they have done (or had done to them) something really bad, massively heroic or eye-catching. It's really worth avoiding this temptation and trusting in the fact your character will have lots of dramatic potential without any such 'special' history attached to them.

In the process of building your character profile, you may well start to get an idea of other characters who are close to the one you've chosen to explore. Simply note what you want about these significant others, but don't so over-whelm yourself with information that you start to lose the feel of what your chosen character is like.

Other strategies for envisaging your character
You may find it valuable to think about whether your character is more of an introvert than an extrovert. It may also help you to think about whether your character is, typically, high energy or low energy, and whether they are men-tally active or physically active, emotionally expressive or emotionally inhib-ited, optimistic or pessimistic. Are they open hearted and generous of spirit or mean minded and cynical? Are they sitting on a lot of anger? Do they need to be in control? Do they have a need to win? Do they find it hard to say 'no' in life? Are they highly imaginative? Are they literal? Are they practical and organised or are they happily chaotic? Are they fearful? Are they very gregari-ous? Are they easily overwhelmed? Do they finish what they start, or not? Do they get dogmatic and stick to their guns rigidly in an argument? Can they stand their ground in a conflict or are they a push-over?

Characters' physicality
It can really help to get a mental picture of your character's physical type and presence. Are they able-bodied? If not, what is their disability and how does that affect them?

Are they long and thin, short and fat, inflated round the shoulder and chest or collapsed? Do they have a piercing gaze, a soft, warm look to their eyes? Are they strong in the jaw, or quite weak chinned? If you think this kind of detail is unimportant I suggest you start observing people's physical types and see how it relates to their energy and typical patterns of behaviour. You may be surprised to notice some definite correlations.

How does your character move? If you watch people carefully you'll see that it's often quite possible to detect a predominant manner of moving and speaking. Exaggerate these a little in your mind and you may find it fits in one of these categories: dabbers, flickers, pushers, pullers, gliders, punchers and slashers. Translated back into questions, is your character tentative, impulsive, insistent, demanding, composed or aggressive?

Again, don't feel you have to nail every single aspect of your character's physicality down, but do as much as feels useful to you at this stage, and in any case do start to watch other people more closely.

If you're wondering how much value there is in getting such a clear picture of your character when all you're going to do is end up expressing them as words on a page which will then, perhaps, be embodied by an actor chosen by a director, I'd suggest the process is a very worthwhile one: what it will help you to do is to give each character you write *individual definition*. A frequent failing in new writers' work is that their characters don't seem to live and breathe as individuals distinct from the other characters alongside them. All too often it's possible to cover the names of the characters over and then find it impossible to know for sure who is saying the lines in question. The process of envisaging so many different aspects and specifics about your character will help you to avoid this trap.

Once you've compiled a character profile in note-form and have had time to get to know your character, it's time to meet up again with the rest of the group doing this exercise with you.

Hot-seating your characters

A very familiar exercise to many actors, this entails putting a chair in front of but at a little distance from the group. Each of you takes a turn at sitting in this 'hot-seat' and being questioned as your character by the rest of the group. This may sound a little daunting to anyone who has not experienced drama or theatre exercises, but in my experience of using this exercise with many would-be writers, any initial nervousness tends to be very rapidly and easily overcome, and people do find the whole experience really valuable in their writing process. It's worth observing a few guidelines.

Keep to a fixed period of, say, 15 minutes for each character.

If you are the one being hot-seated then don't have your notes with you to refer to, although you might want to refresh your memory before you start.

Whilst you are sitting in the hot-seat, you can only be the character and not yourself.

Be the character rather than play at being the character. There can be a great temptation to play-act, to ham up your character rather than doing your very best to portray the character you've built up on paper. It's not important to convey all the external facets of a character (to make your voice exactly like that of an old person, or little boy). It is far more important to get to the essence of how your character is and tell the others all about him or her from that place. It's the knack of *being yourself whilst being someone else* that you want to acquire, and which can help you so much in getting to know the characters you want to write.

Immerse yourself in the experience, and act and react as the character would. If you feel your character would not volunteer information on a certain subject then be true to that impulse.

Stay in character. Don't let anyone's embarrassment or resistance (including your own) pull you away from being the character at all times once you're in the hot-seat. The more continuously and convincingly you can do this, the more you will be met with a convinced and engaged response. Obviously this hot-seating exercise is an artificial situation: if you are male but playing a female character or vice versa, or if you are asked to describe your character's appearance and it's a long way from being like your own, there's going to be a temptation for the others to react to the apparent absurdity of the situation and laugh it all off. If this happens, don't worry, but do get back into the exercise properly as soon as you can. Once you are used to the exercise you'll find such lapses tend not to happen at all. Do remember this is an exercise calling for the sustained use of your imagination – just like writing.

For those asking questions of the hot-seated character, try asking about more than just the factual. Ask how the character feels about this or that; by doing this you give them a chance to flesh out the mental and emotional realms of their creation. (If by some chance you do not have a group of people you can try this with, maybe a friend or member of the family would help you out with the hot-seating.)

Feedback

When each person has finished their stint in the hot-seat, take a few minutes to gather some two-way feedback. Those questioning will have gathered a lot of information, and they should also have gathered some ideas about what this character is like. This will have been deduced from the factual data and also the way in which the character has reacted and responded. Are they funny, or deadly serious; open, or quite secretive; courageous, or rather timid; clever or stupid? How do they come across on the face of it all? What do you think might be going on underneath and why do you think that? Share these first impressions with each other and compare notes with the person whose character you've just hot-seated. Do your impressions line up with what s/he had intended? In any case, how did the person in question feel while they were being the character? Above and beyond the pure facts of a character's life, the questions of *how* a character comes across in the world and what is going on for them beneath the surface, are crucial ones.

Although we need to know at least a little (and more usefully a lot) about *who* a character is in order to start writing them, dramatically it is *how* they act, react and interact in the world which will really tell us what to write. *How* will my character be in the world at any given moment? That's the question you need to be able to answer to write the character convincingly.

Continue with the exercise until everyone has been hot-seated. You will now have several budding characters and there are two very worthwhile writing exercises which you can try to take what you have developed further.

Write a monologue in which your character muses on and tells an imaginary audience all about something which happened to them. Concentrate on getting us to understand what your character is like from the incidents they choose to relate, and the way they relate them. Avoid letting your character make open statements describing the simple truth about themselves. So if they are genuinely a happy-go-lucky sort of character, don't have them appear and say, 'I've always been a happy-go-lucky sort of person'. Illustrate the fact in their attitude to events and the actions and reactions they choose to make.

You may find it very useful to have a look at one or two of Alan Bennett's *Talking Heads* monologues.

When you're happy with the finished version of your writing get together with your group again and read it for them: better still, get someone else in the group to read (it's always illuminating to get some distance between you and your work), and then let the others tell you what they got from the piece, what they thought about how your character came across. Avoid saying anything about your intention until you've heard what they've got to say. It could well be that they don't get everything you've intended to get across to them, but the truth is they will have got just as much as they got – no more, and no less. That's an indisputable fact, and one which can usefully send you back to the drawing board.

PUTTING YOUR CHARACTERS TOGETHER

Another valuable exercise after hot-seating individual characters is to invent credible scenarios in which two or more of the characters you've started to invent meet and interact. Again, don't feel the need to choose an extreme situation or to make something terribly significant happen in some crunch moment between your characters. It can be interesting to find out how a character carries on in a simple situation, with someone they don't, as yet, know well. For example a young woman, Jean, who really wants a boyfriend but who seems to have bad luck in relationships might have a job as a sales assistant in a department store. Another character, Sally, who has just found out she is pregnant by the partner she loves very much comes in to look for clothes. How much do they find out about each other? How does one respond to the other? It could be that the incident would pass off on the surface as completely unremarkable: then again, Jean might really draw her out so as to try for a share of the shopper's happiness by proxy. It depends on what you've found out about your characters, and what they would *credibly* do and say given how they are in the world in general, and then this situation in particular.

Just a couple of further notes on this. Remember the power of action and reaction: your characters do not have to speak all the time. A silence can be quite eloquent. Stillness can have great power.

Don't try and handle too many characters in a scene all at once. When you're starting out, a two- or three-handed scene can be quite enough to manage. Try a two-handed scene with a third character perhaps coming in for just a bit of the time. Only write for as many characters as you feel comfortable with.

You may prefer to put one of the hot-seated characters into play with a character (or characters) they already know very well. As long as you do enough preliminary work on the other character(s) to know how *they* are in the world that's fine and will, of course, allow for a different level of potential contact.

When you've finished writing your scripts, then meet up again with the others, and take turns at casting your scripts and reading them out. Try casting men as women, sometimes, and vice versa. Afterwards take time to gather feedback and, as ever, do this in a supportive, constructive manner. Always try to offer detailed criticism. 'I think that's really good' is of limited value. Try to say what exactly it is that you like about a script and why you like it. Open up a truly constructive, creative dialogue with each other.

Whilst sharing your work with others committed to supporting each other's development as writers can be invaluable, another benefit of working like this is that, in time, it refines your abilities to internalise these exercises and enables you to become your very own workshop: as well as working at the level of the imaginal – fostering the ability to 'see' your drama through – there is also great advantage to be gained by stimulating your ability to 'hear' each character in your head and sense whether they are speaking or reacting in a way which rings true for them. And if by now you're thinking these exercises are fine for actors but a bit silly or unnecessary for someone simply setting words down on the page, there could be much to gain by giving the matter second thoughts. Writing drama is no more nor less than an introjected version of acting. Like it or not, the writer of convincing drama must inwardly enact every moment of his work, and consider it from each character's point of view as he does so, to get the most convincing action and reaction with which to write the story.

There are screenwriting books which detail all the principles of genre, style, story and theme, and which seem to treat actors, if not as Hitchcock once famously suggested they should be treated – 'like cattle' – then certainly almost as an afterthought. And yet the actor's process and the building of character seem to be completely central to the business of constructing convincing drama. Most fiction scripts are intended primarily for actors to work from, so it seems only common sense to examine what actors look for as they take the words their characters are going to speak off the page and bring them to life as a character. It is no coincidence that many writers of drama for stage or screen have had experience of acting. Whether you act, or write for actors, the process of *enactment* at the level of the *vividly imagined* is crucial to producing convincing drama.

IMPROVISING: THE KEY TO UNDERSTANDING CHOICE

Every moment you write in a drama is one chosen from many alternatives. What writers strive for are those choices which seem to flow effortlessly and naturally from previous choices made for that character, and which also give the maximum potential for further dramatic development.

Improvisation can be a truly worthwhile way to explore possible ways forward for your dramas, to try alternative versions of moments and scenes, and a group setting provides an excellent opportunity to experiment with and get used to improvising. There are some very useful books on this subject, and for those interested in developing their skills I'd recommend Keith Johnstone's books *Impro* (Methuen) or *Impro for Storytellers* (Faber and Faber), Chris Johnston's *House of Games* (Nick Hern Books), as well as Augusto Boal's *Games For Actors and Non-Actors* (Routledge). Don't be put off by the fact that these books relate to theatre. If you have formed or can form a support group for your screenwriting, then as well as reading some or all of these books consider regularly turning over some of the group's time to playing with improvisatory technique. However off-putting you find that idea, given an atmosphere of mutual encouragement, I guarantee your sense of narrative and drama, and as a consequence your scriptwriting, can benefit enormously.

Getting used to the idea of improvising scenes will help you internalise what can be a vital asset in understanding how to make a scene go using its own momentum and its own inner dynamic, rather than driving it all from an externally sourced, cut and dried idea of what you want to achieve. When your writing doesn't quite ring true, doesn't seem to have enlivened voice, and when it fails to surprise you at all, it's time to open up different approaches using your inner (or outer) improvisatory skills. To an extent, this is a process all writers of drama draw on naturally; the more experienced you become with it, the better your scripting will be.

THREE VITAL QUESTIONS

In improvisation one is constantly inventing action, reaction and dialogue for the character you have chosen to play. As writers, we make the ambitious choice of playing *all* the characters, jumping from one pair of shoes to another, in order to animate them all as accurately as possible. In order to do this, consciously or not, we ask ourselves, 'What would *I* do (or say) now?' Along with that question are two others which inform it and expand it to keep us on the right track. These are: 'What would *anyone* do (or say) now? (in other words, what strikes me – and therefore others – as most probable?); and, 'What would *my character* do (or say) now?' This can be the trickiest bit of the equation to hold in the balance, and the work and exercises outlined above are designed to help you create a foundation from which to keep answering that part of the combined question.

The inventiveness of your plot, the interesting situations and dilemmas you pose your characters with, will partially dictate the choices you make for your characters. *Who* those characters are, and more crucially *how* they are, will help dictate the rest. What can also help a great deal with the element of character is to know the realms your characters are drawn from.

DEPTH, COMPLEXITY AND A 'CHARACTER COMPASS'

Earlier in this book I suggested that all ideas are *nuclear* in origin and also *unclear*. So it is with character. In their earliest incarnations we may have the haziest idea of character; maybe we've got their gender and their approximate age. Maybe we've got their name. Maybe we know what they do. We are going to build on all this, but the depth, complexity and detail we are going to need to arrive at is determined by what we are writing. I have devised what I call a *character compass* which you might find useful as a reference guide to the terrain we're trying to populate, and therefore the kind of characterisation we need to achieve.

Needless to say, we are rarely if ever operating on just one bearing with this compass. There is a dynamic interaction between all its different aspects.

Nevertheless there may be a predominant 'direction' your character is coming from.

At one 'pole' we have the gods or archetypes. If you're unfamiliar with the concept of archetypes, *The Hero With a Thousand Faces* by Joseph Campbell offers a fascinating study across cultures and through time to show how legends and folk-tales throughout the ages all feature intrinsically identical adventurers, heroes and gods embodying the archetypal quest to arrive at meaning and understanding of the human condition. More recently, Christopher Vogler has written a very accessible book, *The Writer's Journey*, which distils Campbell's findings and links archetypes directly to the art of screenwriting.

A fundamental feature of the archetypes is that they are larger than life yet exist very much in outline, as it were, allowing us to invest them with a lot of generalised meaning. At the other pole, this is also true of caricatured figures. Here, a characteristic or mannerism is again made larger than life, but this time with the aim of diminishing the character. Their tendency to grandiosity is parodied, pointing out their all-too-human failings. At the extremes, characters in these realms (archetype and caricature) scarcely seem to belong to the recognisable, workaday world; and yet, they are immediately easy to identify with, embodying as they do the height our hopes and dreams can soar to as well as the ludicrous depths to which we can descend. They may be Luke Skywalker from *Star Wars,* or the clown who drives into the circus ring in a car with wacky wheels, flaunting his magnificent machine, moments before it drops to bits around him; such characters capture the essence of our questing spirituality or that of our undoubted mortality and relative insignificance. As I said before, we do not need to invest characters drawn at these extremes with so much depth or detail; they will still function powerfully in the right story setting.

Likewise, stereotypes are exaggerated simplifications, conforming to generalised expectations. The brutalised police officer, the middle-aged, male politician – the stereotype is our knee-jerk response to a generalised perception which captures some surface truths.

At another pole of the character compass we have role and persona. Again these are surface images. Role is an externalised definition imposed on a character by the world – teacher, student, writer, lover, manager, brother. There is an immediate common experience embodied in the definition, and a universal expectation of what it means to have this role.

Alternatively one may construct a persona, an internalised image, an aspect of the personality with which to define oneself – ruthless, irrepressible, tyrannical, compassionate. This becomes like a badge by which we easily identify a

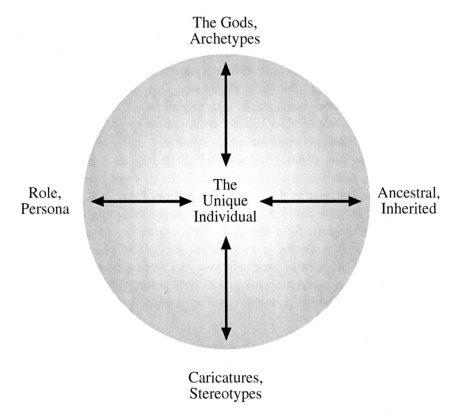

The Gods,
Archetypes

Role,
Persona

The
Unique
Individual

Ancestral,
Inherited

Caricatures,
Stereotypes

Figure 4.2   A character compass

character – a simplification of who they are, highlighting the one aspect of themselves they overwhelmingly choose to show to the world. Both role and persona offer an easily-read surface identity.

At the opposite pole we have the ancestral or familiar. These are inherited traits of appearance and mannerism attributable to our genetic inheritance or imitated by us during our upbringing. Again these can be observed as surface image. Look in the mirror and the reflection is simply who we may see ourselves (or be seen) as, before we (or others) look inside. The seeds of drama can spring from this alone. Take, for example, the idea of a boy who looks just like his father sadly now estranged from and despised by his mother. An immediate tension might also now exist between mother and son because of that superficial truth.

As we craft dramas and populate them with characters, so it can be useful to understand which surface images belong with these characters and how they may be operating.

For example, Del Boy Trotter in the television comedy *Only Fools and Horses* (John Sullivan) is drawn primarily as a *caricature*: a pretentious entrepreneur, a 'dodgy wideboy', a ludicrous parody of the big-time operator. At the same time, his characterisation rests (as with many comedic creations) firmly on the *archetype* of the trickster; ultimately always one step ahead, daring the gods, living off his wits, always managing to seize victory from the jaws of defeat. At the same time, the *role* of elder brother is important to Del. Yet more often than not, he is brother in name only, comically and drastically abusing Rodney or letting him down. (Rodney, Del's little brother is physically a lot taller than Del, which at the surface level of the *inherited* provides another comically ironic dynamic to their brotherly dealings.) And yet, at times, Del can show true compassion and the audience is moved to heartfelt silence as he recalls a tender moment from the past. This requires us to go beyond the surface and attend to a specific and significant slice of Del's history; of course, no sooner is that moment of brotherly love and feeling humanity achieved, then the moment is undercut with a one-liner pulling Del and us back to those surface aspects which powerfully and appropriately drive and define the character.

So what the viewer experiences is a dynamic flow, a movement around aspects of the surface of the 'character world' and an occasional sortie towards the centre, the core of who Del is, which both authenticates him, suggests who else Del might be (given a different context) and also serves to underline his comedic impact.

With an epic myth or action thriller, a training drama, or a drama offered in the style of social realism (like *Cathy Come Home* or *Land and Freedom* (Tony Garnett, Jim Allen)) we may never see far below the surface of the character. That's not the fundamental point of such pieces: they are there to deliver messages or stories of such generalised import that we do not need to become engaged with the individuals concerned in any great individual depth. The universal and typical truths of such stories will reach us despite and also because of the comparatively slight depth of characterisation. At the same time, this allows us lots of room to imagine what they are like and to project ourselves into these creations.

It follows from all this that the more detail, depth and complexity we go into, the more we bring a character into sharp relief. We achieve greater focus and offer them up as unique, living entities.

Specific details generate an air of authenticity, especially where dialogue is concerned. They can underline the particularity we all establish in our lives through the individual choices available to us.

Different types of drama call for different levels of detail and focus in characterisation. Then again, within any individual story, varying depth of focus can be more or less appropriate to different characters. Sometimes a taxi driver is just that in a story; a role, a driver of a taxi, taking significant characters from A to B. And then again, sometimes a taxi driver is Travis Bickle, a highly significant, fully fleshed-out, unique individual, and the main focus of our detailed attention.

NAMING CHARACTERS

I strongly recommend that you get into the habit of naming characters when you write them. The reason I suggest this is two-fold. Firstly, the act of naming a character helps you consolidate the process of *owning* them. You will identify more closely and invest more in their individuality. You are more likely to write them with greater care. By the same token, a named part is one an actor is much more likely to own and invest in. If you write 'second-policewoman' for a character who has, if only fleetingly, some reasonably important things to say or do, you could well get a lacklustre performance from an actor who may, from the absence of a name, assume that you consider the part to have no weight at all in the piece.

There can be a temptation to think of a character purely in terms of a role, and write, for example, 'Mother' rather than the character's name. If you fall into this trap, don't carry on writing them this way, telling yourself you'll give them a name later. Rectify the process there and then and let the character acquire the dimension and depth they need to have.

Obviously there are times when not naming a character over and above giving them a label is quite appropriate. If a character has no particular significance in your story, is a mere functionary, a by-stander, in truth *is* simply an extra, then 'waiter', 'man in crowd' or whatever they happen to be is going to suffice.

CHARACTER AND CONTRADICTION

We all have contradictory qualities. We can be generous and also mean, kind or nasty, industrious or lazy. Even if we can truly say we are one rather than the other, we will still have our contrary moments. The same goes for characters we write. By and large, they should have contradictory qualities. By and large, because there are indeed stories where a monolithic characterisation can be quite appropriate. No point waiting around to see the good side of Cruella DeVil, the Riddler, or Blofeldt, or indeed the bad side of Superman, the Lone Ranger or Noddy. Though I should perhaps qualify these remarks and give a mention to the interesting approach to characterisation adopted for the TV series *Heroes* (Tim Kring). Superman has his very human alter ego, journalist Clark Kent, a shy bumbler lacking confidence and presence. In *Heroes* that age-old concept of human/super-human hybrid is given a fresh outing and in the process an engaging makeover. In the tradition of super-hero comic books, yet at the same time ironically self-referential and reflexive in places, *Heroes* (traditionally enough) plants and plays with the idea of an all too human hero-worshipper like Hiro Nakamura getting the surprise of his life, discovering his own twin-track super-human and Samurai powers and also realising he is destined to make the hero's journey. This series offers a humorous contemporary twist on an old device whilst inviting us to discover in its central characters some depth and complexity. This comes in the guise of frailties, and egotisms coexisting in the same bodies as unshakeable, mono-lithic, super-human heroism or villainy – and without too many obvious 'phone-booth' moments to separate the personae. So for example when Hiro has rescued his best friend Ando from the evil clutches of Sylar in Isaac Mendez's loft and re-materialised the pair of them at his work-station in Yamagato Industries, Tokyo, he tells his friend he must go back alone to face Sylar and defeat him. Ando then lists the contemporary film and comic-book heroes Hiro has always worshipped and wanted to be like, concluding by expressing a belief his friend will one day belong firmly in the midst of this pantheon. Hiro then gives him his ancient Samurai sword as a keepsake to vouchsafe his return - all of this, in traditional heroic style. Ando objects but

Figure 4.3   Masi Oka in *Heroes* © NBC/Universal TV

Hiro reassures him, 'It's not the sword. It is the man. This man is ready'; definitely the stuff of myth, legend and comic book. And then the humorous, modern-day, human touch (rendered all the funnier by its subtitled translation from the Japanese) as a deeply impressed Ando tells Hiro 'you look badass' and disarmingly taken aback Hiro faintly swaggers 'Really?' Laying claim to depth and recognisable 'reality' whilst announcing itself as self-consciously fictional (hence that all too real and contemporary looking Hiro being counted alongside Superman by Ando), the story entertainingly flirts with boundaries of genre and in the process, as mentioned, invites the viewer to perceive a complexity to the characters. It's the kind of device much cultivated by writers in recent years and is of similar ilk to that hilarious, philosophically playful moment in the animation *Toy Story 2* (John Lasseter, Pete Docter *et al.*) when toy astronaut Buzz Lightyear is in the giant toy store and berates the group of Buzz Lightyear toys on display correcting their delusion that they are real and pointing out he is the real thing, they mere toys. How obtrusive such witty escapades can be when not successfully calculated is another matter.

Yet despite moments in *Heroes* such as the end of that interchange between Hiro and Ando described above, or that other at the climax of the first season's shows when would-be President Nathan Petrelli zooms through the sky landing in New York's Kirby Plaza to tell his brother and (super)human-bomb, Peter, that he loves him – and to hear the same back – before, Superman-like, whisking him high into space so they can explode together spectacularly thus, of course, saving the world. Despite these moments of conscious stylistic complexity, with *Heroes*, we are, for the most part, firmly in uncomplicated, archetypal, comic-book – and therefore mythic – territory with these characters. To my mind, there is definitely something embarrassingly disorientating about those climactic moments when the writer to all appearances *without tongue in cheek*, makes these characters try to straddle and belong in both story worlds. Generally speaking the moment we come away from writing at the extremes of the character compass I described earlier, we need to look at multi-dimensionality and in-built contradictions. They help to authenticate the characterisation. They make characters more believably human.

Beyond the contradictions within individual characters, it can be worthwhile checking whether or not the characters you are writing embody between them a variety of human qualities, indeed a range of vices and virtues. If you have an impetuous character, then it can also make sense to have a character somewhere whose greater prudence will frustrate that first character's rashness. If you have a misanthropic recluse, it can make sense to have characters around whose social ease or prying curiosity will challenge that world-weariness. A character's cowardice is all the more interesting in relation to others' obvious bravery. In drama, remember, there is great value in introducing and exploring conflict. I'm not suggesting you go as far as mechanically and obviously parading a range of virtues and testing these against vices, as you would find in medieval morality plays; rather it's a matter of recognising what the strengths and weaknesses of your characters are as you develop them, and seeing where these can be brought into interesting conflict with contrasting qualities which seem to sit naturally with other characters in your drama.

One final note. All these exercises are designed to help you know your characters well, and it's a good idea to feel you have a confident hold on how your characters operate in their world. That said, do leave room for them to sneak up on you in the writing sometimes and surprise you with what they do or say.

Exercises

This chapter has been quite full of exercises already but I'd just like to suggest a few more.

1   Following on from the hot-seating process, a useful exercise is to think about the history, personality and circumstances you have so far outlined for a character and consider the possible ways you can upset one or all of these aspects so as to impel a story. In other words, where would it be best to throw your grenade to cause unavoidable havoc and maximum complication and thus ultimately really put your character to the test. This is a useful exercise to do on your own, and also very valuable to do with others as you collectively consider each other's characters.

2   From a pack of playing cards sort out a variety running from low number to high value and perhaps with one or two values duplicated here and there. In the group, get everyone to choose a card without letting anyone else see what they've picked. At no point until the very end of the exercise are you to reveal what is on your card.

Now allow just two minutes to get round and make contact with every member of the group, introducing yourself and trying to demonstrate where in the pecking order you think you come. So if you have a low value number, think of ways to show this relative to other members of the group. At the end of two minutes, line yourselves up trying to place yourself in precisely the right order relative to the others. Reveal your cards and see if you all got it right. If you want to, discuss the experience!

3   Pick a new card. Improvise a scene where you are all stuck on a train which has ground to a halt in the middle of nowhere. No explanation has been offered, and the strain is beginning to tell. Be more subtle about your character's status this time: don't go out of your way to demonstrate it too explicitly. Work hard to find out where other people are relative to you.

At the end of about 15 or 20 minutes, call a halt to the improvisation and line yourselves up. Reveal your cards and see whether you got the pecking order right. Discuss the experience, noticing the subtle and less subtle things characters do to make their position quite clear.

5
Dialogue

For some new writers, one of the more daunting aspects of crafting drama is handling dialogue. By now I've already sneaked up on you in this book and offered you a couple of exercises aimed at easing your way into the process. The 'hot-seating' exercise in the last chapter will have given you the opportunity to let your character chat discursively, and then the more focussed exercise of placing one or more of those characters in a scene will inevitably have pushed you into actually writing dialogue. So now your feet are already wet, and you can relax: however effective and convincing that dialogue turned out to be, in simply doing the exercise, some of you will have overcome a major hurdle. There is really nothing mystical about writing dialogue; it's simply the process of letting your characters speak to each other. Naturalistic dialogue is a close cousin to ordinary speech, despite the fact it is a studied, distilled, and sometimes heightened version of what we might actually say every day. And most of the occasions you are likely to meet writing for the screen call for naturalistic dialogue.

It was probably also hard, if not impossible, for you to write the exercise following *Two Sharp* without feeling seriously tempted to make one or more of the characters say something. Doing the exercise, it may have seemed like there were moments when characters absolutely needed to speak in pursuit of their objectives. You may or may not have been right about that. Often there are ways of turning what you first think of as speech into dramatic action, and that strategy of trying to do it all through action is a very useful one to hold on to. Screenwriting impacts visually before anything else: actions *do* speak louder than words.

Nevertheless I think it *is* true to say that ultimately characters will feel impelled to speak, if they can, when the conflict arising from a dramatic situation leads them to that point. So that dictum, *characters speak when they have to*, is a useful rule of thumb to bear in mind. Implicit in it is a more important cautionary note – *watch out for characters speaking when they don't have to.* Particularly for those new to dramatic writing (and especially to screenwriting) it can be a big temptation to let characters speak when they don't have to. If you go along with the idea that characters are only going to speak when they have to, then it only remains to crack that tough little nut – *when* do they have to?

In his book, *On Directing Film*, David Mamet asserts:

> The purpose of dialogue is not to carry information about the 'character'. The only reason people speak is to get what they want.
>
> (1992: 71)

What he's talking about here is, in part, the difference between that hot-seating exercise you did and any specific scene you may have written featuring those same characters. While being hot-seated, it's perfectly appropriate for the character to be revealing their biography and chatting about their deeper selves in a discursive manner. Once you put the character into action in a scene, they have a focussed purpose and the scene must be about them pursuing that objective within the scene or be about nothing. When starting out, writers can sometimes be tempted into thinking that characters in plays and screenplays can behave exactly as people do in life, or even as they might do in a raw improvisation; in either case, focus and purpose inevitably slip and slide. This is just not the case with polished and effective drama. Characters move from one mini-goal to the next, pursuing their objective within the scene and their overall objective within the bigger story: so their dialogue must reflect that fact.

CONFUSING SCREENWRITING WITH WRITING FOR THEATRE

Stage writing can afford to take its time more than screenwriting. One scene for a stage play may encompass the amount of material which would fit into considerably more scenes on the screen. There is not the same highly selected focus of a camera shot to worry about, and the story is not the driving force it has to be in many conventionally told screen dramas. As a result of this difference in pace, speeches within individual scenes in theatre can be longer. Characters going off at tangents to the main thrust of the scene are far more acceptable. Where screenwriting looks to compress and condense – to take the straightest line through the story – theatre allows for a more discursive, relaxed approach in crafting dialogue. A theatre audience is taking in the whole scene and selecting aspects of the action to focus on. Audiences watching a screen drama have the focus of attention selected for them; the narrative process drives along much faster, with the relationship of shot to shot and scene to scene an essential part of the process. So lengthy digressions which disrupt that momentum are unwelcome, and it takes a very important speech to hold attention on an individual character for, say, as long as a minute.

Obviously there are TV and film adaptations of classic stage dramas: to sustain audience interest these may depend on cutting the original text quite heavily, introducing a busy and varied visual treatment to provide extra interest, or they may simply rely on an audience indulging them for the separate kind of animal they are. It's quite instructive to look at older television adaptations of classic novels and compare them with more recent efforts. Older adaptations of Shakespeare also make for interesting comparison, say with the more recent productions such as *Romeo and Juliet* (Craig Pearce and Baz Luhrman from the play by William Shakespeare) or *Richard III* (Ian McKellen from the play by William Shakespeare). The increasing influence of cinematic conventions is clear to see.

Writers who move from theatre work to film or TV really need to acknowledge the differences and embrace them. The important trick is to devise ways of combining well described, well chosen action with more concise dialogue to get over everything you need to tell the audience, rather than trying to write theatre for the screen, and then perforce hacking it down to size and bringing it up to speed.

SOME COMMON PITFALLS

Relentless chatter

Perhaps one of the most common errors which new writers can make is to try to fill up the scene with wall-to-wall dialogue. It's as though they know only one way of covering the bare boards of their scene, and that's with fitted carpet throughout. For what it's worth, try considering rugs, or even polishing up those boards. In other words, there are always options, and to fill your scenes with non-stop dialogue is to miss out on the power of action, reaction and significant silences, both long and short.

Writing a radio play is obviously much more dependent on dialogue than writing for feature films (though it's worth noting this is a generalisation and there are exceptions to the rule to be found in both media). That said, the skilful radio dramatist knows how to move into startling or evocative effects, uses music well, and is not afraid to create some silences in their drama. So, if you find yourself cramming every scene full of busy verbal interchanges, stop and think again. Go back to the first exercise in this book and consider how you made a lot happen before our very eyes without the use of any dialogue.

Conversely, a fault some new writers make is consistently to write too little. They have perhaps read a few scripts, observed the economy with which they are written and in an attempt to get in line, produce very terse, mannered dialogue which has no natural ease, and doesn't seem to have the flexibility to vary from scene to scene and match the different situations and characters.

Talk for talk's sake

In the false belief that dramas are all about characters talking to each other, characters are made to talk to each other about nothing in particular. But, unlike people in real life, characters in a good script don't just bump into each other and chat idly; if they are going to do that in a script, then the idle chatter must have an underlying motive which illuminates where the characters are up to in the story. For instance, if one character is in the midst of an affair and shortly after having been with her lover then separately bumps into her lover's wife, an ensuing scene in which she and the betrayed woman chat about nothing in particular will feel authentically motivated and hold a lot of dramatic interest: the fact that the interaction is being held at such a superficial level tells us a lot about the level of contact the guilty woman does *not* want to make right now. (See the section on subtext (p. 181) for more on this.) So always make sure your characters' talk has some point to it. Even the most seemingly mundane of scenes must be about something.

Knowing when to shut them up

The knack of writing good dialogue can chiefly consist in knowing when a character would not say anything. In a film like *The Piano* (Jane Campion) the mute heroine chooses to scribble down notes which are obviously significant, but her silences are frequently just as eloquent, because of what else we see going on for her. Likewise in the film *The Pawnbroker*, tormented refugee Sol Nazerman is so imprisoned by the tragedy of his past experiences that he is unable and unwilling to reach out. In fact, Rod Steiger, who played Sol revealed that he was instrumental in cutting up to one third of the lines his character originally had, in order to amplify the hero's brooding isolation (*Scene By Scene*. Interview with Mark Cousins, BBC2, 16 July 2000). In more extreme cases like these where characters can't or won't speak, the effect of their silences on others is plain to see, and the drama will often derive some of its most powerful moments from how they react to what others say to them. We are particularly focussed on how these characters are so cut off, verbally, and so we scrutinise them to learn what they think and feel. However, the same principle is at work whenever a character withholds speech. Stillness can be as compelling as dynamic movement, and silence every bit as compelling a way of making one's voice heard. Don't overlook the potential for making the setting, the mood or the weather express what is going on in a character's head.

Mistaking the situation for the subject matter

This occurs when writers feel under some compulsion to make reference to the setting. Just because you set a scene in a supermarket you don't have to make the characters discuss the price of carrots. If talking about the price of carrots happens to tie in naturally with the point of the scene, and actually enhances the main subject matter, then fine; otherwise a setting can be just that, and you do not have to make the characters respond to it.

Another common fault can be getting characters to talk about what they're actually doing, perhaps born of an insecurity that the audience just won't understand a situation. If it's obvious, or very soon going to become obvious, that two characters are on a date, why have them talk about the fact? Unless it is relevant to plot or character in some way, let them get on with having the date.

Unnecessary formalities

A very common fault in beginners' scripts is writing in the business of how someone arrived, or getting characters to perform unnecessary hellos and goodbyes. Unless those moments carry some special significance you are wasting ink. If, for example, two characters who already know each other meet but the circumstances are such that they carry on as if they are strangers, that could be interesting. If we know this is odd behaviour, we will wonder why they are behaving in this way, and engage more keenly in the drama. But other than as a way of enhancing intrigue, beware of falling into the trap of making your characters go through unnecessary formalities.

Writing the fight

It's not at all unusual for writers new to drama to fall into creating scenes which are nothing less than verbal brawls. When first starting out, it can be easier to create abusive mayhem than anything else. This may spring from the insecurity I mentioned earlier that unless something obviously dramatic is happening (and what is more dramatic than a fight?) then the scene just will not happen for its audience. But, as many of the examples in this book show, conflict is so much more interesting between characters when it informs their words and actions but is not openly on display; when it actually comes to a fight, which is usually going to resolve conflict and therefore dissipate the interest, then far better that should happen as the climax to a story than that story be told as an unrelenting series of bruising encounters.

So if you find yourself writing a lot of scenes in which characters snipe at each other, shout at each other or worse – then think again.

Language!

There are those who take exception to the use of any expletives, obscene or abusive language in a script. Arguments have always raged around the rights and wrongs of reflecting what some experience as the unacceptable sides of human behaviour, 'bad' language included. My stance on the issue is that any and all dialogue which you create should be right for the character and right for the moment. If a reader or viewer doesn't remark on anything as standing out and interrupting their engagement and identification with your piece then it's probably doing a good job.

That said, there are those few who are so hardened to using or hearing a stream of obscenities as everyday interpolations, that they may carry this over into their writing without a thought for its impact on others. They might do well to pay attention to the feedback they will inevitably get from others and think about broadening their verbal horizons.

Over-liberal use of strong language has the inevitable effect of diluting it. Rather as with dramas which are all fight and no build up, the question arises, 'What have you got left to play?' It really can be far more effective saving extremes for the most intense moments of your drama.

There is also the factor of 'language'-as-lubricator to be taken into account. It's allied to that phenomenon of writing the fight I mentioned above, and can be a sign that a writer has included the strong language as a way of trying to invigorate their process and their dialogue. Very often it's possible to strip out much (if not all) of the stronger stuff without any detriment to the finished piece.

Finally, when you write for performance, publication or public screening, you will at times come up against institutionalised standards and strictures, and you will have to take account of those. My advice is that if you genuinely believe specific words are truly appropriate and integral to your drama, it's most important to fight your corner. But those occasions may well be a lot rarer than some might think.

Over-explaining

The point of characters talking to each other is to pursue what they want, not to describe it, and not to explain why they want it. If the drama is well written, we'll understand why from the rest of the piece. As for characters in a sensitive, personal situation describing what it is they're after – how often do you see people do that in real life? Besides, any situation where you could just come clean, say what it is you want and get it instantly with no obstacles, is unlikely to have much mileage as the meat of a good drama, where conflict and complication reign supreme. If you catch yourself writing passages in which characters explain matters to each other and the audience, they are not getting on with telling us the story, and you'd better have a good reason why that is so: the audience is only truly engaged by the story, and are not interested in circumstantial explanations. Think hard whether the explanation is necessarily intrinsic to your drama. Whenever you find yourself using characters to offer what is, in effect, narration, you are getting them to step outside themselves to support an audience's understanding of what should be made clear *if necessary* by captioned, or voiced-over narration, or more ideally be carried somewhere within the drama as another scene or part of a scene. Always go back to basics and think what you would do if you didn't have dialogue available to you. Deny yourself the option of other devices (voice-over or caption) as well, and see if you can turn that explanation into credible and engaging action. This may help to concentrate your mind on what exactly does need spelling out.

Unnecessary repetitions

These can just be phrases or sentences repeated within a speech or a scene for no particular purpose, or they can extend to re-running the content of whole scenes to no good effect. Sometimes a character will go through an experience and then, two or three scenes later, meet another character and tell them all about what the audience has just actually seen happen to them. Before you fall into the trap of writing a scene which is no more than a narrated version of earlier action, ask yourself *why* this character is relating the events. If there is some particular interest in watching for the reaction of the character being told about the experience (for example, to watch for signs of guilt), then perhaps there is some point to using the device: even when this is the case, ask yourself if there is a real need to relate the whole scene again in your dialogue; would it not be just as effective to join the scene right at the end of that character telling their tale? *Don't try an audience's patience any more than is absolutely necessary.* Progress the plot.

News-sheet scenes

Sometimes you come across what I call 'news-sheet' scenes. These are frequently to be found in some soap-operas, and unlike the well-taken opportunity to remind an audience of a particularly significant event in the story and its impact, 'news-sheet' scenes have characters reporting to each other on events under the thin disguise of giving them an opportunity to comment on those events; in this way they update viewers on what has been happening. There's not a lot of excuse for bad scenes like this at any time, and none at all within the single drama. In soaps, they can come about through a misguided notion that the audience needs and likes a reliable update service within the drama – a sort of in-show teletext. In my view they stick out like such sore thumbs that they completely disrupt the flow of the plot and the characters involvement in events, as well as that of the audience. Avoid even miniature versions of this if you can.

Stooging

All the characters in a drama have emotional attitudes, positive, negative or neutral, and will move through these moment by moment. In different scenes we watch characters make shifts (lesser or greater) which contribute to their overall journeys in the story.

Sometimes, as in life, it's a character's function to react to others. When this is the case it's still important to make them authentic, rather than reduce them to the status of mindless stooge – *unless* that does truly fit their place in the drama. So avoid interchanges like the one below.

EXT. STREET. DAY.

> JACK
>
> Audrey!

> AUDREY
> Oh, hello, Jack. Sorry, can't stop, I'm on my way to hospital.

> JACK
>
> Hospital!

> AUDREY
> Yes, Mike had a fall and managed to break his leg.

> JACK
>
> No!

> AUDREY
> Yes. Last Thursday. Fell off a ladder. Well you know he's been painting the house.

> JACK
>
> Yes.

> AUDREY
> Off he came. Just lost his balance.

                    JACK
Dear me.

                    AUDREY
The doctor said he was lucky not
to have killed himself. They've had
to pin it in three places.

                    JACK
Pin it!

                    AUDREY
Mm. He's going to be in a while.
I wouldn't mind, but we were
going on holiday next Tuesday.

                    JACK
Oh no.

                    AUDREY
Yes. To Andalucia. Well that'll have
to go by the board, I suppose.
Still must dash or I'll miss visiting
hours.

                    JACK
No, you get off, then.

                    AUDREY
I will. I'll give him your best.
Nice chatting, Jack.

I've caricatured the malaise that can set in to illustrate the point. Not that Audrey does anything remarkable, but Jack is a cipher, a stooge allowed no space to live, breathe and react. He's there simply to fill in the spaces and to act as an occasional prompt. It's most important to allow all the characters to take the space they would naturally inhabit, and to let them act and react as fully as they would naturally want to. Concentrating on one character's thoughts and actions at the expense of properly writing the others is a trap the unwary newcomer can fall into. It's important to check you are fully animating all of your characters and doing each one of them justice.

Gestures

I'm using gesture in the sense of rhetorical device here, and want to caution you against giving your characters big verbal flourishes so that they can make their presence felt. It's difficult to offer specific examples out of context, but if you feel that you're giving a character something to say to demonstrate some-thing about them to the world at large, when the more natural action or reac-tion would be more restrained, lower key, perhaps less predictable, then go with your instincts and rein yourself in. Remember the three questions mentioned in the last chapter: 'What would anyone say or do? What would I say or do? What would my character say or do?' You need to write from a cocktail of all three, and gesturing tends to come about when the first two are neglected and the third overworked at and then demonstrated superficially; this can render dialogue inauthentic and distance the audience.

Don't say it if we can see it

An associated trap writers can fall into is that of getting characters to say what we've already seen.

INT. RESTAURANT. DAY.
SOPHIE, a waitress, watches through the window as DAVE parks his car slap-bang outside.

EXT. STREET. CONTINUOUS.
DAVE gets out of the car, glances nervously at the printed parking restrictions, then through the window where he catches SOPHIE's eye.

INT. RESTAURANT. CONTINUOUS.
SOPHIE has started to take an order. DAVE opens the door and hovers. SOPHIE looks over.

DAVE
(to SOPHIE)
Is it okay to park my car
outside like that?

Well, we've seen him park the car and Sophie's seen him park the car; so he could just say:

DAVE
(to SOPHIE)
Will it be alright there?

In fact, this kind of fault, which is far more common than you might think, is a direct result of writers taking their eye off the ball, stopping watching the action unfold in their head as they write it. Instead, the writer has become so focussed on hearing what the characters are saying to each other that they forget what they (and we) are watching, as well as what the characters will have seen, and therefore will not need to refer to. It is very important that you *keep seeing your drama through as you write it*, and be aware of what does not need describing or explaining.

Failing to define character

In Chapter 4, I outlined strategies for forming character. Once you've got hold of them and are busy jumping from one pair of shoes to another, it really is vital to preserve each character's particular voice and characteristic ways of being in the world of your drama. A time-honoured exercise for knowing whether or not you are achieving this is to cover up all the names in a copy of a scene you haven't looked at for a while and seeing whether you can still tell who's speaking. Better still, let someone else who knows the script (but not as well as you) have a go. With practice, you will certainly be able to sustain individual delineated characters, who consistently speak with their own voices. As I stressed in the last chapter, it's really important to name characters, and it can certainly help you carve out individual voices. A sure give away, more often than not, that a script has had little or no character work behind it, is the script which boasts 'Man One', 'Woman One', or 'Mum', 'Dad', 'Policewoman' and 'Gran' in its cast list. I admit there may be scripts where, although this is the case, characters are well defined and formed with plenty of individual detail, and the device of using relative anonymity is a deliberate stylistic ploy. However, with newish writers that doesn't tend to be the case, so watch out for damaging corner cutting.

Naming names

The world being what it is, some new writers may also go to an opposite extreme. Not only will they name all their characters, but they will then insist on all the characters addressing each other by name frequently throughout the script. If you observe how much we call people by name in reality you will notice it is actually quite an occasional business: so it does ring false when you make it a frequent event in your script. In life people tend to call each other by name to get their attention, or to create distance from them, or when they are trying to get a closer connection with them. On the whole, the same rules apply in a drama, certainly where naturalism is concerned. Do watch out for this pitfall; it's really quite a common failing for the newish writer of drama to fall into, and it can also creep up on a scriptwriter who's out of practice or one who's failed to get focussed on the material before settling down to write. If in doubt, err on the side of omitting names. You'll know soon enough on a re-read if the actual calling by name of another character really does have a natural place in a speech.

Straying from character. Beware: 'Writer at Work'

Just as obvious as it sounds but sometimes the easiest thing to miss. Here's an example of what I mean:

EXTERIOR. VALERIE'S GARDEN. CONTINUOUS.

PAULETTE AND VALERIE HOLD A COUPLE OF TENT PEGS EACH, FORMING THE CORNERS OF A STRING RECTANGLE.

> PAULETTE
> I thought you'd planned it all out.

> VALERIE
> I had . . . in my head. Now we're
> out here it just doesn't feel right.

> PAULETTE
> Mother!

> MICK APPEARS, LEANING ON
> THE GARDEN FENCE.

> MICK
> Afternoon.

> VALERIE
> Where do *you* think, Mick?

> MICK
> What?

> VALERIE
> (SURPRISED HE HASN'T GUESSED)
> For the lawn.

> PAULETTE
> She's been watching Charlie Dimmock.

> MICK
> Oh.

> VALERIE
> She's very good.

> PAULETTE
> So Hiroshima here's getting a make-over.

> MICK
> Right.

The problem is in that penultimate line. Paulette is just nineteen. Whilst make-overs would definitely be part of her experience from TV and magazines, it's far less likely that she would have come across Hiroshima. Even if she has heard of that city's devastation at the end of World War Two, it's very unlikely to spring to her lips as analogous to their neglected garden. Unlikely to spring to *her* lips, but not to those of the much older writer. It's such moments when what *you as the writer* would say obscures a clear imagining of what *the character* would say, that you need to watch out for; and often the writer can fall into such moments because he is too attached to something he's dreamed up to be able to hear it doesn't ring true. At second glance, however, the line did stand out as uncharacteristic and got changed to:

> PAULETTE
> (FAKE POSH)
> Yes, we're giving the grounds a
> make-over.

Obviously your aim is to keep a character's words consistently believable and identifiably *theirs*. Specific details can help the credibility of a character. Compare:

> RITA
> Did I mention my eldest Peter's
> moving? He's got a new job. It's
> a research post in Milton Keynes.
> They're developing GM courgettes.
> Controversial, I can tell you.

with:

> RITA
> My son's going to move. Got a new
> job, somewhere down south.
> Researching into vegetables or something.

Which is the more memorable? And therefore, which convinces you that the character has a mind and feelings of their own with which to respond to their world? *Specifics authenticate*, and can very often build a most valuable perspective into the way a character is seeing something. It's all part and parcel of that ever-present drive you should develop as a writer, to focus in from the fuzzy, generalised, and not especially convincing, to the detailed, particular and substantially engrossing.

One of the most powerful ways writers can employ particularities is to give characters quirks or mannerisms. This uses the same principle as a caricaturist might, picking on one special habit or gesture and highlighting it. In Alan Bleasdale's brilliant television drama *G.B.H.*, the author gave political supremo Michael Murray an involuntary twitch. As Murray's power grew and his plotting became ever more grandiose, so the drama's satire strengthened and Murray's twitch almost assumed the proportions of a full-blooded Nazi salute. Peter Sellers employs a similar mannerism for the hilariously sinister eponymous atom-bomb scientist in *Dr. Strangelove* (Stanley Kubrick, Terry Southern, Peter George, based on the novel *Red Alert* by Peter George).

When it comes to dialogue, the same device – a verbal mannerism or catch-phrase, can clearly mark a character out and help define their personality. In comedy, this is a frequently used strategy: *One Foot in the Grave*'s (David Renwick) Victor Meldrew with his 'I don't believe it'; *Steptoe and Son* (Ray Galton and Alan Simpson) has the young Harold's 'You dirty old man'; *Ally McBeal* has Richard's automatic 'Bygones', mumbled after every faux pas. Straight drama can also use these verbal habits to distinguish character; episodes of *Inspector Morse* feel incomplete if we haven't heard Morse trucu-lently bark or complain, 'Lewis!' in that unmistakably incredulous, disap-pointed way he has, and Poirot *will* keep referring to those 'little grey cells'. Just as real friends, acquaintances and colleagues partly become familiar to us through their mannerisms and habits, so our identification with or insights into characters can be strengthened by showing us idiosyncrasies of behaviour, including verbal mannerisms. A word of caution, though: it can be far better to let these come about, rather than dream them up and then impose them on characters. Meldrew's 'I don't believe it' works so well, because it is so much a reflection of his outraged stance towards the world.

Losing tone

Quite simply, if you are writing comedy, then the dialogue needs to hit the right note. It may, and often does, depend on a lot of repartee or banter. This jokey sparring will have a particular lightness and wittiness which could sit uneasily in sombre, tragic, deeply-felt drama. Comedy is often a matter of intellectual recognition, and so both the content of those jokey parries, lunges and revelations, as well as the timing and poise with which they are delivered, need precise calculation: whereas a distraught character bearing his soul about a past tragedy would not display that kind of control (despite the writing process being every bit as calculated). So the cautionary note is to warn you to watch for when the tone of a phrase, a speech or an interchange doesn't have a place in the larger scheme of things. As I suggest elsewhere, there *are* times when contrasting tone can be and is a most effective device to employ.

Losing rhythm

First of all, you've got to have it in order to lose it, and so I suppose this is by way of encouraging you to find the natural rhythms in your characters' speech: find it without letting it outstrip the content. These natural rhythms can be found in individual phrases or lines, within whole speeches, and in the interplay between one character's line and another. The feel and sound of the speech can enhance the flow, can intensify an audience's engagement with a drama, and add considerably to the sheer pleasure they can derive from just listening. But the rhythms do need to fit the tunes being played, as it were. Sometimes dialogue can sound really energised, beautifully sprung and poised, when the content doesn't really merit that level of elaborate ornamentation. In those cases the matter being expressed can feel too dressed up. It's worth remembering that Shakespeare would drop into prose at times, to match the less poetically charged passages of his plays. However, in the main, it can pay great dividends to learn to gauge the 'feel' of your dialogue as you put it down.

Look at the scene between Almásy and Clifton from *The English Patient* (p. 191) and notice how the speech reflects a certain stiff-upper-lipped awk-wardness, accurately conveying both the social background of the characters and the unspoken rivalry between the two men. Notice, too, how the lines are written with beautiful internal balance. They are going to be easy to learn and to speak, and will sound like they belong to the characters. Unless you self-consciously set out to do so (and some scripts and screenplays which have their origins in improvisation or are strongly tilted towards social realism do exactly this) when writing drama you are not aiming simply to reflect every-day speech, in everyday speech patterns: as I said before, although dialogue is a close cousin to everyday speech, it is often a distilled and heightened version, and needs careful management in the writing to ensure it flows easily and commands engagement from an audience.

This business of rhythm is key in constructing a passage of dialogue. As with music there may be an overall rhythm reflecting the gathering or relaxing tension, the intensification of contact or the gradual distancing and release. If you're following the moments for each and every character with accuracy and feeling, then these overall rhythms will end up being there. And along the way there will be the bounce of one line off another, the moments which hang in a well-judged pause, and the run or stagger appropriate within each tiny section. Take this key passage from *Shallow Grave* (John Hodge), in which the three friends shop in a DIY store preparing for the next step in their plan to make off with that windfall of cash they've just stolen – the disposal of lodger Hugo's dead body:

Alex places the screwdriver down on the shelf and walks across the aisle to pick up a saw and hammer.

Now this is what we need. And this.

Alex hands the tools to David, who looks at them with disgust. Alex walks on.

Now what else?

DAVID
I don't know.

ALEX
A spade, we need a spade – I wish
you would concentrate – we need a
spade if we're going to dig a pit.

DAVID
So who's going to do it?

ALEX
Dig the pit, I don't know.

DAVID
No, not that.

ALEX
Then what? Who's going to do what?

DAVID
You know what I'm talking about.

ALEX
Do I? What? What? What are you
talking about?

DAVID
You know what. Who's going to do it?

ALEX
We all are, David, we're all going
to do it. Each of us, you, me, and
Juliet, will do his or her bit. Is
that fair enough?

DAVID
I can't do it.

ALEX
I don't hear this.

DAVID
I won't be able to do it.

ALEX
You're telling me you want out? Already?
You're telling me you don't want the
money? Hugo is going off. He smells. The
flat smells. We can't wait any longer.

DAVID
I'm just telling you, I can't cut him up.

Alex turns away in disgust.

Notice the staccato, hysterical edge to David's lines and the way he's deliber-ately given repetitions to convey that nervousness. Alex is also given repeti-tions part way through as a way of underlining the tension and escalating the conflict between the two of them. When he reaches his longer line with its patient explanation and its ominously funny reference to each one of them doing 'his or her bit', the aggressive undertone is almost palpable. Notice as well how David is given that longer, more deliberate and collected last line to show him trying to stand his ground, and how that non-line of Alex's – the turn away – perfectly fits the piece and disrupts the contact, rounding the scene off to a tee.

You can see, too, how the passage winds itself up, reaches a pitch of antag-onism, and then breaks off, leaving the tension between the two unresolved, our knowledge of what's going on for each character quite complete and our interest in where things will go next fully aroused.

SUMMING UP

I realise there's a long list of 'watch out's' listed here, but they are offered in a genuinely constructive spirit. If you are just starting out writing dia-logue, there's no question but that you *will* fall into traps here and there. That's nothing to be discouraged about. Do look on any shortcomings as opportunities to see your own process that much more clearly. The whole business of writing, and particularly crafting dialogue, calls for frequent re-reading and revision of your work. The process of reflecting on and editing your work is part and parcel of getting to write with economy, impact and 'voice'. No-one I know who has developed their writing skills has escaped that process; experience teaches that practice can only make for improve-ment, and the more aware you can be of what needs stripping away to expose a core of fully powered-up dialogue, the more rapid that improve-ment will be.

Exercises

1   Take a dialogue scene you've written earlier (perhaps from putting characters together in Chapter 4) and revise it, bearing in mind some of the pointers listed in this chapter. If you can do this in a group, discussing the content with each other and considering strengths and weaknesses, so much the better.

2   Pick a non-dialogue scene from one of your previous exercises, featuring characters who you felt at the time of writing could well have gone on to have something to say. Write the scene, or an extension to it, giving those characters dialogue. Again, if you can discuss this before and after, do so.

6

Making scenes, building sequences

All conventional dramas for the screen are built up from individual moments which add up to scenes, or significant events in your story. Although a scene is usually a significant story event in the overall chain of events which make up the bigger story, some scenes are included with the aim of fulfilling other func-tions: they can be there to explore character in greater depth, to establish setting or time, or movement from one setting or time to another, or to provide an interlude or respite from the main narrative drive of the piece. In a short film, there is neither the time nor the need to explore character in any great depth, nor to break off from telling the main story. A feature film, however, provides far more scope and needs to do exactly those things a short film will not allow.

Scenes are built into sequences, and these sequences in turn become the building blocks forming the entirety of your drama. Not unusually, feature films will contain about ten sequences, each containing about ten or a dozen scenes. These sequences, each containing scenes from both the major plot and the film's sub-plots, will be distributed over three acts.

A half hour episode of British soap opera will, on average, contain somewhere around 15 to 20 scenes. Usually these will concern themselves with three separate stories (possibly a much less significant fourth story element), one of which will be the major point of audience interest. These slices of separate story are told in intermingled sequences of four or five scenes apiece. The stories featured in each episode will all be at different points in their develop-ment, and the different story strands are so interwoven as to maintain variety and interest and provide enough ongoing recognisability for an audience to come and go in their viewing habits a bit and always be able to latch onto something they know about or feel at home with.

With episodes of continuing serial drama or series featuring self-contained stories (like *The Bill*) different overall narrative structures are deployed to engage and maintain audience interest. *The Bill* has ongoing interest in the shape of its regular protagonist, the police, but its stories are designed to be effective short stories, one-offs containing their own set-ups, conflicts, climaxes and resolutions. Occasionally stories will extend over more than one episode, but they are designed to resolve sooner rather than later. By contrast an episode of a soap may run a storyline, like the famous Jordache family's 'body under the patio' strand in that erstwhile Merseyside classic *Brookside*, a story designed to take place over many months, featuring, with more or less prominence, alongside more transient story strands.

Although an episode of a soap opera doesn't have act structure in the same way as a feature film, it does work to achieve its key moments. In commercial TV, the scene at the end of part(s) and more particularly the cliff-hanger at the end of an episode are designed to hook the viewer's curiosity and so ensure they'll watch again.

This quick survey of different structures is offered as a way of demonstrating that whatever the piece you're writing, *the key components are scenes and sequences of scenes.* Understanding how to build these is crucial.

Just as there is an overall structure to an episode or a self-contained drama, so each and every scene must also have a clear structure with its own beginning, middle and end.

SCENE STRUCTURE: SOME USEFUL RULES OF THUMB

A well-worn and nevertheless vital truism about writing scenes for the screen is that you join the scene as late as you possibly can and leave it as early as you can. In other words, as soon as the scene has delivered what it's there to deliver, it's time to get out and get on with the story. By and large this is a very useful rule to abide by, although it is *only* a rule, and certainly, as with all rules, is to be departed from whenever appropriate. For instance, when writing a pivotal scene, full of big emotion, it may well be right to allow sufficient time for the mood to be established and the business of the scene to feel fully resolved. A scene of this sort may really need more space than others to breathe. That said, being concise and dynamic can and most often will pay great dividends in screenwriting. In particular, avoid wasting time going through the motions of mechanically bringing characters into a scene and going through laborious formalities or introductions between characters unless the way they're shown doing all this is significant. Wherever you can, simply *find* your character where you want them. And don't be worried about leaving them rather than contriving ways in which they physically have to leave the scene. Of course we're all so familiar with these techniques you will have seen what I'm talking about a thousand times.

However it is a fact that, for many, when they try their hand at actually writing scenes, they do fall into the trap of giving their characters unnecessary entrances, exits and mechanical niceties to get through. Remember, screenwriting is unlike writing for the stage: the medium is highly mobile, and shot-changes can re-focus interest in a second: much of the art of screenwriting consists of telling the story through the sequencing of shots and the cuts between scenes.

To state the blindingly obvious, the beginning of most scenes relates directly to the end of the preceding scene, and vice versa. Therefore, beginnings and endings need careful attention, not only in terms of whether they satisfy the needs of the scene itself, but also in terms of how they build the relationship between one scene and another. No scene exists in isolation from others, and in particular from its closest companions in your script. Where you have just come from, as well as where you are about to go to directly affects the choices you make for beginning and ending your scenes. As we look in more detail at a storyline, a little later on, we'll see examples of how this principle is to be borne in mind.

HOW TO BUILD A SCENE: BEGINNING IN THE MIDDLE

Having stressed the importance of beginnings and endings, you may be surprised to know the way I recommend you write a scene is to start somewhere in the middle. As I said at the start of the chapter, for the most part each scene is a fresh event, and so its purpose is to build on what has gone before, taking the story on to another stage. So, for the most part, each scene is *about* something new, and the entire contents of your screenplay should be reducible to a fairly simple list of progressively developing events on camera. There is a useful way in which starting off with this approach can really help you focus on defining each scene. If you cut to the heart of what the scene you're dreaming up is about, reduce this to a one-liner, note this down and then build the rest of the scene up around it, you won't miss the scene's meaning or leave it unfocussed.

Identifying the 'headline' which is the heart of the scene can give you an ideal platform both to build on and, in due course, also to check the resulting scene against: does it end up being about what you intended it to be about? Just to clarify what I mean by 'heart' here, I should point out that the key moment in a scene doesn't have to lie at its physical centre, more or less half-way through. Life would be very predictable and boring in some ways if this were the case. What I mean by 'heart' is the major moment which the rest of the scene builds to and revolves around.

Here's the storyline for a scene from a vintage episode of *Coronation Street*.

A man of his word, Percy turns up for dinner as expected. As Maud has gone to so much trouble Percy eats the meal she has made but there is clearly something wrong. Percy and Maud discuss their trip to France and Maud's visit to a particular graveyard. Percy has since talked to Maureen and discovered that Maud had an affair with an American soldier, and that he is Maureen's real father. Percy and Maud talk about it but Percy sees what Maud did as a terrible betrayal of her husband while he was away serving his country. Percy calls their engagement off.

A scene all about Percy's pride, the key moment in this scene, as storylined, is the last one, also the climax of the episode. What this scene is about is Percy breaking off the engagement. The rest of the scene is simply the run up to that moment when Percy's principled, angry reaction to the truth about Maud's past proves an insurmountable obstacle. So 'Percy calls their engagement off' is the headline for the scene – the one-liner core which the rest of the scene must be built around. That his decision is already made is signalled by his unease with sitting down to eat the meal, and the fact that his talk with Maud is not going to be about wanting to really hear her side of things. The storyline doesn't tell us he wants his mind changed. He thinks she was wrong.

The next thing to note is that it's Percy's scene. Just as stories have their protagonist, so too, scenes are very often driven by one character. It is that character who wants something and will try their best to get it. So, going back to the headline, it's clear what Percy wants – to break off the engagement. Beyond that, the deeper driver at work in Percy is his attachment to old soldierly pride and the black and white virtues of unquestioning loyalty.

So, Percy's overall objective in this scene is to finish the engagement. Why not just get him in there, let him tell Maud, and then wind up the scene? Because, just as with the telling of the whole story, conflict and narrative tension are the life-blood of its individual scenes: it is these which ensure the audience stays engaged and identified with the piece as it unfolds. Besides, the scene becomes a great deal more emotionally authentic once the writer acknowledges that there are contradictory emotions at play, and that this is a difficult process for Percy. He and Maud are not simply friends. In the end, writers look to play scenes (and especially big scenes) for all they're worth.

Maud is the antagonist in the scene, and she is going to fight to preserve their engagement. The interest in the scene isn't just going to be about how it turns out (though that, of course, is its chief interest): each emotional step should hold our interest and have us gripped.

EMOTIONAL JOURNEYING

For the scene to work fully, both characters need to have travelled from one emotional state to another, and in the process taken us with them. At the start of the scene Maud is trying to mollify Percy. She is guilty and feels sorry. Percy is stuck in self-righteous indignation, is nursing a grievance and obviously feels very angry. By the end of the scene, both are going to reach a point of resignation and deep regret. But they are going to get there by a carefully thought out route. Here's the very moving scene Patrea Smallacombe wrote from the storyline.

> SCENE 17 INT 1845
> SET MAUD'S HOUSE
> PSC
>
> PERCY. MAUD.
>
> PERCY EATS HIS MEAL IN SILENCE.
> MAUD NEEDS AN ANSWER ON HER
> FUTURE.
>
> MAUD:
> (OF THE FOOD) I'll have to remember
> that dish if you like it?
>
> PERCY:
> (NON-COMMITTAL) Mmm.
>
> MAUD:
> (SORRY) I was planning on telling you,
> Percy.
>
> PERCY:
> (DOUBTFUL) And when would that have
> been?
>
> MAUD IS UNABLE TO ANSWER. PERHAPS
> SHE WOULDN'T HAVE TOLD HIM.
>
> PERCY:
> You know, thought of coming home to
> wives and young ones were all that
> kept some blokes going.
>
> MAUD:
> (EVEN) But not all of them came back.
>
> PERCY:
> So some of you took out a
> bit of insurance just in case.
> (CHALLENGING) Is that how it was?
>
> THIS IS THE FIRST OPENING PERCY GIVES
> MAUD TO JUSTIFY HER BEHAVIOUR OF

SOME FORTY-ODD YEARS AGO. SHE
ISN'T ABOUT TO.

MAUD:
(DEFENSIVE) You weren't all so innocent,
either.

PERCY:
Are you referring to your Wilfred?

MAUD:
(QUIETLY) No. Not that I know of.

PERCY:
(POINT PROVEN) No . . .

MAUD:
(BITING BACK) I never asked. And if I had,
who knows if I would have
got the truth the way you all
stuck up for one another. Yes, you
were all in it together. And didn't
we know it. When you came back
it were like some secret society – one
us women could never be part of.
Fifty years on and it's the same.
You only have to go down t'Legion
and you can still feel it.
(ANGUISHED) Endless remembrance
ceremonies and D-Day celebrations.

PERCY:
Commemorations.

MAUD:
Don't any of you just want to forget?

PERCY:
(BETRAYED) It were you who used my trip
to Normandy to remember the war as you
saw it. You who've got the constant
reminder in your Maureen.

MAUD IS STUNNED INTO A CRUSHED
SILENCE. SHE DIDN'T SET OUT TO USE
PERCY OR HIS TRIP, BUT IT SEEMS FUTILE
TO EXPLAIN.

PERCY:
I saw blokes receive letters such as
the one I presume you wrote
Bombardier Grimes.
(TEARS BEGIN TO ROLL DOWN MAUD'S
CHEEKS.) They didn't think 'Oh, well, on to

the next one!' News of wives and
girlfriends giving themselves to the Yanks
killed 'em as sure as any gunfire.
Even knew of some willingly walking to
their deaths thinking they had nothing
more to live for.

MAUD BREAKS DOWN AND SOBS. SHE
DOESN'T WANT TO HEAR ANY MORE,
DOESN'T TRY TO DEFEND HERSELF OR
HER ACTIONS.

PERCY:
(ANGRY) Your men were young, frightened.
They were out there risking their lives
for you and that's how you
repaid 'em.

MAUD:
(DISTRESSED) We were frightened too.

PERCY:
(PULLING BACK) I'm not saying you
weren't. (EXHAUSTED) I suppose we all
dealt with it differently, that's all.

MAUD:
Maureen was part of our future – mine
and Wilfred's. He loved her. Loved me.

PERCY:
Then you were very lucky. But I'm
telling you, it wouldn't have been
my choice.

MAUD:
(COMPOSING HERSELF) And now?

PERCY:
Can't say as I feel any
different now as I did then.

MAUD:
(BRAVE) And neither do I.
(RESIGNED DIGNITY) So that's it then?

PERCY:
Aye. (WITH DIFFICULTY) I suppose it is.

WITH GREAT SORROW, BOTH HAVE
COME TO THE REALISATION THAT THIS IS
THE END OF THE LINE.

END OF EPISODE 2712

Going through the scene, it is worth noting some of the key moments and major shifts both characters pass through in pursuit of their objectives. The first couple of interchanges down to Maud's uneasy silence see her offer him the chance to forgive and forget – to carry on as if nothing had changed. When it's clear he doesn't want to know, she becomes regretful, trying to appease his anger. He is determined to punish her. With that in mind, he goes on the offensive. She stands her ground and with that line, 'But not all of them came back', is trying to plead mitigation for her infidelity. She's asking for him to see it her way. Percy ploughs on with his offensive, determined to get her to admit her guilt. The best means of defence being attack, she strikes back, trying to minimise what she did all that long time ago by referring to the disloyalty shown by men during the war years. Not to be deflected, Percy brings it right back to her doorstep, personalises the issue and asks whether her husband ever gave her cause to doubt him. She is forced to admit that he didn't and we reach the first point in the scene where Maud could admit defeat. But she rallies and renews her attack on the secret conspiracy of men with their endless 'celebrations' of war. He corrects her, pointing out that they're 'commemorations'.

Although the point of the scene is Percy breaking off the engagement, the following interchange forms the emotional heart of the scene, discovered by Patrea in the writing of it, and supplies the *reason* behind Percy taking this step. Maud's betrayal of her husband all those years ago was bad enough in Percy's eyes, but now he accuses her of a double betrayal; as he sees it, she used his recent trip to Normandy to betray him as well, by visiting the 'Yank's' grave. A secret lover she'd also kept a dark secret from him. Given that she's done that, how can he trust her now? It's an unimpeachable reason for dropping her. And from here on, Maud is unable to defend herself as Percy presses home the attack as he once might have made a bayonet charge (even though he was in the catering corps!). He accuses her of playing with Wilfred's life. It's the killer blow and pushes Maud to break down. Still he can't resist kicking her one more time, and in that moment Maud finds it in her to speak the simple truth – she was frightened. It touches a nerve with Percy, who comes to himself, comes back to the present, relents and finally shows some compassion. She breathes again. Perhaps he will understand and forgive. In the hope that she can free them both from the past, and save their future now, she refers to the way Wilfred came to terms with her waywardness and forgave her. The implicit invitation to Percy is clear; he shouldn't throw away what they've got. But he has already made his choice and at the crunch moment (Maud's 'And now?') he sticks with the past, leaving Maud to retrieve what's left of her dignity with an implied assertion she was (and is) only human, and has always been true to her feelings. They have reached the end of the road.

Throughout the scene, she has done her best to save the relationship, and he has stuck to his guns and accomplished what he set out to do – finish it.

It's a terrifically well-written scene, constantly moving Percy and Maud on from one stage to another, escalating the conflict, opening possible turning points, and in its touching conclusion, ringing absolutely true to character. You can see how nothing whatever has been left to chance here. Every stage has been thought through, crafted to flow naturally from the last, and calcu-lated to set up the next. It is especially true of this sort of TV drama that writers occupy themselves with the minutiae of characters' feelings from one moment to the next. These tiny brush-strokes form the substance of what these dramas are about. Crucial to this process is the writer's ability to *inhabit the emotional truth of each and every moment.* Indeed, I would say this is a corner-stone of all good dramatisation.

Just a couple of incidental points on this scene. You will notice with many of the lines Patrea has specified, in parentheses, the characters' intent, or their tone of delivery. On the whole this is a practice I'd discourage; write a line with clear enough intent and the actor should then be able to understand it, too. Obvi-ously, where there's room for misunderstanding, it can be very helpful to offer clarification. As for manner of delivery – which really relates to the emotional charge of a line – actors are skilled at working out an interpretative line through their characters' parts, and it can be no bad thing to leave them to do just that. *Their* way may not be the same as *your* way, but may be just as (if not more) effective. In the same way writers need a movie in their heads to write the script of a drama down, so they also need to hear their characters speak in their heads as they get their lines down; but, they needn't make the mistake of thinking that has to be the way it is all going to sound in production. So, why then would a very experienced and talented writer incorporate so many instructions on the page? I have several possible suggestions.

One is to do with the nature of high-pressure TV production undertaken to a tight schedule, where actors and directors have very little rehearsal time, and where the writer may well not be present to iron out any queries. These addi-tional pointers woven into the dialogue and action are offered by way of defini-tive and helpful clarification. Another reason may be that, just as TV companies have differing house-styles on the printed page, so too they may well have indi-vidual cultures and conventions on how much or little writers are encouraged to specify their 'vision' and intent. Clearly, with *Coronation Street* (as with many high-volume TV dramas) it is quite acceptable to be this prescriptive.

Finally, writers are individuals and do not all conform to a set of rules; they have personal preferences about how specific or not they want to be in their instructions. My personal recommendation is that you weigh the pros and cons; definitely clarify and supply supporting information where there's a need for it; and, at the same time, also allow for interpretative freedom of expression. In the end it's going to be your decision how much or how little you want to interfere or pin it all down. However, do try and differentiate between what *you* needed to create in order to make the scene live in your mind so as to write it, and what *others* may then want or need to do to bring that page to life on the screen.

Having looked at the thought, feeling and speech in this scene so closely, a word on the visual aspect. Often scenes rely for their first impact on what we see, and here we are offered a special meal – a clear sign that Maud has gone to some trouble for her man, and a visible sign of her bid to make a particular effort. This context underpins the poignant irony of the scene's outcome for the pair.

Experience teaches me that, having read all the analysis above, some people will now be saying to themselves, 'That's all very well, but surely to goodness writers don't *actually* think about all those things when they're writing a drama!' Well my clear opinion on that is that they absolutely do – and they absolutely don't. How much of it is a self-conscious process by the time a writer has become experienced at the craft is, indeed, a good question. But one way or another, I do believe that talented and experienced writers constantly perfect their skills in making the most of whatever it is they are writing. Whether it happens in the planning, during the actual doing, or in the reflective editing and honing of their work (and it's usually a mixture of all three) is really beside the point. Effective scripting is, as I said at the outset of this book, not an accident, and the more conscious you make yourself of what you are setting out to achieve, the more potential you will be able to fulfil.

CONSIDERING OPTIONS: WHAT IF ... THAT SCENE HAD BEEN WRITTEN DIFFERENTLY?

A well-written scene will always flow off the page with energy and presence. It may seem effortless and that things just couldn't have happened any other way. However, if the storyline for this scene had been given to another writer, the finished product would not have been the same; that much is a certainty. Just where, and to what degree, another writer's version would have varied, or how significant those differences would have been, is immaterial: the important point to grasp is that *you can always do it differently*.

With this in mind, it's important to note that your first thoughts are not always the ones which are going to make for the most effective or engaging version of a scene; before you get going, as well as throughout the writing process, it's going to be important to keep considering your options. It's also equally important *to make and commit to choices* having considered several different ways of writing your drama; without that commitment, the end product will retain needless ambiguities, and may well be short on clarity, presence and impact.

So, for the sake of a specific, concrete example, let's just look at the scene between Maud and Percy afresh, considering the kinds of different choices a writer could have made. Once a writer has been given the storylined version of a scene, they will very often work strictly to that outline. After all, if the storyline writers have done their job well, they will have grafted hard, presifting many possibilities. They will have tried to offer the one which fits the mood and tone best and also has most to play (offers the characters most conflict and potential for complication). However, as a matter of fact, apart from safe-guarding the continuity of the episode (that's to say, not overturning events in a way which will re-write history or go against character), episode writers often do make changes to storylined scenes in the process of making them their own.

For the sake of argument, let's consider total freedom to revise the elements of this scene, working to the single simple headline '*Percy breaks off the engagement*'. How might this have been written differently? To illustrate this I'm just going to track a few of my thoughts and see where they lead me.

Characters

Just who is going to be in a scene is one of the fundamental questions to be answered. Percy wants to break off the engagement. Does he have to do this in person? What if he writes a letter? What if he does this over the phone? What if he were to use a go-between? There is both the question of dramatic potential, as well as characteristic behaviour to look at here. First and foremost, Percy is no coward and it's very hard to believe that he wouldn't do this face-to-face. Scenes played out remotely tend on the whole to be much less dramatic than face-to-face encounters. Reaction is at least half the business of any scene between characters and can be the overwhelming interest. Certainly Maud's reaction to Percy's onslaught is affecting, and whilst she could get a letter and break down reading it, actually seeing him watch her distress has far more dramatic interest and impact. So it both fits his character and makes for better drama to bring them face-to-face. This also gives her a fighting chance to hang on to her man, which is, in part, what the scene is about.

It's always worth considering whether a scene would benefit from the addition of any other characters dipping in to help out or make life more difficult.

With the scene set in Maud's house, the answer to this question seems clear enough. If it was in a more public setting then the constraining influence of others nearby or the reaction of strangers to unchecked emotion could be an interesting and powerful addition. If, say, Percy were trying to control the meeting, and avoid uncomfortable shows of emotion by choosing a semi-public setting, and if Maud did her best to find privacy within that setting, the scene might offer an interestingly ironic take on the question of Percy's courage.

Setting

Where a scene is set is one of the most basic questions to address. Here it was decided to set the scene at Maud's. But what if . . . ? Well, what if the scene were set at Percy's? Given that he is a lodger at Emily Bishop's, there is the question of how much Percy's place *is* his or not to take into account. Not an insurmountable problem (it's always possible to get other characters out of the way) but definitely one to bear in mind. In any case, inviting Maud round is probably not a good idea and not credible. He wants to finish the relationship, and is also feeling angry; so he's going to want to be able to walk away as and when that feels right. He is not going to want to have to deal with any difficulties any longer than he has to.

However, what if he were coming from a different place emotionally and breaking this relationship off more in sorrow than in anger? What if he could see why Maud did what she did all those years ago, knew it really didn't matter in the grand scheme of things, and yet still just couldn't bring himself to carry on with the engagement? Given that as emotional background, maybe it *would* be very strong, dramatically, to invite her round to his place.

But that isn't the case. Percy's character is such that he *is* inflexible and what's more he *has* made up his mind. He is black and white in his opinions, and to make him change now would be unacceptable meddling in continuity; unless we were given some compelling reason, viewers would simply not believe another version of Percy. Even if he were still struggling with whether or not to carry on, it would still be stronger for him to be able to walk away. (It can be very useful to consider the question of a character's power in a scene and characteristically how much they are able to retain it or not.) In this scene, Percy is going to have to be strong, and we know he can be. It will not be easy but he must break off the relationship.

Well, if not at his place, what about on neutral ground? What if he's decided he must break off the relationship, and doesn't want the embarrassment of being looked after or made to feel at home? Where would be a good setting; the café or the pub? These are rather too public a setting for an intimate talk of this sort.

What about an outing to the park? This offers the possibility of safe, neutral ground where they can credibly find a quiet corner. Perhaps they have an awkwardly polite cup of tea in the park's café, not full of other Weatherfield regulars, yet still a constraining atmosphere. Maybe they then go and find a quiet spot before getting to the heart of the matter. What's more, that quiet corner might be not too far removed from the war memorial; tangible reminder of those other betrayed parties – Maud's dead husband and Percy's fallen comrades. Or is that too obvious? Hm . . . definitely worth thinking about: a sneakily subconscious move on Percy's move to turn the screw and punish a conscience-striken Maud? It has its appeal as long as that memorial is featured to just the right degree – not too much, not too little.

However, the park as setting would be putting them both in a place where things were already clearly cooler between the two of them. The scene as storylined chooses to have Maud believing, or at least telling herself, that the situation is retrievable, and the way to Percy's heart is via the time-honoured alimentary canal. This is a way of her demonstrating she really wants to hang on to him.

Where you can go to in a drama, depends largely on where you have been. So both character and plot play their part in dictating what you must play next and where you must play it. You can't just leap over stages: if Percy and Maud are relatively estranged at the start of this scene, we will need to know how that came about, and preferably to have seen it.

Finally, this scene is about home-truths, and where better to tell them than in Maud's home? Here, where she should feel safest, she comes under attack. It is an intimate environment for intimate dealings and as such is totally appropriate. My alternative thoughts about the park and the war memorial would be all well and good if it fitted where the characters were up to with each other, but I wonder if it could ever have the same impact as an intimate domestic setting: since the scene has to be the cliff-hanger, the major emotional moment on which we leave the characters and the episode, I wonder how much a strange setting would limit that all-important atmosphere. Perhaps it would be just a different kind of scene with a different kind of final moment. Percy falling silent and looking away, Maud doing the same, disconsolate, holding back her tears – the two of them tellingly framed against the backdrop of that war memorial.

Action

As you can see, the choice of where to play a scene is not unimportant and can have a real bearing on the action. As for the action itself, to repeat the point, as long as you are true to the characters and to the events which have impinged on their lives to date, then the rest is really up for grabs. What you have to watch for is which option offers the most potential. As we have seen from the finished scene Patrea Smallacombe wrote, there is a great deal going on for each of the characters and they both pursue their objectives as far as they can to a point which will not be reversed: end of story. (Well, until she tries to propose to him in the future! However, he did think she had to be joking. So to all intents and purposes the story of their romance is at an end.)

I've suggested there might be one or two alternative scenes to play – the café and park; or, building on that idea, say, for instance she has invited him for a meal, he has rung and cried off. She guesses what's happened and goes round to explain she was going to tell him about the past when the moment was right. With Emily lurking in the background, this is a highly embarrassing conversation for both and so, reluctantly, he agrees to take a walk so they can discuss the matter.

Then again, perhaps there's a scene in which Percy has made up his mind, calls round to return a gift Maud gave him during the engagement period. Whatever the choice you make, any alternative scene must take account of Percy's immovability and Maud's refusal to be rail-roaded into begging forgiveness for her behaviour in the past: she may be sorry not to have told Percy about it, but there's no sign that she is ashamed. (History tells us that she can be every bit as dogged and perverse as Percy.) So, even if we design a scene where she is forced to take the initiative in order to try and keep him, it's still important to be true to her character.

Remember, Maud's bottom line is still that she will not be shamed, Percy's that he needs to feel righteous: knowing what he does about her, she is almost a fifth columnist now, and whatever else you might do, you do not sleep with the enemy. The emotional attitude of each character must ring true to how they would behave under such pressures, and those emotional attitudes must be respected in the telling of the story.

KEEP ASKING QUESTIONS

Once again, the suggestions I've run through are by no means intended to be an exhaustive list. However, I hope they serve to illustrate the importance of constant self-interrogation. Like a good chess player, you have to try to plan ahead, scrutinising different possible runs of moments, to find the one which offers the greatest possible conflict, complication, the most satisfying resolution, and of course, through all this dramatic interest – entertainment. Whilst sorting through the different possibilities in your head, and focussing in here and there to test how you can make them solid, it's important to keep an open mind. Until you actually do commit to a choice, keep turning over possibilities. Don't be afraid of turning an idea through one hundred and eighty degrees just to see whether it plays more interestingly. Don't be worried about flirting with even the most outlandish of possibilities at the planning stage: some of the best, most worthwhile and eminently workable fragments are often discovered in the middle of otherwise unpromising ideas.

I stress the importance of all this because for some, once they have started involving themselves with and attaching themselves to particular ways of outlining a story, they then find it very hard indeed to see it another way. Yet, along with the capacity to visualise your drama, this capacity to pan for gold, as it were, is one of the most valuable assets you can develop as a writer of screen drama. All of which said and done, in the end it's just as important to be able to recognise which moment and which way of playing a series of moments really do speak to you, for those are the ones you're going to be able to give life to most convincingly.

THE FINISHED PLAN IS ONLY EVER A START

I remember talking to a writer friend after I had settled on the idea for how I was going to write a new play. I was full of enthusiasm and bubbling with excitement, even though there wasn't a word of the play as yet written. 'Enjoy the feeling,' said my friend. 'It never gets better than this – just harder'.

There is a cruel irony embedded in the fact that, just as you settle on a good outline which definitely can bring its own feeling of reward and completion, you realise you have to write it, and inevitably the writing of the piece will have its ups and downs, and even throw up one or two problems. Nonetheless, that vital planning stage, and the detailed step outline, within individual scenes as well as between those separate larger steps, will have assisted your process enormously. Make sure each step of the way builds on the previous steps and keeps carrying the story forward. Make sure the parts all relate to the whole, and vice versa. Keep telling the story, and telling the story means revealing what's going on each and every step of the way for all the characters involved, and even where that may be similar to what has gone on for them before, making sure it is still somehow different.

And if, at any stage, it all gets to feel too easy, you forgot to turn the engine on, and wherever you think you are, you're still sitting in the car park.

BUILDING SCENES INTO SEQUENCES

As mentioned earlier in the chapter, screen dramas are made up of interwoven strands of separate (though often related) stories. So how one builds each of these story strands, as well as how one chooses to inter-weave them, merits some close attention. It can be quite a complicated process, and depends on both craft skills and instinctive feel. Principally, there are two considerations at work. How do you build a run of scenes within an individual story strand so as to develop it to best effect? And then, how do you place each scene from one particular story strand amongst scenes from others, also to maximum effect?

Building an individual run of scenes

This essential process of constructing sequences is, of course, common to drama for both television and cinema. However to illustrate it here I'm drawing on another *Coronation Street* storyline. (Just to clarify one or two potential queries: on *Coronation Street* there has always been a strict convention of stating the precise time of day; there's also a convention of listing all the characters featured in a scene directly beneath the scene heading; finally, 'PSC' stands for 'portable single camera', and appears in the headings of scenes to be shot on location.)

Rather than reproduce all of Episode 4116 here, I'm going to pick out the main story strand and then look at how parts of that story strand were woven into a couple of short sequences using scenes from other story strands. At the top of this storyline, the four strands featured in this episode are summarised in headlines:

ANNE KISSES CURLY, MAXINE GOES FURTHER.
ASHLEY TAKES DON HOME.
TRICIA FINDS OUT ABOUT THE CHILD SUPPORT AGENCY.
LIZ HOLDS OUT ON JIM.

As the bold print suggests, Curly Watts' story is the main one featured in this busy edition of the soap. He is about to leave the street having been disappointed in love. The scenes (or parts of scenes) forming Curly's story in this episode are as follows:

SCENE 3 PSC THE STREET 1230
MAXINE. FIONA. CURLY. LIZ.
Back from shopping, Maxine notes that having a new man has certainly perked Fiona up, and she reluctantly admits that she misses Tony – she's *always* had a bloke in tow. Liz passes. Fiona tells her that she got a Christmas card from Steve – how is he? Well – has Fiona got five minutes?

Curly's off to the pub. He asks if he can buy these three a drink tonight, but they all decline. Rejected, Curly heads off. Maxine feels sorry for him.

SCENE 4 ROVER'S BAR CONTINUOUS
JACK. VERA. CURLY. TRICIA. FRED. NORRIS.
Curly expects to be the centre of attention but no-one seems interested. Vera hardly

gives him the time of day. Miffed Curly is unaware that Vera's pulling out every stop to make sure tonight is a success.

SCENE 6 PSC THE STREET 1330
CURLY. ANNE. EMILY.
Curly heads home, he's got a lot on today. Emily spots him – he hasn't forgotten that she's giving him dinner tonight has he? Curly bluffs that he certainly hasn't – he's looking forward to it. Anne's knocking on his door.

SCENE 8 WATTS 1345
ANNE. CURLY.
A present from Anne – a practical Swiss army knife. She eventually confesses her feelings – she's glad he's going, it will make life much easier for her. She's always carried a torch for him. If only things had worked out differently. She kisses him. Startled, Curly responds. Anne has to go before things go too far.

END OF PART

SCENE 10 WATTS 1910
EMILY. CURLY.
Emily tells Curly that dinner will be ready in about half-an-hour. Curly's reflective and considers the enormity of what he's doing – he's burnt so many bridges, and who knows what this trip has in store for him? He's looking at Raquel's star chart – what should he do with it? Kind Emily will look after it for as long as he likes. They set off for Emily's.

SCENE 11 PSC THE STREET CONTINUOUS
EMILY. CURLY.
Emily suggests a quick drink for old time's sake. Curly's not too keen, but she insists. She pops into the house with the star chart which leaves Curly standing alone in the deserted street. He takes a long look round.

SCENE 12 ROVER'S BAR CONTINUOUS
JACK. VERA. CURLY. DES. LIZ. JIM. MAXINE. FIONA. EMILY. ALAN. ANDY. ANNE.
TRICIA. NORRIS. FRED. MAUREEN. MIKE. ALMA.
The pub's packed with hushed regulars when Curly and Emily arrive. Surprise! He's truly gobsmacked and his eyes fill with tears. Jack says a few kind words and hands over the present – a camera, bought with the proceeds of a whip-round. Maureen beams at him. Andy confides that Anne's responsible for all this. Curly's touched, she *really* is a remarkable girl.

Fred and Norris can't help regret Curly's rashness, but they're smarmy to his face – he was on the point of being admitted to the Inner Rectangle! Another crevice to fill.

SCENE 14 ROVER'S BAR 2045
MIKE. ALMA. JACK. VERA. CURLY. LIZ. JIM. MAXINE. FIONA. EMILY. ALAN. FIONA.
ANDY. ANNE. TRICIA. NORRIS. FRED. MAUREEN.
Maxine's cornered Curly. He must be so upset about Raquel – is that why he's leaving? Curly would rather change the subject, but Maxine's intent on being 'sympathetic'.

SCENE 16 ROVER'S BAR 2045
JACK. VERA. CURLY. LIZ. JIM. MAXINE. FIONA. EMILY. ALAN. FIONA. ANDY. ANNE.
TRICIA. NORRIS. FRED. MAUREEN. DES.
Des is surprised to find all this going on – he had no idea Curly was leaving.

Vera and Tricia are celebrating their victory over Baldwin. Tricia goes to serve and Curly
tells Vera that there's something she ought to know. If Tricia signs on, the Child Support
Agency will track down Terry and tell him he's a daddy again . . .

Fiona reckons Maxine is drunk – can she get Alan to run her home? Maxine's going
nowhere. In that case, Fiona has other fish to fry – she leaves with Alan.

Curly bumps into Des at the bar. Des expects the worst, but Curly keeps his powder dry.
He feels sorry for Des. He dumps one woman and moves on to the next. He'll never
know what it's like to really *love* someone. Like Curly loved Raquel. Des finds this hard to
deny.

SCENE 18 ROVER'S BAR 2240
JACK. VERA. CURLY. LIZ. JIM. MAXINE. EMILY. ANDY. ANNE. TRICIA. NORRIS. FRED.
MAUREEN. DES.
The gloss has been taken off the evening for the Duckworths. Terry finding out he's a
dad can only mean one thing – trouble.

Time for Curly to go. Tears are shed. There are kisses from Anne and Maureen – neither
knowing how the other feels. Maxine's sitting on her own and gallant Curly wonders
how she's getting home. Fiona told her to get a taxi but she's not sure if she's capable.
Curly will sort her out. With Maxine clinging on to him he takes his leave of the Rovers.

SCENE 19 PSC THE STREET CONTINUOUS
CURLY. MAXINE. DON. ASHLEY.
Maxine fancies a night-cap – has Curly got anything in? He has – but just one, mind. In
the background, Ashley and Don cross the street.

SCENE 20 WATTS CONTINUOUS
CURLY. MAXINE.
Maxine would rather forget about the drink. She pulls Curly close and snogs him within
an inch of his life.

END OF EPISODE

Curly's story forms the spine of this episode, a major one for the character. As
such, it gets both the lion's share of the programme and is unsurprisingly given
both the end of part, and end of episode scenes. In addition, the first scene of
the episode establishes the preparations for the surprise of party so that, from
the beginning, the audience can savour the irony of what they know but Curly
does not. Curly's potential for fatal naïvety is what the episode plays off: there's
a surprise party and he hasn't got a clue it's coming; and then there's also the
question of Curly's innocence in the women department. Both of these are

explored with comedy and pathos – traditionally a hallmark of the *Coronation Street* ethos, tears and laughter often keeping close company.

So, from that first meaningful moment when he slopes off to the pub alone and 'Maxine feels sorry for him' in scene three, we may have more than an inkling of what she's got in mind, but Curly most definitely does not.

The first three scenes all build on each other to let us know that Curly clearly wants a get-together, a farewell drink, however informal, with friends and neighbours in the Rovers. He wants to feel that people care that he's going. He wants to feel he'll be missed. A casual invitation to Maxine, Fiona and Liz leaves him feeling snubbed and the next scene moves on to intensify Curly's feelings of rejection as people in the pub (including Vera, an erstwhile land-lady of his, and therefore closer than most) make a show of more or less ignoring him in the interest of maintaining surprise. Pretending that he has too much to do to linger, he heads home, and meets decoy Emily (his very first landlady on the street) who reminds him about her dinner invite. His bluffed reply underlines where he'd really rather be that evening, and empha-sises his sense of isolation. So Anne's appearance is timely; by now he is a man in need of consolation. And it arrives in the form of a Swiss army knife – a present which lets us know, whatever Anne's feelings are towards Curly, she's a practical sort of soul, not given to romantic impulses. All the more surprising for us, and for him, when she can no longer keep it all in, and comes clean about her feelings, giving him a kiss. Unsurprising, however, that just as he gathers his wits and responds, she reverts to type and runs off. Her fantasy is far safer than the real thing and Curly's left holding his knife. Par for the course. In fact, the writer of this episode had the good judgement to change the knife to a torch, both symbolising what she's been 'holding' for him in her heart, and also the perfect present for a man so frequently left in the dark where his dealings with women are concerned: now who's holding the torch? (In fact, in the end it was decided to go with just one present from everyone and neither the knife nor the torch made it through to the broad-cast episode – a reminder that the writing process is just that, a process.)

We leave part one intrigued and amused, wondering if this will come to any-thing. It's perfectly in character for Curly, so often disappointed in love, to find himself sitting alone in scene ten, pondering the wisdom of his action in leaving, and raking over a few regrets. The previous scenes have all built beau-tifully to this moment where he can open his heart to dear, kind Emily, pretty much a mother figure to him. So here we see the lovelorn husband holding his errant wife's star chart and openly wondering about what's to come: we could not have a clearer sign of how much he had seen his future as bound up with Raquel's. It is also a graphic reminder of how ill-starred Curly has been in relation to her, if not with women in general. Finally, for those who remember it, that star chart also reaches back to Curly's origins on *Coronation Street*. (Before he arrived on the street many years ago, he had turned down a place at university to read astronomy, an interest which, from time to time, he has in fact pursued.) We are invited to ponder with Curly, not only his place in the street, but in fact his place and meaning in the cosmos! If there's more than a hint of wry humour in the scene, there's also a good deal of sympathy for the character at work as well. Curly's helpless attachment to that star chart tells us where his heart is really tied up, and Emily's gentleness and sensitivity in offering to take care of the chart for as long as he wants, is a truly touching acknowledgement of his feelings and his deepest hopes. Handing it over to her for safe-keeping, is also a sign of beginning to let go, and of relinquishing those hopes.

In just five scenes Curly has been moved progressively from bonhomie, through disappointment and annoyance via bewilderment and further disappointment to reflective sadness: a journey from wanting to reach out, to needing to reach inwards. And so it feels quite natural that by the time Emily tries to get him into the pub for the party, he'd actually rather just spend a quiet evening with her, nursing his feelings. To get him to this point of melancholy solitude is perfectly judged, and maximises the impact of the overwhelming kindness he's about to be shown. We feel with him. The story has taken us along with his hopes that he is cared about and that he will be missed, and as he steps into *The Rovers* it fulfils those wishes. He, and we, are moved and satisfied.

The story can now shift up a gear and click back into the comedy of errors which makes up Curly's love-life. So Maureen can beam at him, a reminder for those who remember of her tenderness towards him, their ill-fated one-night stand when things were rough between her and Reg, and also of Curly's definite tendency for being used as a shoulder to cry on. So it was with Raquel, and so it is perhaps about to be with Maxine, who homes in, apparently offering her own shoulder to comfort Curly. Curly resists the invitation.

What we see is him being increasingly buoyed up by the drink and the mood of the party. That vulnerability we saw just prior to his arrival at the party has vanished and he's in warrior mode. And it's in this frame of mind that he deals with Fred and Norris smoothly over what they secretly see as his ill-judged defection; then he rains on Tricia and Vera's parade by pointing out the snag about the CSA, and reminding us what a good guy he is compared to Tricia's wastrel of a man, Terry Duckworth; finally, loins definitely girded for the occasion, he squares up to Des, responsible for so much romantic mayhem in Raquel's life. A fatal triangle these three, with Curly's love for Raquel being just like hers for Des – never truly reciprocated. So there's a lot of history behind this little tête-à-tête, and it's completely true to character, though scant comfort, for Curly that he would now claim a moral victory where Raquel is concerned.

The writing continues to take this expansive, empowering line with Curly, showing him surrounded by women who've all got a soft spot (or more) for him. But he's sorted; his life is free of complications, and he stands poised to ride out of town. On the face of it, he's just showing his usual, caring nature in offering to get Maxine back home safely: in fact, of course, he's succumbing to his unavoidable flaw, and is about to be taken in all over again. Maxine started circling him that very morning and is now going to snap Curly up in those gaping jaws, a veritable shark to Anne's minnow. We could be celebrating with Curly since he ends up going home with tonight's star prize, but somehow we already know, given Maxine's history, this is not about making *him* happy.

Now you can see how carefully orchestrated this story is, it's also worth picking out one or two key moments in the writing to show how they enhance what's going on. The crunch moments with Anne and Maxine are placed at the ends of the respective halves, book-ending the party and illustrating, by contrast, how Curly is fated to fall in with the wrong woman. At the end of part one, we wonder what, if anything, Curly will do about Anne; at the end of part two, we wonder what Maxine will do with Curly. When Andy promotes Anne's cause, in scene twelve, Curly can be touched but not enthralled. The next time we see him, Maxine already has him in her clutches. Despite the best of intentions, when it's his call, Curly is destined to make the wrong choices.

There's also a telling moment at the end of scene eleven. The writers have carefully engineered the moment to give us a desolate Curly lost in memories against the backdrop of the street. The cut is to a hushed expectant throng, and the contrast is effective. Cold, dark, lonely and excluding cuts to warm, bright, excited and inclusive, moments before we see Curly make the transition from one to the other. We know they are waiting for him; we also know what the impact is likely to be on him.

WEAVING STORY STRANDS

There are many pressures in the making of a soap opera which impinge directly on its writing. A major story is going to dictate its own inclusion; that said, there may well be a pressure to let a popular story run over a long period suspensefully, and so the question of when, and how often, to deal with a story becomes a matter of strategic judgement. Earlier in the book I mentioned *Brookside*'s Jordache family's 'body-under-the-patio' story as an example. Often in soap there are no major events to be writing about, and then when there *are* more important developments, as with this episode, they can threaten to overwhelm the rest of the storyline, squeezing the rest of the script into a corner, if not handled carefully.

Which other stories can be run is also affected by actors' availability; where scenes can be played is affected by the number of available sets and how much exterior shooting is available – so there are a number of logistical considerations to consider, which are going to govern the material storyline writers may have available to work with.

Clearly the art of the storyliners consists of doing their best to combine story elements where they can play off each other, or at least find their prompting from within one another, rather than just seem like an arbitrary assembly of events, piled up one beside another. All this must be done whilst also keeping an eye on the feel of sequences, their rhythm, allowing enough time to elapse between scenes so that it doesn't jar against the actual time which needs to have passed in the action of the drama. A further, seemingly simple consideration is how many characters are involved in runs of scenes; it can, for example, become very monotonous to have scene after scene, each with just two characters inter-acting.

In this script the chance encounter between Liz and Fiona in scene three gives Fiona the opportunity to mention the Christmas card from Steve; it's a perfectly credible pretext for her enquiry after him and for Liz to take the chance to unload. Their next scene together and, thus, the inclusion of that story, has been woven well into the fabric of the episode. It probably has least resonance with Curly's story and so needs to find its place; it is given least prominence of all the four story strands (one scene, plus one telling moment in the party) and is kept well away from the central story.

Don Brennan's story, on the other hand, offers more potential. The aftermath of a suicide attempt (his second), and especially Don's depression offer a sombre atmosphere, totally at odds with the party-planning going on down the street. The contrast is such that they work well against one another, seemingly having nothing in common. However, when we get to scene seven, sitting between the Curly–Emily and Curly–Anne scenes, we see it has been placed there with good reason. This is the scene:

SCENE 7 1315 PLATTS
MARTIN. DON.
Martin tackles Don. The smoke will have done some damage, carbon monoxide poisoning can have disastrous effects. He's *got* to have a check up. Don's one step ahead – Martin's talking about a psychiatrist isn't he? Martin comes clean; yes he is. Don will have none of it. Can a psychiatrist pay his debts, wind back the clock and stop his life

from falling apart? No way is he going to see a shrink. He blames the medical profession for saving him the last time. They should have left him to die like he intended.

Don is that much older than Curly, well into his fifties, and thoroughly embittered. The point of dropping this scene in here just after we've followed a rejected-feeling Curly home from the pub, is to offer us the comparison with Don. Will he end up like Don, isolated and desperate? The fact we've just seen Anne hovering by his door offers us hope that he will not; however, the resolution to the next scene with Anne, makes us think that it's a possible risk. Nothing ever seems to flow happily for Curly in his personal life. It's certainly a theme picked up in the second half of the episode, and explored up to the point where he stands alone and sad taking that long look round the street. At the same time, we know Curly is capable of bouncing back, and so is quite a different character from Don: the question left hovering is whether this will always be the case. The proximity of that scene about Don suggests, perhaps, that there but for the grace of God, perhaps, walks Curly. If we look at later scenes in the Don story, we can see how the theme is further developed and the comparison between Curly and Don used effect-ively. Just after Curly has had his moment of truth with Des at the party, we cut to scene seventeen in which Ashley, Don's lodger – shocked on his return from a trip away to discover what's been happening to Don – has now found him at the Platts'. So we go straight from Curly telling Des that he doesn't know the meaning of real love to:

SCENE 17 PLATTS 2210
MARTIN. GAIL. DON. ASHLEY.
Ashley wants Don to come home. Don wonders why Ashley should care one way or another. Ashley's answer is simple. He cares because he *cares about* Don. He's grown fond of him and can't bear to see him like this. Don is struck by Ashley's sincerity and eventually agrees to go home with him.

The scene demonstrates a depth of care and loyalty Curly knows about too, and sets up the idea of returning home which we are about to cut back to at *The Rovers*, where Curly faces the prospect of doing exactly that. If only he could find someone truly worthy of his attentions – someone who'll really care about him. Ironically, of course, he's about to 'find' Maxine.

And this link between the two stories is concluded with a deft little touch: as Maxine wangles her way into Curly's house, in the back of shot we see Ashley being a true friend and escorting Don home, having found a way through his depression and past his defences. The contrast in motives between Ashley and Maxine – selfless and selfish – forms an effective counterpoint. The moment also highlights the fact that both Don and Curly are emotionally vulnerable types. (Curiously enough, by the way, it won't be that long to go in *Coronation Street* history before Maxine and Ashley are married!)

STORIES WITHIN STORIES

Coronation Street, in common with other long-running series, is a never-ending story, whose chief concern tends to be about the relationships between the characters. So there are, as I outlined earlier, the characters' ongoing, longer-term stories in the series, as well as the stories we get offered, short-term within any one episode. Those individual, immediate stories also observe the rules of classic story telling.

In this episode, Curly is the chief protagonist. A dominant feature of his life on the street is that he wants happiness in his future, and love to work out for him. The longer-term version of this story has featured several women, and in particular Raquel. Although this episode clearly does relate to those longer-term events, it also offers us a shorter-term story concerning Maxine and Anne.

Curly wants happiness and love to work out for him. The obstacles to this are his naïvety and the fact his affections are still tied up with Raquel, who has gone. Does he get what he's after *within this episode*? Yes and no. The antagonistic forces at work mean that he cannot get it together with Anne so he falls foul of Maxine's predatory attentions. So he does end up with a desirable woman, but not the one he wants and at altogether the wrong time. The other thing he wants, a clean get-away, is compromised in the process. It's both a satisfying self-contained resolution, and one which leaves us enthusiastic to learn more. Such is the art of good soap; constantly paying stories off whilst managing to leave their audiences wanting more.

This does mean, as we have seen, that the arrangement of stories, their internal sequencing, and their patterning within the grander scheme of things – as with all good screen writing – does need careful planning.

In pointing out the artfulness of some of that patterning – how and where moments and scenes are placed in relation to each other – you may already have realised there are some reasonably reliable principles you can draw on to make effective transitions between scenes. Pointing up strong similarities or differences can ease your path, as can exploring resonance.

SIMILARITY

Earlier in the chapter I mentioned that beginnings and endings of scenes deserved special attention in terms of how they relate to the beginnings and endings of adjacent scenes: indeed, this can also apply to the beginnings and endings of sequences.

Cutting between similarities can feel like a very natural sort of transition, and there are different sorts of similarity to move between.

Identical dialogue

A line delivered at the end of one scene and then repeated at the beginning of another can be most effective. Consider this scenario.

A man, let's call him Ray, goes to take up a labouring job he's been offered by the local authority. He encounters Doug who's unaware of this development because he's not bothered to answer his mail. He doesn't like the idea and tries hard to deter Ray who sticks to his guns, insisting he's been appointed. He is only taking the job to please his partner, Kath. In grandiose mood, Doug insists this was sneaked in behind his back and he would never have agreed to the appointment. Finally he 'softens' and with obvious mischief in mind offers to 'interview' Ray the following day. Ray goes ballistic but remembering how important this is to Kath reluctantly agrees. As a parting shot, Doug tells him to get a good night's sleep because there'll also be 'a practical'. 'Practical?' Ray queries, totally flummoxed. We then cut to the next scene where Kath immediately repeats, 'Practical?!', shaking her head and oozing incredulity.

In a flash we've got the fact that she's had the whole story from Ray, and is not impressed with the fix he's got himself into. The cut graphically demonstrates and emphasises the rock and the hard place between which Ray is being squeezed.

Similar or identical action

Cutting between two actions, with one part happening in one scene and the other in the next, can help tie together scenes, and this device – the action cut, a favoured film editing trick – is also useful for the screenwriter to think about. It can be as simple as a character raising a glass to their mouth in one scene and a different character who has just finished drinking (in an apparent continuation of the action from the scene before) putting their glass down in the next. This kind of cut can also be a useful way of making a transition backwards or forwards in time. For example, a young girl bounces a ball against a wall. We see the girl, we follow the ball and see it strike the wall and then see the girl catch it. She throws it again, we see it strike the wall once more, but this time years have passed and we see a woman (obviously the same character but older) catching an almost identical ball.

Similar or identical imagery

Matching a particular image at the end of one scene and the beginning of another can be a useful device. The same house, landscape, boat, homed in on and matched perfectly via a rapid dissolve, can also take us from one moment backwards or forwards to another. A clock zoomed in on and then pulled out from can reveal the same setting at the same time of day, but weeks, months or years apart.

Then again, the juxtaposition of two very similar, but non-identical images can also help us move easily from one scene to another. For instance, a locomotive enters a tunnel at the end of one scene; at the start of the next, a matched shot of its toy counterpart, seen as if life-size, emerges from the tunnel on a model railway enthusiast's lay-out. The compressed similarity and difference between the two images surprises, combines and contrasts all at once.

Similar subject matter

It can also be useful to use a coincidental topic of conversation – though between totally different characters in a totally different time-frame – to move between scenes, making a virtue of the coincidence and allowing it to be the opportunity for the juxtaposition. Or, perhaps at the end of one scene, characters speak of a particular dream or fantasy, a world-cruise maybe, and at the start of the next scene we see that same cruise . . . with another character doing the cruising. As with the seeming absurdity of all coincidences in fiction, you need to be sure it fits the tone enough not to jar the audience out of its engagement with the piece.

Resonance

As we have seen with the Don and Curly storylines above, one can invite the comparison between characters or moments without trying to depict them as identical or even strongly similar. In the case of Don and Curly there are lots of differences; Don is much older and depressive, embittered, pessimistic and really quite a loner. Curly has plenty of friends flocking to show support, is bright and energetic; he always seems to manage to get on his feet again and start over. Yet, temporarily, there is a resonance of mood between the two, and the suggestion that Don's fate might just foreshadow that of Curly. There are times when the ripples spreading out from one scene can mingle with those from another, inviting some valid comparisons and tying those two scenes together.

Pace, tone and feel

It can be very effective to tie scenes together with moments of similarity in pace, tone or feel. The earlier extract from *Some Mother's Son* (p. 51) is a good example. The urgent pace of the dancing, its tone of traditionalism, as well as its feel of drilled precision, all marry well with the demeanour of and values held by the IRA team fulfilling its mission. Whereas the pace of action is observable and obvious, the mood, tone or feel of a scene can be a more subtle commodity, and calls for the writer to stay alert to what they are creating on the page beyond just the straightforward speech and action.

Another way of carrying over mood or intention from one scene to another, and tying scenes together, is via the music and effects tracks. Cinema has always recognised the power of a good music track, and where television drama has had the budget and the daring to follow suit, the gains have been tangible, and the well-timed reprise of a theme or motif can suddenly bond moments together or carry over the mood from one scene to another. Where lavish costume dramas had ploughed right in and copied from cinema, on the whole, smaller-scale, more domestically proportioned dramas had been more hesitant to follow: probably a matter of money, convention, the fact that TV tends to be relatively dialogue intensive and may not leave much room for an elaborate sound track, and of course, until recently, the inferior quality of sound reproduction available for TV have also been deterrents. It is interesting to note how some soap-operas, *Neighbours* for one, drew on a very cheap and cheerful version of this device to highlight heightened moments. The cross-over between cinema and TV drama, which became ever-more pronounced from the 1980s, and especially such ventures as *Twin Peaks* (Mark Frost and David Lynch), drove a horse and carriage through that sense of small-screen reserve and paved the way for a sizeable tranche of (especially, but not exclusively American) TV dramas to be quite elaborately orchestrated. Good examples of this are to be found in *Ally McBeal* (David E. Kelley) and *The Sopranos* (David Chase).

Carried-over sound effects or dialogue

Foreshadowing the first images of the subsequent scene by including their accompanying sound at the end of the preceding scene is a very common device used to pull the two story events together. So, at the end of one scene a character may announce their intention to get away somewhere, then while they're still talking about it or preparing to go, before we leave the scene, we will hear the sound of the train, plane or car used in their journey.

Similarly with a character recalling a scene from their past, it can be an effective device to include the sound from the first action of the following scene (the actual flash-back) quite audibly within the last moments of the preceding scene. Conversely, it can help to carry the last of the dialogue or effects from the preceding scene into the one following, letting it run out over the first images of what comes next.

These devices employed to anticipate or recall the contents of immediately adjacent moments in the story (though they may be far from immediately adjacent 'in reality') helps to maintain narrative tension and can serve to emphasise the link between events, or may help to expose the ironic gulf between them.

Similar but different

Sometimes you can juxtapose two moments which are similar but different, creating an interesting effect in the process. Take the example of a couple, Kevin and Pauline, who have gone out for a drive in the country. They start bickering and then have a full-scale argument. Finally Pauline demands to be let out of the car. In no mood to compromise, Kevin complies, and to her astonishment he then drives off. Much later, and seemingly oblivious to her fate, Kevin is taking a nice hot shower (in a glass-sided shower cabinet) and singing to himself, using the shower spray as a microphone. From here, we cut to a shot of a wet and miserable Pauline huddled in a phone box at night, trying to call home, the rain lashing down outside.

The overall images are similar; both Kevin and Pauline enclosed in glass cabinets, both holding handsets, one for the shower and one for the phone, whilst water cascades around them. And yet, of course, the differences are there to be appreciated as well. One is happy, warm (bathed by a soothing hot shower) and also safe at home, whilst the other is wet, unhappy and still miles from home, facing the prospect of an uncomfortable walk through the pouring rain. The superficial similarity between the shower cabinet and phone box only serves to emphasise the irony of the situation – an unbridgeable gap between both characters' circumstances.

Definite differences

Stark differences can also generate a lot of interest and can make for a powerful way of juxtaposing scenes. A total contrast between someone's stated intention and their subsequent behaviour can be an engaging combination. If someone tells their partner there's no way on earth they're going to go to *that* party with them, and then the very next scene we see them in tow, falsely beaming away at all the other party-goers, the gap between their firm stated intention and their actual behaviour makes us smile; this gap is intensified by the contradiction being made immediately apparent.

A similar device is at work when someone's voiced-over thoughts are saying something quite at odds with the pictures we see at the same time. In this case their actual or pretended self-opinion is set against the observable truth, and, again, the gap is illuminating, if not fascinating to the audience.

As with similarities of tone, pace and feel, pronounced differences between any or all of these can invite interesting comparison, and so make for powerful transitions. In *Network* (Paddy Chayefsky), the story revolves around a disenchanted news anchorman who is fired and promptly announces his intention to kill himself on air a fortnight hence. His show becomes compulsive viewing after he goes on air again – supposedly to apologise and say his dignified farewells – only to rant and (obviously unbalanced) indulge in apocalyptic truth telling. Newly-appointed director of programming Diana Christensen sees her chance to capitalise on events, make the show a huge hit for the station, UBS, and in the process do herself a big favour. Here is her moment of truth:

INT. UBS BUILDING, LOBBY
Howard Beale, bleached white by the GLARE of the CAMERA LIGHTS, is obscured by the CRUSH of cameras, REPORTERS, SECURITY GUARDS.

> HOWARD
> Every day, five days a week, for
> fifteen years, I've been sitting behind
> that desk. The dispassionate pundit . . .

INT. DIANA'S APARTMENT, BEDROOM
Diana, naked on the edge of her bed in a dark room, watches Howard Beale's impromptu press conference on television.

> HOWARD
> (*on TV screen*)
> . . . reporting with seemly detachment the
> daily parade of lunacies that constitute
> the news . . . and . . .

Also on the bed is a naked STUD, who isn't really interested in the news. He is fondling, fingering, noodling and nuzzling Diana with the clear intention of mounting her.

> HOWARD
> (*on TV screen*)
> . . . just once I wanted to say what I
> really felt.

The young stud is getting around to nibbling Diana's breasts.

> DIANA
> (*watching the TV set with single-minded intensity*)
> Knock it off, Arthur.

The juxtaposition of stark differences speak volumes. The noise, glare and turmoil of the bustling press conference in which Howard is laying his soul bare, contrasts strongly with the dark, peaceful cocoon in which Diana watches him. Here she actually is warm and naked, but is starting to show herself as cold, veiled and dangerous; we know from watching Arthur that her real thoughts and feelings are a million miles away from the apparent intimacy and vulnerability of her setting. Howard may be intent on saying what he really feels; it is questionable whether Diana even knows what she feels, and very doubtful whether she would ever say it. *In extremis*, Beale has set about reaching out, the best way he can, to all his faceless viewers: watching him do this, Christensen couldn't be less interested in the immediate human contact she actually has on offer, right there in her bedroom. It's clear what she *doesn't* want, and by implication we are invited to guess what really does turn her on. The darkness of her setting also suggests the secrecy of her scheming and the ruthless, dark nature from which it springs. The contrasts between the individual scenes underline a third level of meaning beyond the literal level of what's going on in either scene, and this third level is made available to us by comparing them both.

Differing tones

As mentioned earlier in this chapter, contrasting moods or tones can also make for arresting transitions. Perhaps chief amongst these is the juxtaposition of pathos and comedy. In *Brassed Off* (Mark Herman), set in the depressed northern English town of Grimley, the local miners' brass band battles towards and (eventually) wins the national competition, despite the closure of the pit, economic hardship, domestic tensions all round, and the illness of Danny its musical director. Danny's son has very bad luck, and faced with the threat of his wife and children leaving, he puts on his Mr Chuckles clown outfit to go and do some work as a children's entertainer. At real crisis point for Phil in the film, we suddenly cut to him in the middle of an abortive suicide attempt, dangling in mid-air dressed in the costume. The cut is doubly shocking – both because of his despair *and* because he's dressed like a clown, which only serves to underline the fact that Phil's bungled the attempt. Later, there is a scene in the hospital where his father is struggling with pneumoconiosis, still arranging parts for the band and determined to make those finals at the Albert Hall. The scene builds gently and the mood is sombre. Suddenly there is a rapid cut to the hospital corridor where Phil, still dressed in the ludicrous costume, is passing Danny's room. The contrast is shocking and effective – comedy and pathos tempering each other and proving a potent mix, reminding us of the complicated mixture of emotions life throws up.

Nurse Betty (John C. Richards and James Flamberg) has a most extraordinary shift of tone in it, and one which has a crucial function with regard

Figure 6.1   Renée Zellweger in *Nurse Betty* © Abstrakt/Gramercy/IMF/The Kobal Collection/Birmelin, Bruce

to the plot. Betty Sizemore lives in small-town Kansas working in a local diner and unhappily married to selfish, unfaithful car-salesman husband Del. She comforts herself reading romantic fiction and most of all by avidly following hospital drama *A Reason To Love* whose heart-throb surgeon, conveniently and just recently enough bereaved David Ravell, Betty dotes on. The film opens gently and amusingly on Betty's thirty-first birthday anatomising Betty and Del's awful marriage and showing both Betty's coping strategies and also the fact that she is not without spirit and initiative, as she secretly manoeuvres to borrow the Buick LeSabre she wants and deserves to go out in with friend and neighbour Sue Ann to celebrate her birthday, rather than the car Del has foisted on her. In the event Sue Ann can't get out to play and so Betty stays in to indulge herself secretly by watching an episode of her favourite soap, a habit which Del derides as 'people with no lives watching people with fake lives'. Unaware she is at home Del comes back with a couple of men whom Betty has seen and served as customers in the diner and who she assumes, from what Del has told her earlier, are potential customers for one of the Buicks. In fact Del has decided to try his hand at some unauthorised drug trafficking, fallen foul of the dealers and the two men, Charlie and Wesley, are father and son hit-men sent to retrieve the drugs and mete out retribution, which the younger man, Wesley, does with appalling violence when he scalps Del in retribution for an insulting remark about 'Injuns' and in order, as Wesley puts it, 'to make a statement'. The build up to this shocking scalping which is described, and was filmed, in graphic detail is interspersed with scenes from the soap episode Betty's watching in which Ravell has rejected the advances of scheming nurse Chloe, because he is not ready and knows there's 'something special out there for [him]', only to be accused of sexually assaulting her, putting his career at risk. Her attention finally drawn away by Del's cries of distress Betty looks through to the dining room from the den where she is watching and sees the scalping and Del's subsequent agony before he is put out of his misery by Charlie shooting him. It is anything but a gratuitous use of violence designed as it is to shock the audience sufficiently for them to believe the incident is enough to put Betty into deep post-traumatic shock and induce a level of dissociation in which her fantasy soap world now becomes a reality for her:

CHARLIE
JESUS CHRIST!!!

Wesley steps back, staring at the dripping scalp in his hand, as if wondering how it got there. Betty is transfixed, horrified.
Charlie re-enters. The two men look at each other over Del's MUFFLED SCREAMS as he plows headlong into the wooden panelling, a china cabinet, and finally back toward them near the breakfast counter. Del bashes blindly into it.

CHARLIE (cont'd)
(to Wesley)
What the fuck is the matter
with you?!

Wesley is practically foaming at the mouth, still rushing on what he did. Charlie draws a silenced pistol and mercifully SHOOTS Del through the head. The big man stops suddenly, blinks once or twice, topples over.

INT. BETTY'S HOUSE-DEN-NIGHT
Betty points her remote at the dining room and clicks it, as if trying to make the image disappear. Finally she gives up, slowly turning away from the carnage and aims at the TV. A Reason To Love pauses on the face of David Ravell and Betty sits in absolute silence.

The natural flight response Betty has to witnessing her husband's brutal killing is about to be transformed into a mission. Betty is about to become Nurse Betty, one time fiancé of David Ravell, and will suddenly take off for LA in pursuit of her one and only true love.

The plot of this comedy thriller develops with enormously entertaining ingenuity, 'art' (in the form of soap opera) and reality constantly vying to outdo each other, all underpinned by that imperative of comedy to be too much and keep delivering more. That switch of tone described above, though by no means the only one in the film is incredibly effective and the whole script really worth studying, demonstrating as it does how bold conjunctions of, and variations in, both mood and matter can excite surprise, arouse interest and intensify engagement.

Differing pace

Intercutting radical contrasts in pace can be a useful strategy. In the extract quoted earlier from *Some Mother's Son*, you may remember that just as the rocket was about to be launched, the girls were suddenly seen dancing in slow motion. Where there has been an unimpeded rush in a sequence, such a moment can herald the climax of an action sequence. It can maximise tension, just before all hell breaks loose. It can also eloquently counterpoint the reality of what's going on, taking the viewer out of time, as it were, aping the effect that shock has in actual moments of extreme crisis, to seemingly elongate time. In this case it also heightened the lyricism of those last moments of dancing. Equally, brief moments of frenetic activity seen cut against outwardly reflective calm, notably when moving into a flash-back sequence, can create a startling counterpoint and can also provide an effective transition into an extended sequence of that busier recalled activity.

These few examples are by no means meant to be an exhaustive survey: I hope they help to illustrate the importance of being aware of what kinds of transition in sense, content, feeling, tone and pace you are making in moving from one scene to another, and how those transitions – created by the moments you choose to move between – are *essentially* part and parcel of the business of writing. I do recommend that you read screenplays and, more importantly, pay close attention to the films and programmes that you watch, examining them closely to see what kind of choices have been made in joining up scenes, and to see how these choices do (or do not!) work to enhance the structure and meaning of the drama.

Exercises

1   Storyline a different scene for Percy and Maud in which he's persuaded to continue their engagement, and let Maud be the driving force in the scene. Perhaps try writing the scene. As ever discuss your ideas with a writing partner or the rest of your group.

2   The morning after for Curly and Maxine. Storyline the scene between them over breakfast. Storyline the next scene for both of them once they have parted.

Possibly as part of this, Anne comes round to say goodbye, only to find Maxine there. Go on to storyline the next scene for her as well, once she has left.

3   Pick a scene you particularly like the look of and write it.

Once again, where possible, cast your work and read it, then discuss what you thought.

7
Adaptation

A really useful practice which can help develop screenwriting skills, and in particular the ability to visualise scenes and sequences in action, is to try your hand at adapting a short story. If you are struggling to create any kind of a narrative through-line, then with this exercise there is, of course, the in-built advantage that the raw material is already there for you to take off from and work with. That said, it will still offer scope for invention and will also require you to reflect on the existing material and select with an eye to what will make for engaging and effective screen drama. Above all, as I've emphasised throughout the book, you will need to *visualise* the story as it already exists before translating that into a short screenplay, visualising it afresh and editing and augmenting image and action in the process as best fits your emergent script. In this chapter I will discuss both a short story and its screen adaptation. First though, a few general observations about the business of adaptation.

Any number of screen dramas have been adapted from short stories, novels, novellas and plays. A contentious acid-test often applied in assessing the success of the venture is whether or not the adaptation was 'faithful' to the original, and many's the time writers (and directors) of screen versions have been criticised for changing the original source material out of all recognition. Writers and perhaps more particularly directors can differ widely in their approach to this issue of keeping faith, or even in what way they choose to understand that idea. Hitchcock for example, when asked by Truffaut how many times he had read Daphne Du Maurier's short story 'The Birds' whilst preparing to make his film version, blithely retorted:

> What I do is to read a story only once, and if I like the basic idea, I just forget all about the book and start to create cinema.
>
> (Quoted by David Thomson, in the Virago edition of
> Du Maurier's short stories, 2007).

And of course it showed. The action was shifted from depressed, post-war, rural Cornwall to Marin County, California; the central character translated from a disabled ex-soldier, now part-time farm-worker, struggling to protect his wife and family, to a glamorous, philandering lawyer who, at the start of the film, is caught between three decidedly non-working-class women all competing for his attention - one of whom (shades of *Psycho*) is his clingy mother! The original story (published in 1952) hovers adroitly between the birds' mass attack standing as an allegorical, Jungian evocation of dark, unconscious forces, or more transparently as the manifestation of incipient Cold War paranoia, rooted in recent experiences of Blitzkrieg, and foreshadowing a feared Soviet-bloc invasion. After the first attack in the story, hero Nat Hocken warns his wife:

> 'There are birds in there,' he said,' dead birds, nearly fifty of them. Robins, wrens, all the little birds from hereabouts. It's as though a madness seized them with the east wind.'

And later a farmer asks him:

> 'Well what do you make of it? They're saying in town the Russians have done it. The Russians have poisoned the birds.'

(Ibid., pp. 6, 19)

Figure 7.1   The Birds © Universal/The Kobal Collection

Clearly Hitchcock was having none of that. In the film there is a jokey, flirtatious opening set in a pet shop, a romantically comedic love-tangle, scarcely a mention of the wider world outside Bodega Bay (and that only fleeting and local); this in stark contrast to the original story's use of BBC news bulletins specifically describing an unfolding national disaster. In the film the emphasis is on straightforward entertainment throughout. Du Maurier's original story closes with Hocken and family bleakly besieged, most probably doomed, only ominous silence from the once comforting wireless, Hocken's wife plaintively enquiring:

> 'Won't America do something? They've always been our friends, haven't they? Surely America will do something?'
>
> (Ibid., p.38)

Ironically perhaps, given that last quotation, and by way of stark contrast, with the Hollywood film we are unsurprisingly offered the central characters' escape and the anodyne prospect of a return to happy, privileged normality just around the corner.

But of course what Hitchcock did get hold of was that core element of massed birds and the terror of their attacks, realised most brilliantly on film. And as renowned master of suspense he improved no end on the pacing of that key component. In the book the first attack happens almost immediately; in the film, timing and intensity of the build up are gradual and judged to perfection.

In other words Hitchcock knew exactly what he was after – surprising and spectacular suspense-cum-horror – took that element and with the technology available to him in the late 1950s he worked it to perfection. And knowing what you want to do with a chosen story over and above simply translating it into dramatic action, is a very important part of the process of adaptation.

Another striking example of an adapter deliberately assuming a fresh point of view and inventing so as to deliver it to his audience, can be seen in Andrew Davies's TV adaptation of Jane Austen's *Pride and Prejudice*. Davies was very aware that 'Austen gave herself the limitation of never seeing D'Arcy on his own or with other men' (interview, BBC Radio 4, 5 August 2007) and decided to invent material which filled this gap so as to 'write a pro-D'Arcy' version of the story. Of course adapting a novel for serial drama is different from writing a feature film based on a novel. The latter will often result in the writer, as Diana Ossana neatly puts it, 'cutting a path through thickets of prose in order to shape a powerful screenplay while maintaining the essence of character and story' (*Brokeback Mountain, Story to Screenplay*, p.145). In contrast creating scripts for several hours of television drama can offer more latitude for invention and exploration. Indeed Davies took satisfaction in writing new scenes and making his audience believe they were penned by Austen.

Of course Jane Austen is no longer around to comment on how she feels about Davies's changes...unlike Susan Orlean, author of *The Orchid Thief*, the book about a plant collector which was the basis for Charlie Kaufman's brilliant screenplay *Adaptation*. The screen rights were originally optioned on a magazine article and subsequently the book which grew out of that article. Whilst the article clearly had the raw ingredients of a mainstream film, a fascinating central character, interesting and unusual subject matter as well as a crime (plant stealing), producer Edward Saxon had a creative challenge on his hands when the book was finished. As he put it, 'You couldn't take a highlighter to the book and say "There's our movie".' He did think it 'a fantastic book which needed a little glue to join it together as a movie...maybe a lot of glue' (http://movies.about.com: Susan Orlean and Edward Saxon interviewed by Rebecca Murray and Fred Topel). In fact Kaufman's screenplay takes considerable and, at first glance, unlikely looking liberties with its subject matter. Cheekily he uses a reflexive conceit and puts himself in the screenplay, one story strand tracing his tortured struggle to find a way of adapting the book, whilst his twin brother Donald (an entirely fictional creation!) breezes his way to newcomer screenwriting glory. And if that wasn't enough Kaufman goes on to include the character of writer Susan Orlean, in the script roundly (and fictitiously) defaming her as a drug-taking adulteress unethically involved with Laroche, the plant-hunter/thief subject of her journalistic assignment. Fortunately for the film makers Orlean proved to be a very game participant who (after some initial resistance) not only tolerated Kaufman's poetic licence and consented to her inclusion, but was also, ultimately, full of admiration for his skill:

> The book isn't a linear conventional story...it's not really about this crime, plant stealing – it's using the crime as a way of looking at issues of passion and desire and how you figure out your life...That's the irony of course, that it is actually an extremely faithful adaptation of what the essence of the book was for me.
>
> (http://movies.about.com: Susan Orlean and Edward Saxon interviewed by Rebecca Murray and Fred Topel)

If we take her at her word, and there's no reason not to, then it's clear that Kaufman's screen adaptation goes way beyond whimsical and hilarious inventiveness, insightfully probing the thematic heart of the piece and ingeniously laying it bare. There are, as they say, more ways than one to skin a cat, and that question of faithfulness to source material is less straightforward than it might at first appear. Perhaps there are several possible interpretations we can give that word 'faithful' as it applies to adaptation: faithful to the events and characters of the original story; faithful to the themes and ideas it explores; faithful to the story it relates; faithful to the tone in which it is told; faithful to what you perceive as the 'spirit' of the piece; or faithful to your own vision of what any or all of those criteria just listed might mean as they fit the adapted piece you create. However you choose to look at it, there are judgements and choices to be made if your adaptation is to engage readers effectively and clearly show the potential to make for engaging viewing.

In contrast to that case I cited of Hitchcock's *The Birds*, it is not uncommon for writers to read and re-read the original piece carefully before setting about the business of adaptation. This process of close scrutiny is aimed at thoroughly understanding the story, identifying essential characters and plot; noticing particularly in the case of novels (the very length of which usually calls for compression) whether events and characters can be conflated or omitted; or conversely, in the case of a short story being adapted into a feature film, noticing whether there is a need to invent extra material. And there does seem to be a general consensus around the importance of safeguarding the essence or true spirit of whatever is being adapted; lining up with the author's underlying intention is a crucial part of the task. So all of that said, I wonder what you make of this (very!) short story 'Encounter' by Norwegian writer Roy Jacobsen, translated by Frankie Shackleford.

ENCOUNTER

Arvid had delivered the fish to the packing plant and returned the boat to its moorings. It wasn't much of a catch, a half crate of cod, three big coalfish, and some rosefish – from forty nets! Still it was no worse than expected. It was a bleak time, with bleak expectations.

He rowed ashore in the dinghy and put the coalfish in the wooden crate on his moped. He always kept the biggest coalfish for himself. You can't get much for it, and besides, it tasted better than cod. He walked the moped past the drying rack and up onto the road, brushed wet snow off the seat, and put on his driving goggles.

From the packing plant it was twelve kilometres home on a country road, straight across a flat swamp. It could be a tough trip in the winter, but Arvid just bent over the handlebars when the weather got too bad, didn't push down on the gas so hard, and made sure that he stayed in the middle of the road. He got up at five every morning, and drove the twelve kilometres to take the fishing boat out to sea. In the evenings he drove back. It was a nice rhythm. His parents had been farmers, but Arvid was a fisherman. He liked the sea better than the soil.

Figure 7.2   Encounter © Joe Tucker

He started the engine.

Up on the swamp he shifted into third gear and accelerated. It was a gray day with no wind, so he could drive fast. When nobody was looking he sometimes leaned forward over the handlebar even though it wasn't really necessary.

After driving a few minutes he caught sight of a small figure at the other end of the world. It was moving towards him on the narrow ribbon of road and resembled a man on a moped, his own mirror image almost. . . Arvid didn't understand what this could mean. There was only one moped on the island and that was his. Once in a while there was a warm mist over the swamp that distorted one's vision, but that was only in the summertime.

He gave it more gas and leaned even closer into the handlebars. The figure was getting larger. It really was a man on a moped. Arvid moved over to the right a bit, but not much, so that his opponent had to yield more than he did. They passed each other. The man on the other moped was a black man.

Arvid sat up straight. He drove 230 meters into the darkness before he managed to brake. He stopped and looked back. The black man continued driving as though nothing had happened, kept getting smaller and smaller and threatened to disappear completely.

Arvid pulled himself together, turned the cycle around and went after him as fast as the moped would go. Fortunately the black man wasn't going very fast - he was the type who sat upright and looked around at the scenery while he drove. And slowly but surely Arvid caught up with him, glided up next to him and looked at him. They looked at each other. The black man smiled. He, too, had a crate on his baggage rack. Arvid signalled that he should stop. They stopped.

Arvid got off his moped and walked right up to the man.

"What are you doing here?" he asked.

"I be selling books," said the black man and patted the crate.

Arvid couldn't imagine anything more meaningless. The man talked just the way the blacks talk in the Donald Duck comic books...

"I came by ship," he said. "Many be buying books here on the island."

"By *ferry*," Arvid corrected and was forced to laugh. "You came by ferry. This afternoon?"

"Ja,ja," the black man continued to smile. He said he was a student from Ghana and that he had to sell books to finance his studies.

Arvid had never seen a stranger man. He took off his goggles and moved even closer. The black man took off his goggles, too.

"What kind of books?" Arvid wanted to know and slapped the crate.

"You be interested?" asked the man cheerfully and got off his moped. "Fine books."

He opened the crate and paged through a book, since Arvid's hands were too dirty to touch it himself. The book was red on the outside. On the inside there was a lot of text and Arvid saw several pictures of Jesus. The book was called *Gleams of Light*. He wrinkled his nose. He didn't like Jesus. They had a church in the community, but it was only used for confirmations and funerals. The black man laughed at him and pulled out another book. It was green and much thicker. It was a cookbook. Arvid looked at the colored pictures of the various dishes. He didn't like cookbooks either. But he didn't want to abandon this mystery so soon.

"Will you manage to sell this stuff?" he wondered

"Ja, ja," said the black man. "I be going over there now."

He pointed at the farm of Martin Grønli, which they could barely see smoke from at the other end of the swamp. Arvid thought that though Martin couldn't read, he was probably just dumb enough to buy a book.

"Don't you have anything else?" he asked.

The black man happily pulled out one more.

"This be a novel," he said and displayed a thick book with nothing but writing. It was called *Moby Dick*.

"I've heard of that," said Arvid and was suddenly embarrassed. Maybe it had something to do with the name *Moby Dick*, but maybe it was just that he felt sorry for this person from the other side of the world who didn't realise how ridiculous he was.

"I'll take it," he said.

"Buying?"

"Ja,ja, buying."

But it was a premature act of charity, for Arvid had only a wrinkled wharf invoice in his pocket and nothing else. The black man looked at him.

"Fish," he said and pointed at his crate. And Arvid could, of course, have offered him the coalfish, but it sounded as if the man said "fish" just to show that he knew the word.

"I don't have any money on me," he said. "but you can come to my house afterwards, and I'll pay you then."

He explained where he lived, but they weren't able to communicate well enough, so he had to draw a map on a piece of paper that the black man gave him. He wanted to give him the book right away too. He could pay later.

"Take it," he said.

Arvid hesitated. He wiped off his hands and held the book with his fingertips. It was heavy and nice to hold. He stuck it under his overalls, closed the zipper and looked around. There wasn't really anything else to say.

"Ja,ja," he said and was on the verge of exploding with laughter. The black man was laughing too. They got on their respective mopeds and started the motors. They put on their goggles, lifted their thumbs in greeting and drove off their separate ways.

Arvid steered straight ahead in the middle of the road without leaning over the handlebars. He was stiff. After several hundred meters he stopped and looked back. The black man was just a little figure on the other end of the swamp. Arvid stood still and watched him disappear. The only thing left of him was *Moby Dick* heavy against his chest.

The story has one or two qualities which immediately make it an attractive proposition for adaptation into a short film script: first there is its own brevity and the palindromic neatness of its ending; then it has an evocative setting, a wintry landscape of working fisher-folk's coast and, at its heart, the moody, mysterious limbo of a seemingly endless stretch of swampland at twilight perfectly fitting that 'bleak time with bleak expectations' described in the very first paragraph; and also it has the immediately entertaining, highly intriguing, synchronous coincidence of the near identical mopeds ('his own mirror image almost') fated to meet in that archetypal wasteland, and Arvid catching sight of that 'small figure at the other end of the world'. In itself this is a strongly evocative image redolent of one of the most famous shots in cinema that of Sherif Ali's famous long, slow approach towards camera out of the heat haze across the desert in *Lawrence of Arabia* (Robert Bolt and Michael Wilson). It is a comparison further summoned up by that mention of occasional mirages in summer on this stretch of swampland; yet in this Norwegian story that memorable moment of high romance blends with the much more absurd evocation of Arvid, a latter day Don Quixote, charging for the joust. And beyond those associations there simply is the curious contact between black man and white man, at one level almost as if a printed filmed image was meeting its photographic negative.

Then there is the story to consider and what it might be taken to mean. It is certainly a piece which resonates at different levels - that of the unfolding, literal action but also carrying religious and cultural associations all within a definite air of the allegorical with clearly more than a hint of looking at what it means to 'meet yourself coming the other way'. But before looking at that any further let's see how Joe Tucker approached the business of adaptation:

ENCOUNTER

1. EXT. COAST. EVENING.

ARVID, a young, bearded fisherman in his late twenties, is out at sea in a small, rusting trawler boat. He hauls in a meagre catch and throws it into a crate. The spasming fish barely cover the crate bottom. He selects the largest fish and inspects it, before slipping it into the front pocket of his overalls. We see its head poking out.

2. EXT. FLAT SWAMPLAND. EVENING.

The title fades up over the following:

ARVID is riding down a long, straight road on his moped. He is wearing goggles and a helmet. He leans over his handlebars rather unnecessarily. We see the fish head poking out of his pocket.

3. INT. ARVID'S HOUSE. NIGHT.

ARVID sits alone in a sparsely furnished and dourly decorated room, eating his fish. His wet clothes dry in front of the fire.

4. INT. TOILET. NIGHT.

ARVID sits on the toilet reading an old comic book. The comic book caricatures black people as racial stereotypes, with over-sized lips and wide, wild eyes. He smiles as he reads.

FADE TO BLACK.

5. EXT. FLAT SWAMPLAND. EARLY EVENING.

ARVID is travelling home on his moped. Again a fish head peeks out from his top pocket of his overalls. In the distance, another character, also on a moped – almost ARVID'S mirror image – catches his eye. ARVID shakes his head in disbelief and goes for another look. Sure enough, we see a rider on a moped headed towards ARVID. The rider is a young, black man named EZE. They pass one another at close quarters, almost colliding. ARVID stops and looks over his shoulder in disbelief at the stranger who rides off into the distance. Turning his moped round, ARVID pursues EZE. EZE drives in a relaxed manner, sat upright and looking around at his surroundings. ARVID signals for him to pull over. He obeys and remains seated, smiling as ARVID dismounts and approaches him, out of breath.

> ARVID
> What are you doing here?

> EZE
> I be selling books. To finance my
> studies. Many be buying books here
> on the island.

ARVID looks in total disbelief and bewilderment at EZE.

> ARVID
> What kind of books?

> EZE
> Fine books. You be interested?

EZE opens one of his books and begins to flick through the pages. We see only text, then suddenly and very briefly a picture appears. As EZE watches the pages turning, ARVID gingerly takes the opportunity to study the stranger's face. EZE looks up and ARVID quickly breaks eye contact.

> ARVID
> Turn back.

EZE turns back the pages and when he reaches the picture ARVID puts out his hand to stop the pages turning. It is an image of Jesus. ARVID wrinkles his nose in displeasure. He points at another book.

                    ARVID
            What about that one?

EZE begins to finger through a second book for ARVID. It is a cookbook and ARVID is disinterested. EZE moves to get back on his moped.

                    ARVID
            Will you manage to sell this
            stuff?

                    EZE
            Ja, ja.

                    ARVID
            Don't you have anything else?

EZE spots the fish poking out from ARVID'S overalls and happily reaches for another book. He produces a copy of Herman Melville's 'Moby Dick'. It has a large image of the white whale on the front.

                    EZE
            This be a novel.

                    ARVID
            [Excited]
            I've heard of that. [Pause] I'll
            take it.

                    EZE
            Buying?

                    ARVID
            Ja, ja, buying.

ARVID pats his pocket in search of money. EZE points to the fish.

                    EZE
            Fish.

                    ARVID
            I don't have any money on me.
            You can come to my house
            afterwards. I'll pay you then.

ARVID points behind him to a lone cottage in the distance.

                    ARVID
            [over pronouncing his words]
            My house, see? You understand?

                    EZE
            [offering the book]
            Take it. Please.

A pause, then ARVID wipes his hands and takes the book. He removes the fish from his pocket and places it into his crate. He puts the novel in its place. The white whale's head on the cover of the book pokes out over the top of his pocket as the fish did.

                        ARVID
                [holding back laughter]
        Ja, ja.

EZE nods and laughs too.

                         EZE
        Ja!

ARVID climbs on his moped and starts his engine. EZE starts his engine and they both put on their goggles. ARVID lifts his thumb in greeting and EZE does the same in response before riding off. ARVID rides away in the opposite direction.

ARVID looks over his shoulder and we see EZE disappear over the horizon. Finally we see a close-up of the book against ARVID'S chest, the white whale's head poking out from the pocket.

END CREDITS.

The first thing to notice is the way Joe Tucker changes the opening, inserting a scene actually showing Arvid out at sea fishing. It is really not at all uncommon to make such a change, introducing interesting action at the start of an adapted screenplay to hook the audience's interest, cinema thriving on landscape and movement of characters, camera or both. For example, in another famous and remarkably faithful adaptation of a Du Maurier story, *Don't Look Now* - already mentioned in an earlier chapter, screenwriters Allan Scott and Chris Bryant invent action to dramatise what is back-story in the original piece – the death of a little girl. The original short story opens with John and Laura Baxter in a Venetian restaurant on holiday trying to recover from the shock of this tragic loss. They are about to have their first contact with a pair of elderly sisters one of whom is psychic and has a message for them from the dead little girl; dramatic prospect though this is, the scene itself is very sedentary and driven by dialogue. By way of adaptation Scott and Bryant introduce new material showing a fatal accident – (in the story she has already died of meningitis) – in which the little girl drowns whilst playing. The build up to this is intercut with John and Laura happily installed in a warm interior after a lovely lunch – before that cosy scene is shattered by John's sudden premonition and desperate ill-fated dash to save his daughter.

Though 'Encounter' is certainly a long way from 'Don't Look Now' in content and tone, Roy Jacobsen's story also starts a lot less cinematically than Joe Tucker's adaptation. Lively action will usually play better on screen at the start of a film, and work to establish atmospheric mood. Not only is the same information conveyed but for screenwriting purposes Joe improves on the original. We see Arvid is a fisherman, but in a very small kind of way; Arvid is alone and notice that the trawler is described as small and rusty. This eye for telling, specific detail can be so important in screenwriting and is clearly at work here. Given what I'll suggest is a running theme of fishing in the story and in particular the way in which *Moby Dick* features, it is poignant to compare this down-at-heel, unromantic and unworldly figure with that of Captain Ahab. And from the off, with Arvid, still at sea, popping that coal-fish (a very miniature whale indeed) in his breast pocket, the ironic contrast is effectively drawn. That moment with the fish is also of course Joe Tucker's invention. In the story the fish is taken and thrown into a wooden crate on his moped. It is left to near the end of the story for the reader to hear about *Moby Dick* and then retrospectively reflect on the comparison between Arvid, unassuming hero of a tiny short story, and Captain Ahab the driven, demonic, vengeance seeking centrepiece of Melville's huge epic. In his adaptation Joe sets that comparison in train from the start, revising the action to highlight the theme and create comedic tone. There is something incongruously funny about popping a fish (still alive, as that curiously coined 'spasming' tells us) in your breast pocket, almost as if it were a pen; a tamer comparison to harpooning and running after a giant whale would be harder to find. Of course the idea of putting the fish there also sets up the impact of this short film's final image, and quite possibly was inspired by the image of the book against Arvid's chest already in the story. In the following chapter on metaphor, I will discuss in some detail how consciously structuring and plotting the imagery in a script is an essential part of effective screenwriting and further pick up on that aspect of this adaptation. But for now, by way of further illustration, I'll mention in passing a small, very significant change made by director Nicolas Roeg to the scripted version of that opening sequence of *Don't Look Now* mentioned above. In the script, Baxter's little girl, Christine, as 'seen' by psychic Heather is wearing 'a little blue dress'. In the film (as Mark Sanderson notes, BFI, 1996) Roeg elaborates on the existing image of the girl's red ball popping to the surface of the pond as she drowns, taking just the colour and giving her a hooded, bright red PVC coat; this also reverses the colours of coats worn by Laura and Christine in the original story, and is all part, not unconventionally, of establishing red as a consistent sign of danger in the film. Crucially, though, it also sets up a direct correspondence and deliberate confusion with the red-coated, murderous dwarf who is to be John Baxter's nemesis in the dark back streets of Venice. The power of an adjusted or elaborated image and invention around how it is included can be considerable, and Joe's fish-in-the-pocket image (fishing in any case being close to Arvid's heart) amounts to just such a device.

The second scene in Joe Tucker's script is also a new one, though again credibly dramatised from action which is reported in Roy Jacobsen's story. Showing a travelling shot of Arvid making his regular journey home has the immediate merit of continuing the moving action. Moreover it establishes and rehearses that regular 'rhythm' of Arvid's work-life mentioned in the story, one which we're told he is well accustomed to and likes. In addition Joe takes the opportunity to amplify the comedic element he has already introduced. The goggles mentioned in the story are now supplemented by a helmet, the full motorcycling monty being quite simply funnier to look at. Given the fact Arvid's metal steed is a tiny moped, the scope of his high-speed, daredevil fantasies – indicated by that leaning forward over the handlebars – are decidedly at odds with reality; Arvid is a far cry from being any kind of Marlon Brando or Peter Fonda. Above all, that image of the fish head poking out of his pocket lends the shot an absurdly amusing twist. It's worth pondering the irony of Arvid's judgement on the student visitor in the story, the moment when he 'felt sorry for this person from the other side of the world who didn't realise how ridiculous he was'. Just who is the more ridiculous figure here is a question Jacobsen is inviting the reader to engage with and one Tucker also explores in this script. Finally, taking the opening titles over this shot is not only aesthetically appropriate (and a commonplace for road movies), it also foreshadows exactly where that encounter of the title is going to take place.

The next two scenes are also invented by Joe Tucker, and this time completely from his imagination but again predicated on strong likelihood. The transition from cold, noisy exterior to gloomy, near-silent interior is a distinct and effective switch of scene and mood, underscoring Arvid's solitary existence and implicitly suggesting his circumstances and environment hardly invite company. He is shown as subsisting, surviving in a restricted little world rather than happily thriving; fishing for a meagre catch and then consuming part of it so he can go and do the same again. All of this builds a picture of his daily existence, a normality which we will in due course measure against that of an adventurous, enterprising student far from his homeland taking practical steps to raise money to support himself and his studies.

The next scene showing him reading a comic-book whilst on the toilet is unexpected, earthy and immediately amusing, again working to build Arvid's character. Taking his cue from that mention of the Donald Duck comic books, Joe Tucker conjures this entertaining moment. It suggests something about Arvid's reading habits, a level of childish playfulness and possibly of limited literacy too, certainly hinted at later in the story, and in retrospect it's a moment which will again ironically contrast Arvid and Eze, given the latter's status as a student and easy familiarity with books. The book's illustrations depicting stereotypical black characters pre-figure and explain Arvid's ignorant and prejudiced condescension towards the Ghanaian when they meet. There is also an intriguing, incidental prescience about those illustrations, in tune with the haunting coincidence about to unfold.

The opening sequence allows Joe to jump time after the fade out and we rejoin Arvid as he returns from work the next evening, that fish in his pocket being all the explanation we need. And with no further ado we are at the heart of the action.

So something really to notice here is the way simple description, thought, or reported action can all provide inspiration and raw material for scenes which actively explore character, setting and tone whilst moving the story forward.

Though the script from here on in follows the story fairly closely, there are one or two changes worth noting. (Incidentally, just on a technical level the next block of action is not paragraphed into possible shots, but I doubt that it was all being envisaged as one shot. As I pointed out earlier, how a script will be shot is the director's prerogative; nevertheless there is nothing to stop the writer blocking the action into possible shots.)

That said, most of the significant moments in the story are highlighted, and one or two are pointedly omitted. Arvid's astonishment on encountering what he at first takes to be his reflection is there, actively underlined by the inserted double-take, which also indicates that Arvid thinks he may be imagining what he is seeing, perhaps building on that mention of occasional, optical illusions made in the original.

In the story it is clearly implied that Arvid plays a game of chicken with the stranger:

Arvid moved over to the right a bit, but not much, so that his opponent had to yield more than he did.

In the adaptation Tucker pointedly omits this moment, substituting it with:

They pass one another at close quarters, almost colliding.

It is not an unimportant change. In the story Arvid has a patronising, bemused attitude to the stranger who, as mentioned earlier, he clearly considers laughable. In the story he is torn between ridicule and pity; when he decides to buy the copy of Moby Dick it is an 'act of charity'. Quite unaware of his own prejudice he assumes a position of superiority, that of the native islander who belongs and knows all, as opposed to the naive, incongruous outsider trying his luck; and this delusion is reinforced by that comic-book scene we have already watched. Positioning himself dominantly on the road is clearly an aggressive manifestation of that perception. So Joe Tucker's decision to omit the moment decidedly tones down the dynamic at work, and this odd couple's near collision which Eze simply rides on from, apparently with perfect equanimity, now reads as if Arvid's driving is no more than absent minded, induced by his total surprise at the encounter, and then amplified at the last moment by a xenophobic reflex as he gets a close-up look at the stranger. In fact the overall tone of the piece dwells more on the whimsical than the satirical, though the latter is certainly still there to be discovered.

The fact is that Eze, as Joe names the Ghanaian – lending him a specific individual identity he does not have in the original story – becomes more an object of curious fascination (notice that stolen moment of close-up scrutiny by Arvid inserted in the adaptation), than the potential butt of Arvid's supercilious assumptions, chief amongst which must be just who has got the better of whom by the end of this encounter. That fascination I just mentioned is there in the original. We are told Arvid prolongs the encounter because 'he didn't want to abandon the mystery so soon', and the screenplay dramatises that nicely by having Eze giving up on a sale and making to move off before Arvid stops him by showing continued interest.

The reference to Martin Grønli is lost from the adaptation. It would have been possible, if difficult, precisely to dramatise Arvid's scepticism or amusement at the prospect of a sale to his illiterate neighbour, but the inclusion of that moment would only have served either to establish Arvid's unfavourable judgement of an opportunistic, exploitative student, and to explore further the heavy irony Jacobsen injects into the story; after all it is clear Arvid himself is more responsive to pictures than text and may himself not be much of an intellectual power-house. Tucker sums all of this up in that moment of Arvid over-enunciating the simple direction to his house, when it is clear by now that this student is far more intelligent than the simple fisherman is able or willing to credit. Put this together with Arvid needing to see the picture of Jesus before the penny fully drops that he is looking at a scriptural text and the ironic reversal of the time honoured 'Christian missionary-and-gullible-native' story is complete.

And the adaptation inserts another telling moment which further explores that theme of religiosity. As Eze flicks past the page with the illustration of Christ, an invented moment is inserted with Arvid putting his hands dirty from fishing out to stop the pages turning. The image is an arresting one, graphically demonstrating Arvid's lack of reverence and providing a telling contrast with the way he wipes his hands on his overalls before taking delivery of the novel. The right image will often serve to synthesize or crystallise layers of meaning in a way which will work on both the viewer's conscious and subconscious, not only delivering essential theme or meaning in a way which is appropriate to the medium. A fisherman's dirty hand holding down a picture of Christ is just such an image.

The important change made in the adaptation is that fish-in-the-pocket image finally replaced by a picture-of-huge-fish-in-pocket image. On one level this is in itself enough to explain the barely suppressed laughter between the two characters which then breaks through as they catch the funny side of the swap. At another level, as I suggested earlier, it's all about suggesting some one-upmanship at work. In the story Arvid stops and looks back at the disappearing stranger. In the adaptation he merely looks over his shoulder and presses on. This avoids breaking the flow of action and allows for attention to move fluidly between that look over the shoulder, to Arvid happily pushing on home, and thence to a big close up of that comical image of the whale peeking over the top of his pocket. Ironically the story ends with Arvid having been sold a dream of wild seafaring adventure, the story of Moby Dick, which might feed some sense of grandiosity but which he is unlikely (probably unable), to be able to consume as fiction, let alone get anywhere near emulating in real life; meanwhile the stranger rides off with 'the one that got away', a flesh and bone fish which he will certainly eat and be nourished by. But before the viewer makes any sense of the film's final moment or puts any reasoned conclusion into words, (s)he will simply be struck and amused by the sheer absurdity of an image wittily calculated to make a lasting impression. And it is the ability to recognise (as well as invent) those images which hold potential to carry weight and summarise meaning or layers of meaning which is central to the business of adaptation.

Though Roy Jacobsen's story is a very compressed affair, I hope you can see both the scope it offered for an interesting adaptation and also the care and intelligence with which Joe Tucker attended to the choices and changes he made whilst clearly telling the story.

Last but not least, I should mention the business of acquiring rights. Any story which is out of copyright is fair game and you can simply adapt and film a script from such a work. (Do note that UK copyright extends seventy years after the death of the author – US sometimes longer.) If a story is still in copyright and you have any intention of publishing or filming your script, then you need to acquire the right to do that. This can be done by contacting the rights department of the publisher who may deal with it themselves or more likely will give you further details of whom else you need to contact to get permission. Bear in mind that rights to dramatise may already be held elsewhere or may quite simply be unavailable. Having said which don't jump to the conclusion that a well-known writer is going to turn down your request; I know of at least two students who approached very celebrated writers and acquired film rights for short stories. And of course if it's your intention to adapt a copyright story as a writing exercise pure and simple with no other goal in mind, there is nothing to stop you at all.

Exercises

1   Read the short story 'Encounter' again identifying the tone or meaning you take from the piece, which could be quite different in places from what I have written about in this chapter. Try outlining moments and scenes which work to express your different way of looking at the story.

2   Pick a short story you like then take a paragraph which is all about a character's interior process, reported action, or which is simply heavy on description. Now dramatise this paragraph, omitting, changing or inventing material as needed to make an effective screen drama.

3   Read some other short stories with the business of adaptation in mind. Pick out one or two and put them into screenplay form.

8
Metaphor and moment: deepening your drama

Having previously spent some time looking at the finer detail of scene construction, it's time to take a look at the bigger picture once more. In the last chapter I touched on the topics of imagery and theme. In this chapter I'll discuss these aspects of screenwriting in more detail and explore how careful choice and judicious management of both can really help you achieve greater impact and depth of meaning in your story telling for the screen.

If you cast your mind back to *Two Sharp*, you'll remember that the imaginative impulse for that story was the idea of a pencil in need of a sharpener. In summing up the story I said that, following my first instinct, and letting the story unfold, it turned out that first image proved to be a potent metaphor, without going into any detail. Now it may be useful to look at the idea of metaphors in more depth, with the aim of understanding how you can draw on them to deepen your story telling process, and lend your writing moment: the very thing we're trying to create in effective drama is the moment; as well as 'an instant', this same word can also mean importance. It is the creation of a succession of instants or brief periods of time which carry significance and impact, that is the dramatist's business.

In *The Poetics* (trans. Malcolm Heath) Aristotle tells us:

> . . . the most important thing is to be good at using metaphor. This is the one thing that cannot be learnt from someone else, and is a sign of natural talent.

Well I think I'd quibble with the notion that you've either got it or you haven't in the metaphor department. As Aristotle goes on to say, handling metaphor is essentially 'a matter of perceiving similarities'. The way I prefer to look at matters, consciously setting out to make yourself aware of the ways in which expressive devices are used in dramatic writing can be a very powerful step along the path of starting to use them effectively yourself. It may also waken up your own readiness to 'perceive similarities'.

So what is a metaphor? The word itself comes from Greek and means 'to transfer'; what it boils down to is one thing standing for another as well as for itself. A metaphor combines both a literal and a symbolic level of meaning. It is the concurrent co-existence of both levels of meaning which give metaphors their power. Here's a script by Joanna Smith which illustrates clearly how a well-chosen metaphor can be pressed into service:

THE GREENHOUSE EFFECT

FADE IN:
EXT. STREET OF TERRACED HOUSES. MIDDAY.
MAUREEN (mid 40s) dressed in a supermarket overall with a coat over it, and carrying shopping bags is walking down the street. Tired and preoccupied she reaches an end-terrace house and walks up her front path. Along the passage at the side of the house she catches sight of her husband, DON (late 40s). He is intent on laying out the sections of a self-assembly greenhouse in the small back garden and doesn't notice her. MAUREEN pauses, puzzled and irritated, trying to make sense of the scene.

>   MAUREEN
>   Don?

DON looks up, giving a little wave and a sheepish smile.

>   DON
>   Alright, love?

MAUREEN walks down the passage and over towards where he stands surrounded by all the pieces of the kit, taking it all in very quickly.

>   MAUREEN
>   What the hell are you doing?
>   DON
>   It's a greenhouse.
>   MAUREEN
>   (sarcastically)
>   Oh, really? (BEAT) And where's it come
>   from?
>
>   DON
>   Off Pete. He'd had it for a
>   while, but never got round to putting
>   it up. So he give it
>   to me.
>
>   MAUREEN
>   He *gave* you a greenhouse?

> DON
>
> Well, no. I paid him fifty quid
> for it. It's brand new.

MAUREEN responds with speechless exasperation.

> DON
>
> What? It's still in the packing, look. He's
> not going to give it away, is he?

> MAUREEN
>
> No, of course he's not. Not when
> there's an idiot like you to give
> him fifty pounds.

> DON
>
> I know things are a bit tight,
> but I thought –

> MAUREEN
>
> No, you didn't.

MAUREEN turns away abruptly and starts to walk back down the garden path. She looks back over her shoulder at him.

> MAUREEN
>
> I don't believe you, I really don't.

DON is left standing amidst the pieces, looking after her retreating back. She goes through the back door and slams it. He sighs and dejectedly picks up a section to carry on with his building.

INT. KITCHEN. CONTINUOUS.
The table is still covered with breakfast things. Washing-up is in the sink. No attempt has been made to clear up. MAUREEN's face is set with suppressed anger. She slams around, throwing food into cupboards. She starts to clear the mess from the table over to the sink, where she catches sight of DON through the window, busily intent on the greenhouse. She exhales angrily, watches him for a moment and then continues clearing up.

DON enters the kitchen. MAUREEN ignores him and carries on. He hovers in the doorway, watching her.

> DON
>
> I'll put the kettle on, shall I?

MAUREEN continues her activities noisily and doesn't look at him.

> MAUREEN
>
> Oh, do what you like.

DON continues watching her and doesn't move. MAUREEN turns the tap on violently and the water gushes into the sink. She squirts the washing-up liquid in angrily.

> DON
> I know it's fifty quid, but –

> MAUREEN
> You don't even like gardening.

> DON
> That's not true. I've never
> had the time.

> MAUREEN
> Rubbish. I used to have my work cut
> out getting you to mow the lawn
> on a Sunday. And now all of
> a sudden it's a bloody greenhouse!

> DON
> Well, I was working then, wasn't I?

> MAUREEN
> This house is over-flowing with your
> abandoned 'hobbies' and 'interests'. You
> never finish anything. You go off
> half-cocked, leaving a trail behind you –

DON looks away from her and stiffens. He interrupts her with controlled anger.

> DON
> Well, I've got plenty of time now!

Abruptly he leaves through the back door. MAUREEN pauses for a moment, then goes over to the door and calls after him.

> MAUREEN
> But no time to do the dishes
> or clear up I see. More important
> things to do.

EXT. BACK GARDEN. CONTINUOUS.
DON stops in his tracks, pauses, but doesn't turn or respond. He continues resolutely to his greenhouse kit. Shaken, MAUREEN crosses to the kitchen table and slumps into a chair. Distressed, she fumbles in her bag, takes out and lights a cigarette. Quietly she starts to cry.

EXT. GARDEN. CONTINUOUS.
DON sets to his task with grim determination.

INT. KITCHEN. CONTINUOUS.
The doorbell rings loudly. MAUREEN starts, scrabbles in her bag for a tissue and rubs at her eyes. The doorbell rings again.

> MAUREEN
> Alright, alright.

INT. HALLWAY. CONTINUOUS.
MAUREEN comes down the hall and opens the front-door, to her daughter JACKIE

(early 20s). The smile of hello drops from JACKIE's face as she takes in her mother's distress.

> MAUREEN
> Oh, Jackie.

MAUREEN's face crumples as she starts to cry again.

> JACKIE
> What's up? What's happened?

JACKIE enters and puts her arms round MAUREEN.

> MAUREEN
> He's bought a greenhouse.

MAUREEN pulls away gently from JACKIE and goes back down the hallway back into the kitchen. Closing the door, JACKIE follows, perplexed.

> JACKIE
> What? What are you talking about?

> MAUREEN
> Your Dad.

> JACKIE
> (trying to take it in)
> You're crying because Dad's got a
> greenhouse.

> MAUREEN
> Yes. No. I mean, it cost fifty
> pounds. We can't afford to throw away
> fifty pounds. What does he want with
> a greenhouse? He hates gardening.

> JACKIE
> Well, maybe he thinks it'll give him
> something to do.

> MAUREEN
> He shouldn't be pottering round with a
> watering-can. He needs to get a job.

> JACKIE
> He knows that, Mum. It's not easy.

> MAUREEN
> Oh, I know. It's just . . . it's been
> six months now, and nothing, not even
> an interview. How long's it going to
> take? I'm worried he's never going to
> get another job.

JACKIE

So's he. But he's still looking, isn't he?

MAUREEN nods.

JACKIE

Well, then, he hasn't given up. That's
what counts. And if this helps . . .

MAUREEN

I know. It's just money we haven't
got spare. A greenhouse of all things!
What possessed him?

JACKIE squeezes her hand. MAUREEN smiles back.

JACKIE

I'll go out and see him.

JACKIE leaves the kitchen, walks down the path to where DON is so deeply immersed in his construction he doesn't notice her.

JACKIE

Alright, Dad?

DON looks up, pleased to see her, and stops work.

DON

Hello, Jack. You alright?

JACKIE

Yeah.

They both stand looking at the part-assembled greenhouse for a few moments.

JACKIE

This is it, then.

DON

Mm. Your Mother still mad at
me, is she?

JACKIE

She's calming down.

DON

I know it probably sounds daft, but –

JACKIE

Dad, you don't have to justify yourself.
(pause) How are you getting on?

DON

Oh, alright. The instructions are missing, but

it seems fairly straightforward. Although this
bit's foxing me, I must admit.

He picks up a section and starts fiddling again. JACKIE watches him. He carries on
working, his face a picture of concentration. They stay in silence for a few moments.

> DON
>
> I can't win.

> JACKIE
>
> What?

> DON
>
> Whatever I do it's wrong. I used
> to do stuff around the house, try
> and help out. But that got on
> her nerves cos I didn't do it
> right, or I put the plates back
> on the wrong shelf or something.
> I don't know . . . so I thought,
> right, best if I don't interfere.

> JACKIE
>
> You know what she's like, Dad. She's
> got her set way of doing things.

DON pauses from his work and looks up at her.

> DON
>
> But what am I meant to do?
> Where does that leave me?

He resumes his work.

> So I got this. I thought that'll
> give me something to do. Maybe grow
> some tomatoes and that. Keep out
> of her way a bit. But then
> that's wrong too. I can't win.

> JACKIE
>
> She doesn't mean to take it out
> on you. It's her way of coping.
> She's scared, Dad.

DON pauses in what he's doing but doesn't look up.

> DON
>
> So am I, Jack. So am I.

JACKIE puts her arm round him and hugs him. He smiles weakly.

MAUREEN has come out holding a cup and saucer, and is watching them from just
outside the back door.

MAUREEN

Jackie.

JACKIE

Yeah?

MAUREEN

Ask Alan Titchmarsh if he wants
this cup of tea.

FADE OUT

The greenhouse is, of course, the metaphor. An important thing to notice is that it has a strongly credible place in the story *at a literal level*. It is entirely believable that Don would have bought such an item. He has got it in a bid to occupy himself and to fill the time he has on his hands. As he also says he aims to grow a few things, perhaps some tomatoes, and so be productive; in itself symbolically important to a man who has lost his job, and whose daughter has grown up and left home. And on top of these reasons there's also the fact that he now finds himself getting under Maureen's feet and feeling like he's nothing more than an irritant to her. So, at the literal level, we can believe in this turn of events, and also see how buying the greenhouse has only served to fan the flames between him and Maureen: the greenhouse is not only an extravagance in Maureen's eyes, she may well also perceive it as a sign that Don has given up trying to find work, thrown in the towel and settled for a premature (if enforced) retirement.

The greenhouse is also working hard for its keep at the level of deeper symbolism. Consider the qualities of a greenhouse: fragile, brittle, hot, transparent and therefore exposing. Don's vulnerability and the hothouse atmosphere between him and Maureen (one in which only distance and friction seem able to flourish) are mirrored in the qualities of the kit he's trying to assemble. Moreover, Don is discovered standing amongst the pieces of this greenhouse. As the story progresses, we understand how his working life is also in pieces, how his domestic life is threatening to be, and how he is trying to 'put the pieces together' in more ways than one; again, the literal and the symbolic are tied together. In other words, Don standing amongst the pieces is a graphic illustration of what he is literally trying to build, as well as what things have come to. There's a cleverly judged moment in the writing when daughter Jackie asks, 'How are you getting on?' He chooses to understand her question as applying purely to the job in hand, but his answer ('Oh alright. The instructions are missing') also carries on the symbolic level of meaning. Handling unemployment, with its damaging knock-on effects, does not come with its book of instructions either. Revealingly, once he has deflected the true intent of Jackie's question and she has given him space to do so, he starts to open up about his fears and his difficulties, something he has been unable to do with Maureen. We have seen him rowing with her in the kitchen, where significantly he gets no further than hovering in the threshold: it's clear he isn't feeling welcome in his house and so there is an additional poignancy to Don's efforts to construct another 'house' to go and spend his time in.

I suggested at the beginning of the book that stories often achieve mythic or proverbial resonance: this one may well put the viewer in mind of the saying, 'People in glass houses shouldn't throw stones'. Certainly, the story develops in line with this proverb. At the start of the film, Maureen is seen returning from work, carrying shopping – clearly the breadwinner. Given this, it's doubly frustrating for Don who hasn't got a leg to stand on when it comes to fighting his corner. Again this is very well picked up on in the writing:

> MAUREEN
> This house is over-flowing with your
> abandoned 'hobbies' and 'interests'. You
> never finish anything. You go off
> half-cocked, leaving a trail behind you –

DON looks away from her and stiffens. He interrupts her with controlled anger.

> DON
> Well, I've got plenty of time now!

Abruptly he leaves through the back door. MAUREEN pauses for a moment, then goes over to the door and calls after him.

> MAUREEN
> But no time to do the dishes or
> clear up I see. More important
> things to do.

EXT. BACK GARDEN. CONTINUOUS.
DON stops in his tracks, pauses, but doesn't turn or respond. He continues resolutely to his greenhouse kit.

Finally, Joanna had the wit to use her title 'The Greenhouse Effect' to pull in yet another level of meaning; global warming, or rather over-heating, is the consequence of the 'greenhouse' gases depleting the ozone layer and rendering our world vulnerable to natural disaster. Plainly and simply, the overheating between this couple is what is placing the world of their marriage in danger, and it's notable that the story ends on the hopeful cooler note of truce and conciliation.

From all of this, it should be plain how well-chosen the greenhouse has been as the occasion for a short story. It serves as both totally credible pretext for the conflict visibly acted out between Maureen and Don, and as potent metaphor carrying a layer of meaning which symbolises the unspoken undercurrents and overtones surrounding their relationship. It is this secondary layer which nudges us into a greater understanding of what is going on and makes the drama both an emotionally transferable and a fuller experience.

Getting the balance right, so that a metaphor is *equally* poised between the literal and the symbolic is crucial. Very often metaphors are made obvious, if not extremely obvious to an audience, and as long as the balance of significances is right this obviousness helps rather than hinders the processes of understanding and emotional engagement. In Lasse Hallström's film *My Life As A Dog*, we follow the story of a young boy coming to terms with his mother's impending death. To allow her peace and quiet he is sent away from home to stay with an uncle and aunt; his father is 'away', Ingemar believes, working as a sailor on a banana boat, though the strong implication is that the separation is a more permanent one. Ingemar is now also separated from his own dog, Sickan. The film is also interspersed with moments when Ingemar reflects on the fate of Laika, the dog sent into space by the Russians

Figure 8.1   My Life as a Dog © 1985 AB Svensk Filmindustri

and left up there to die. Early in the film we see how closely he identifies with his own dog. After he and Sickan are separated, he never stops asking after the dog, and asking when they can be reunited. Near the end of the film it becomes necessary to move Ingemar again, making him stay with an elderly neighbour, in a sense sending *him* out to kennel yet again. He agrees, on condition that he can have Sickan come to stay with him. Shortly after, Ingemar discovers his dog has been put down and his uncle has lied to him. In his distress he seeks sanctuary on a freezing night in the ramshackle summer house he has helped his uncle build. When his uncle comes looking for him, Ingemar plays a familiar game of escape, pretending to be a dog, barking and warding off contact. His uncle leaves food and drink outside for him and Ingemar finds a warm coat to put on. When his uncle does get in next morning, he finds the boy crying his eyes out. In a superb piece of writing Ingemar asks for reassurance that he didn't kill her, that it wasn't his fault – and his uncle thinks he is talking about the dog; in fact, Ingemar is finally starting to grieve for his mother.

By the time the film shows us Ingemar in the thick coat barking like a dog in the summer house, the metaphor could not be made more explicit, and indeed the title of the film is there all along prompting us to draw the parallel. The reason that the metaphor is not *too* obvious is that the literal chain of events holds true throughout, and is entirely credible. The metaphor has its secure place at the *literal* as well as at the *symbolic* levels of the piece.

Another fine example of metaphor at work can be found in *Driving Miss Daisy* (Alfred Uhry).

Spanning the years between 1948 (just prior to the American civil rights movement) and 1973, *Driving Miss Daisy* traces the relationship between Daisy, a rich, elderly and irascible Jewish widow and Hoke, an unemployed black man, who proves to be patient, dignified and loyal, hired against her will by Daisy's son to chauffeur her around once it becomes clear she's no longer able to drive herself.

The story moves from downright hostility and rejection on her part springing from pride, humiliation and quite possibly unconscious prejudice, to a position of acceptance and equality. An early scene shows Daisy refusing to be driven, whilst Hoke follows, urging her to allow him to drive her. The final moment of the film (in the old people's home, Daisy now aged 97) shows her genuinely caring about Hoke's welfare and letting him help her with her food.

Central to the journey which both characters make is the Hudson car Hoke chauffeurs for Daisy; or rather a series of cars, as they are updated over the years, with previous models passing into Hoke's ownership.

At the literal level, the car stands for personal independence and mobility. At the symbolic level the car stands for social independence, status and mobility. In one key scene, for example, Hoke is driving Daisy to the synagogue and they are forced to turn back when they find out the temple has been bombed by racists. It is a sobering moment for Daisy (who, we have seen earlier in the film, is very uncomfortable with the idea of being seen to have a chauffeur waiting for her at the synagogue), as she now wrestles with the idea that she and Hoke are fellow travellers in more ways than one.

On one level the story is about circumstances throwing two unlikely characters together, and the sparks that fly as a consequence; at another it can be seen to explore ideas of racial and social tension and inequality; and at yet another, the story is about a journey – both actual and metaphorical – (chauffeured by Hoke) in which Daisy travels from unbending pride to openness, humility and the acceptance of common humanity. *Driving Miss Daisy* turns out to be a powerfully personal piece of drama as well as one which speaks to much broader, universal concerns.

Brokeback Mountain, is another story centred on deeply held prejudice, this time amongst the rural dispossessed of Wyoming. E. Annie Proulx's stunning short story, adapted by Larry McMurtry and Diana Ossana and magnificently directed by Ang Lee also makes use of a well-chosen and superbly effective metaphor. If Joe Tucker's short screenplay makes much of its last image so too does *Brokeback Mountain*. The story of forbidden and ill-fated homosexual love between two latter-day wranglers in Wyoming culminates with the killing of Jack Twist. When he eventually gets to hear of his lover's death Ennis Del Mar makes a journey to Twist's parents. Left alone in Twist's room he spots a shirt of Jack's in the closet, still bloodied from a nosebleed he, Ennis, incurred in the rough and tumble of a passionately playful encounter. The shirt is 'stiff with long suspension from a nail'. He takes it out:

> The shirt seemed heavy until he saw there was another shirt inside it, the sleeves carefully worked down inside Jack's sleeves. It was his own plaid shirt, lost, he'd thought, long ago in some damn laundry, his dirty shirt, the pocket ripped, buttons missing, stolen by Jack and hidden here inside Jack's own shirt, the pair like two skins, one inside the other, two in one.
>
> (*Brokeback Mountain, Story To Screenplay*, p.26)

A perfect metaphor for the hidden love between the two men the shirts in the closet appear at the beginning and just before the end of Proulx's story. The final moment of the screenplay is lifted almost verbatim from the short story with the addition of two moments:

And there on the back of the closet door, WE SEE THE SHIRTS, on a wire hangar suspended from a nail, and next to them, a postcard of Brokeback Mountain, tacked onto the door.

He has taken his shirt from inside of JACK'S, and has carefully tucked JACK'S shirt down inside his own.

He snaps the top button of one of the shirts.

Looks at the ensemble through a few stinging tears.

ENNIS

Jack, I swear…

Stands there for a moment.

Then closes the closet door.

He looks out the window, at the great bleakness of the vast northern plains…

(Ibid., p.97)

The additional moments inserted in the screenplay are that snapping of the button which speaks of caring intimacy and the look out of the window which summons emptiness and despair. The shots carry devastating emotional power on screen and work predominantly through the haunting image of those empty shirts in mute embrace.

At the start of this book I talked about the importance of recognising when an image, or a moment, held the potential to make a story: I also pointed out that stories have power for us *because* they are metaphors. Therefore, developing this ability to recognise when a setting, image, or event provide both the occasion for a totally believable, engaging narrative at the surface level, *as well as* carrying the potential for deeper meaning is a key asset in a dramatist's armoury. It is a skill which, when used well, can lend your screenwriting greater richness and a considerably enhanced power to communicate with your audience, pulling them into a stronger level of identification with your story.

Running imagery

An image with metaphorical resonance may have just momentary impact in a story, or its meaning may be explored time and again throughout the story. Sometimes the momentary impact is very much to the fore, as with the torch it was planned Anne should give Curly in the *Coronation Street* story quoted earlier. The gift has a symbolic resonance, but isn't meant to evoke particular moments of history from previous stories: the star chart, in his scene with Emily, is also primarily a momentary metaphor, tragi-comically summoning up Curly's 'star-crossed' fate in regard to Raquel; however, faithful, long-term viewers may get extra value from the moment, remembering as they might his fascination with star gazing, and those career hopes (pilot, astronomer) shelved long ago. But it really doesn't matter whether or not these associations register for that moment to work.

When symbolic imagery is threaded right through a piece of drama, it can serve to underline and illuminate the emotional significance of the story for both its characters and, by association, its viewers. My Life As A Dog uses the running imagery of dogs, and Ingemar's relationship with this imagery, to explore ideas of caring, love and loss. In that film, we also see Ingemar travel to his relations during different seasons of the year. The seasons are used here (as they are often used in films) to mirror the emotional state of play. So it is in winter that Ingemar experiences his descent into actual loss and starting to experience grief whilst the flash-back reminiscences of times spent with his mother at the seaside are drenched in summer sun. As the film ends and Ingemar starts to recover and embark on a new phase of his life, so the season turns to spring. Changing weather is also often used to express interior emotional states. My Life As A Dog is a film rich in running imagery. The cold exteriors are contrasted with sunny flash-backs and also with the warmth of the furnace in the glass factory, very much at the economic and social heart of this community. On several occasions characters fool around after accidents, playing dead, although on each occasion there is a moment when you believe they could indeed have come to grief; these 'rehearsals' for the real thing remind the viewer what Ingemar's journey is all about – accepting and getting used to the idea of loss. Ingemar and the other children play at boxing, and in particular we see several sparring sessions and bouts. The climax of the film coincides with Ingemar Johansson's world title fight with Floyd Patterson. As he triumphs, the locals run into the street to celebrate, and the radio commentary declares: 'Ingemar didn't let us down!'. The final shot of young Ingemar sees him snuggled up asleep on the sofa with his sparring partner and would-be girlfriend, now no longer fighting but at last able to accept a loving embrace in this, his new life. That radio commentary applies to both Ingemars. He wasn't knocked out by his terrible loss. He will come through and win.

A good example of a single image repeatedly explored is that of the red rose in American Beauty, the title of which is itself the name of the very popular variety of American rose grown by Carolyn Burnham. The image is used at different points in the film to summon up a whole variety of associations: love, romance, sexuality, beauty, blood, danger – all are there:

EXT. BURNHAM HOUSE – MOMENTS LATER
CLOSE on a single, dewy AMERICAN BEAUTY ROSE. A gloved hand with CLIPPERS appears and SNIPS the flower off.

CAROLYN BURNHAM tends her rose bushes in front of the Burnham house. A very well

Figure 8.2   Mina Survari in *American Beauty* © Dreamworks/Jinks/Cohen/The Kobal
Collection/Sebastian, Lorey

put together woman of forty, she wears colour-co-ordinated gardening togs and has lots
of useful and expensive tools.

LESTER watches her through a WINDOW on the first floor, peeping out through the
drapes.

LESTER (V.O.) That's my wife Carolyn. See the way the handle on those pruning shears
matches her gardening clogs? That's not an accident.

And a little later, when Jim #1, one half of the gay couple next door, appears:

> *Lester watches all this from the window.*

CAROLYN: Good morning, Jim!

> *Jim #1 walks towards the fence to greet Carolyn.*

JIM #1:   I just love your roses. How do you get them to flourish like this?

CAROLYN: Well, I'll tell you. Egg shells and Miracle Grow.

Jim #1 and Carolyn continue to chat, unaware that Lester is watching them.

LESTER (V.O.):   Man, I get exhausted just watching her.

Lester's POV: We can't hear what Jim and Carolyn are saying, but she's overly animated, like a TV talk show host.

LESTER (V.O.):   She wasn't always like this. She used to be happy. We used to be happy.

We are invited to contrast Carolyn's suburban obsession with surface appearances and with control (not to mention the uncomfortable associations called up by those pruning shears in the first shot!) with Lester's wild, instinctual fantasies about daughter Jane's friend Angela, in particular the one which finds her posed seductively in a bath-tub full of red roses. This is the fantasy Carolyn wakes to discover Lester enjoying, moments before we see how 'thorny' she herself has become to him.

Projected images of beauty and the actual experience of it (sensual and spiritual) are called up time and again through reference to the rose image and, of course, by our memory of the title. And if you think I'm overstating the case, consider these moments from the end of the film, coming as it does, hard on the heels of Lester's refusal to 'pluck' that young rose-bud, Angela. They are having a friendly talk in the kitchen. Angela goes to the toilet and Lester, feeling very at one with himself, picks up a family photo:

LESTER crosses to the kitchen table where he sits and studies the photo. He suddenly seems older, more mature . . . and then he smiles: the deep, satisfied smile of a man who just now understands the punchline of a joke he heard long ago . . .

LESTER: Man oh man . . .
(*softly*)
Man oh man oh man . . .

After a beat the barrel of a GUN rises up behind his head, aimed at the base of his skull.

ANGLE ON an arrangement of fresh-cut ROSES in a vase on the opposite counter, deep crimson against the WHITE TILE WALL. Then a GUNSHOT suddenly rings out, ECHOING unnaturally.

Instantly, the tile is sprayed with BLOOD, the same deep crimson as the roses.

You could not have a clearer example of all the associations summoned up throughout the film being tied together, and bounced off that image of the red rose.

Fish and fishing are dominant images threaded right through Roy Jacobsen's 'Encounter' and Joe Tucker's adaptation of that story. I've already mentioned the ironically symbolic significance of *Moby Dick* in the piece, the demonically driven Ahab and the vastness and strength of the whale providing a vivid and ludicrous contrast with Arvid and his coalfish. And I pointed to the way that contrast externally illustrates the spirit of ambition or adventure and how this is at work in the stranger and not in Arvid. Beyond all that there are religious associations at work. Arvid is a fisherman as were the first disciples. The fish, indeed, is an age old symbol of Christianity. The first book Eze tries out on Arvid is a religious one. As he is selling his own books to raise money this incidentally raises the probability that the Ghanaian student has certainly had an interest in Christianity, may still have an affiliation, and might even have some evangelical intent in offering this book first. If so he quickly drops it when he sees Arvid's response to the book – a wrinkled nose and then a dirty hand resting on a picture of Jesus. This particular fisherman is in no way a disciple, and that moment of the hand on the picture holds all the distaste Arvid has for Christianity described in Jacobsen's original story. I mentioned earlier the overtones of 'missionary and native' transaction at work in this encounter, playfully and ironically subverted. Beyond a humorous recognition of the switch-around, a deeper point is being made. It is about faith and optimism. That 'bleak time with bleak expectations' is graphically depicted in the paucity of Arvid's catch and the glimpse of his austere, impoverished existence we are shown. Eze, on the other hand has prospects. He certainly has initiative, calm assurance and good humour. These speak of a spiritual repose. Arvid has routine, survival, comic books and as far as we can tell nothing much else.

When Eze takes the fish off Arvid, swapping it for the book, it's a moment which functions at three levels: Arvid feels he has completed doing this 'ridiculous' outsider a favour and so can bask in some misguided sense of superiority; in fact, Eze has won out and proved himself the better fisherman 'catching' a fish he wants and letting go of a whale (story) he has no need of – one which is useless to Arvid. At a much subtler yet nevertheless powerful level Arvid has not just lost the last vestige of his meagre catch, that lonely coalfish also standing for the sense of hope and religious connection which is so eroded in his community and presently absent from his own life -'a bleak time, with bleak expectations'. It is a state of affairs implicitly standing for and reflecting on a wider malaise afflicting the developed world, one which is often perceived as having widespread casualties amongst those who are materially advantaged but spiritually impoverished. As he rides home, book in pocket, we should remember *Moby Dick* does not exactly turn out well for Ahab.

Another film with a potent recurring religious image is *Crash* (Paul Haggis, Robert Moresco). With its multi-stranded weave of stories, sandwiched between the framing device of two road traffic accidents, *Crash* has a title which refers not only to those actual accidents in question, but also to a serial collision of cultures and values in multi-racial Los Angeles, and the complex fall-out from these intricately plotted (if often highly coincidental), interconnecting conflicts all of which unfold over the thirty six hours running up to Christmas.

One of the story strands follows a pair of young, black carjackers Anthony and Peter. Each time they steal a car, Peter takes a St Christopher figurine out of his pocket and attaches it to the top of the dashboard, to act as talisman for the duo's unholy activities. In mid-stream this story strand reaches a pitch of high tension when they carelessly hijack the car of Cameron Thayer, a successful, black TV director, he unexpectedly resists the attack and then chooses to stay in his car with them holding him at gunpoint. In the midst of this minor mayhem, the police happen on the scene and give chase to Thayer's car. Finally forced to stop, instead of telling all and handing Anthony, the remaining carjacker (Peter having run off), over to the police, because he too is black and along with his wife a recent victim of police harassment himself, Thayer shows solidarity and chooses to protect the boy by abusively confronting the police; an act of foolish bravado he gets away with due to the intervention of one of the officers present (earlier involved as an unwilling accomplice in that episode of racial and sexual harassment) who now claims to know Thayer and intercedes on his behalf. An added irony is layered into the scene by the presence of a large Santa Claus decoration further up the driveway Cameron has finally pulled up on, and which is clearly visible in the back of the shot; for the young carjacker Christmas has definitely come early. That Santa Claus also links into the strand of religious iconography.

Later in the film the resolution of the car-jackers' story-strand links back to the start of the film. Chastened by Thayer's defiance and seemingly having decided, for the moment at least, to go straight, Peter hitches a lift from a passing motorist, who unbeknownst to him just happens to be the same patrol cop, Hansen, now off duty, who has had such tangled dealings with Thayer and who is hence doubly motivated to do a good deed now by picking up Peter, a young black man on the wrong side of town and offering him a lift. As conversation develops between them, a level of prejudice and suspicion arises in Hansen. Finally he thinks he is being ridiculed and angrily pulls over to eject his lift. Confused and also angry, Peter reaches into his pocket to show him something. The cop is sure it's a gun and very agitated by now tries to stop him. Peter however carries on deliberately ignoring the warnings and certain he is about to be held at gun-point the cop shoots and kills the young man. After he has shot him, the cop discovers what his victim was getting out of his pocket; it is, of course, not a gun but the St Christopher figurine, being fished out on this occasion with purely innocent intent in response to the amusing coincidence of Hansen already having the self-same figurine on his dashboard.

The bitter irony could not be clearer; St Christopher, patron saint and pro-tector of travellers, has failed twice over. The deeper message being conveyed here is that whilst affiliations and loyalties to religious, cultural and ethnic groupings and traditions can offer identity and a sense of support and belonging, these same groupings and the prejudices which attach to them can also be anything but redemptive, stimulating fear, mistrust and open hostility between neighbours.

In the case of young carjacker Peter's story, irony is then piled high on top of irony when, a little later on, the film picks up on that car crash we see at the beginning of the film. One of the cars involved had slowed for standing traffic and been run into from behind. Its driver is a detective who is none other than the dead boy's older brother, Graham Waters, a rising star in the LAPD. As his girlfriend gets out of the car and takes issue with the other driver, Waters wanders off, his attention caught by the nearby police line and crime scene. He chats to a colleague and asks what's going on. Hearing it's the homicide of a young man he casually slips into professional mode and starts examining the evidence. Within moments he is pole-axed as he catches sight of the victim and sees it is his brother Peter. Elsewhere in the film we have seen the older brother trying to tend to his drug-addicted mother who takes him to task for not looking after his delinquent younger brother. The final beat of this story strand underpins this chain reaction theme of carelessness at work both here and more generally in the film. About to quit the scene and go back to his car, something catches Waters's eye half-buried by the side of the road. It is his brother's St Christopher figurine and he bends to unearth it, holds it in his clasped hands resting his thoughtful head on them in a prayer like pose. Whether or not he recognises it as belonging to his brother its ironic resonance and overtones are far from lost on him; a moment of bitter awakening.

A final example of running imagery is taken from *The Fisher King* (Richard LaGravenese). The story is a modern day re-interpretation of the Grail myth and is suffused with rich use of imagery throughout. I touched on the story earlier in the book but to recap and elaborate, it concerns the fate of Jack Lucas, a celebrity radio shock-jock, who discovers his contemptuous and cav-alier treatment of a regular sad-case caller results in that same caller going out shooting innocent drinkers in a bar, before killing himself. What Jack has told Edwin (the caller) about Yuppies, that 'they must be stopped', seems to have been all the encouragement he needed to go and perform these killings. Jack's career falls to bits and he takes to the bottle, and it is at this stage of the story that we see his quest unfold. In the depths of his despair and on the brink of suicide, he is saved by street bum, Parry (a modern-day Parsifal) who, by the kind of extraordinary coincidence we will easily tolerate in a modern-day myth, turns out to be none other than the husband of one of the women killed in that very same shooting. Parry (once a medievalist and lecturer) has been totally deranged by the shooting, but is now going to be instrumental in the process of Jack's redemption: Jack, in turn, will be instrumental in Parry's return to sanity and society. In Jack's bid to make amends, he begins a journey which will entail facing the truth about himself and opening his capacity to love both himself and others.

Figure 8.3   Jeff Bridges in *The Fisher King* © Columbia/Tri-Star/RGA

So much for the broad outline. At the very beginning of his quest, as Jack stumbles around the New York streets, despairing and drunk, a child carrying a Pinnochio doll crosses his path, and most strangely gives him the doll to keep. That doll keeps Jack company throughout his adventures. At the very start of his quest, just prior to his suicide bid, he has a drunken 'conversation' with the doll:

> JACK
> You ever read any Nietzsche? . . .

The smiling Pinnochio clearly has not.

> JACK
> (continuing)
> Nietzsche says that there are two kinds of
> people in this world . . . People who are
> destined for greatness like . . . Walt Disney
> and . . . Hitler . . . and then there's the rest of
> us . . . He called us the Bungled and Botched.
> We get teased. We sometimes get close to
> greatness but we never get there. We're the
> expendable masses. We get pushed in front
> of trains . . . take poison, aspirins . . . get
> gunned down in Dairy Queens . . .

He drinks from his Jack Daniels bottle . . .

> JACK
> (continuing)
> You wanna hear my new title for my
> biography, my little Italian friend . . . 'It Was
> No Fucking Picnic – The Jack Lucas Story.'
> Like it? . . . Just nod yes or no . . .
>   (tries it in Pig-Italian)
> 'Il Nouva Esta Fuckin' Pinicko' –
>   (he smiles)
> You're a good kid . . . Just say no to drugs . . .
>   (he nods and drinks)
>
> Ya ever get the feeling sometimes you're
> being punished for your sins?

CUT TO:

21 EXT. EAST RIVER, NEW YORK CITY – NIGHT

> CLOSEUP of two feet standing beneath the railing overlooking
> the East River. Taped to one ankle is a brick. Taped to the other
> is a smiling Pinnochio doll.

This alliance with Pinnochio will endure throughout the story, despite an attempt to give the doll away, and at the end of the tale when all is well and love has triumphed, Parry and Jack lie on the grass in Central Park at night, cloudbusting (moving clouds by the power of thought alone). Between them lies the Pinnochio doll.

The Pinnochio story is all about the need to stop lying. *The Fisher King* is a story about facing up to the truth, dropping delusion and getting real. In the Pinnochio story, when he stops lying the doll becomes a real boy. In *The Fisher King*, when Jack has fully undone the lie his life used to be, he is free to be a real man.

The Pinnochio doll strongly prompts the audience to draw that comparison. Unlike the greenhouse in Joanna Smith's script, the doll is a device very much imposed on the plot, and yet given the mythic realms which both source and *The Fisher King* are inhabited by, its introduction fits the appropriately improbable tone of the piece. It has a secure position in the literal chain of serendipitous events offered at what is the mystical level of reality depicted in this story.

Exercises

1   Make a note of some metaphors or running images in some of your favourite films and TV dramas. Discuss these with a writing partner or in the group, and consider how they are set up to support the meaning of the drama. How successful do you think they are?

2   Think up a story and design it around an object which is going to have metaphorical power. Write a short screenplay. Cast these and read them in the group or with a writing partner. Discuss what you thought and felt about how the idea worked.

9
Subtext

'Then you should say what you mean,' the March Hare went on.
'I do,' Alice hastily replied, 'at least – at least I mean what I say – that's the same thing you know.'
'Not the same thing a bit,' said the Hatter.

Alice in Wonderland, Lewis Carroll

If metaphor can radically step up the engine capacity of your writing, then creating an interesting subtext can really super-charge the process. One of the most interesting facets of us human beings is our capacity to withhold what we really mean from each other. Often we carry on with others at a comfortable and convenient level leaving it up to them – in London Underground parlance – to 'mind the gap'; that gap being the space between the apparent meaning of what we say or do, and the hidden or implicit meaning. In reality our capacity to dissemble and disguise can lead us into all kinds of pain, inconvenience and difficulty. 'What a tangled web we weave when first we practise to deceive', is often true enough about the consequences of being less than fully open and honest. In the realms of making good fiction, and especially writing interesting drama, our potential for lack of candour is nothing short of a god-send.

In making hidden messages, submerging real meaning beneath apparent meaning, we can create ironic distance. Our audience is boosted to a privileged position from where they can compare what is actually being said and done with what they know remains *unsaid* and *undone*. Not only that, as a spin-off, we create all kinds of potential complications and tensions between characters, the very stuff of any good drama. If you as writer are ingenious enough to create telling subtext then your reward will be more satisfied viewers whose engagement with the story has been intensified as they work hard to uncover the real meaning, recognise all those complications, and feel clever to have done so.

Another simple fact about withholding is that, whilst it can be uncomfortable to do, or to be on the receiving end of it in real life, for an audience watching this behaviour unfold in a drama, it really can be a most enjoyable experience. Watching people lie can be great fun. It can, of course, also be deeply moving, as there are a variety of reasons *why* we withhold information from others; subterfuge can take the shape of *avoidance, denial, defence,* or *manipulation.* These may well overlap, or be served up in interesting combinations. To expand on them a little more, under one or more of these headings come those times: when there is an unacceptable conflict of interests between people; when ignorance (sometimes even pretended ignorance) is taken to be bliss, or 'what you don't know, can't hurt you' become the watchwords for withholding information. Then there are those times when fear of being exposed is driving devious behaviour, and we want to minimise risk or save our own skins; there are also those times when fear of a conflict is at work; times when one hides the truth to save another's feelings, rather than reveal unpalatable truths. Finally, there are occasions when people operate covertly as a means of manipulation, in order to disguise their real goals.

Back in the Trembling Trout (in Chapter 3) you may or may not remember, Eric promised to have a quiet word with Bernice.

INT. RECEPTION AREA. A LITTLE LATER.

BERNICE sits with her back towards ERIC key-boarding away intently. he makes for his office, changes his mind, creeps up, moves HECTOR and perches on the edge of her desk. it takes a moment or two before she notices.

> BERNICE
> Ooh, Eric! You frightened the life
> out of me.

> ERIC
> Well that makes a change.

A moment, then she gets it and pushes him playfully.

> BERNICE
> Get on with you.

> ERIC
> Anyway, how are you settling in
> with us?

> BERNICE
> Fine thanks, Eric. I love it here.

> ERIC
> Good, good. How long's it been now?

> BERNICE
> Six months.

ERIC

Six months! Would you believe it?
Bit of an old hand by now,
aren't you? Still it is nice isn't
it when you get over all those
little teething problems. When you know
where everything is, who's who,
and exactly how people like
things done.

BERNICE has been following every word.

BERNICE

(Vehemently) Oh yes. You're dead right there.

A pause. ERIC throws a pointed glance at his pile of work.

ERIC

Not too much for you, is it,
looking after the two of us?
I mean the work-load's not
too heavy?

BERNICE

(With a big, sunny smile) No, no. You're no trouble
really. Either of you.

ERIC

You know I really like that about
you, Bernice. You're a really happy
sort of individual. Always got a smile
on your face.

BERNICE

Oh, stop it, Eric. You'll have
me blushing.

ERIC

It's true. Always ready with a smile
and a friendly word for just
about anyone.

BERNICE

That's what you're like too.

ERIC

I know. Been my downfall sometimes, that
ready smile. Too ready some might say.

BERNICE

Oh no, I think you get it
just right. I much prefer outgoing people,
don't you? Between you and me it
wouldn't do Adrian any harm to smile
a bit more often. Takes fewer muscles
you know.

                                    ERIC
                    Yes . . . (Helpfully) I've found everything has to
                    be just so for Adrian before he
                    lets the sun come out.
                                    BERNICE
                    (Commiserating) I know. Gets on my wick.
                                    ERIC
                    But if you do your job well,
                    then he really does lighten up.

BERNICE looks very doubtful even though ERIC underscores this covert encouragement
with some cheerful 'it's-true' type head nodding. He stands and pats the pile of papers.

                                    ERIC
                    Do you know, I once went to
                    a conference, and the title they gave
                    one of the sessions was 'A busy
                    desk is an empty desk'. Food for
                    thought that, isn't it?

This one goes right over BERNICE's head but she smiles politely even so.

                                    ERIC
                    Well I've enjoyed our little chat.
                                    BERNICE
                    Me too. Ooh, you're dead nice,
                    you, Eric.
                                    ERIC
                    I'd better leave you to get on,
                    hadn't I? See you now.
                                    BERNICE
                    Yeah, see you, Eric.

He goes, she turns to the key-board. We see a satisfied smile on his face. When he has
rounded the corner the phone rings and she answers it.

                                    BERNICE
                    'Chelle, hiya. Guess who was just
                    dead nice to me?

Though the real purpose of this conversation eludes Bernice, while Eric considers it a job well done, the point to notice here is the motivation for his not just coming straight out with it. While dropping a broad hint, he wants to save her feelings, a common enough motive for disguising the truth. This scene also illustrates a common outcome of the scene carrying subtext – characters will be left with very different perceptions or levels of understanding about what has passed between them, and the audience will inevitably know best.

Here's another example of subtext at work, a script by Ian Mayor which, though written as an exercise, stands well as a self-contained piece, illustrating ingenious and appropriate use of both metaphor and subtext.

A Right Pair

FADE IN:

INT. FRONT ROOM. OLD TERRACED HOUSE. NIGHT.

The sound of rain lashing at the windows and a persistent knocking on the front door. TERRY (early 50s) opens it. RICHARD (26) stands in the downpour soaking wet and shivering in his hoodless jacket. He is holding a sopping wet jumble made up of an assortment of his clothes and trainers. Some of them are muddy. He grins weakly.

INT. FRONT ROOM. LATER.

Dressed only in his boxer shorts and socks, RICHARD sits in a well-worn comfy chair drying his hair with a towel. In front of the gas fire is a clothes rack draped with clothes and RICHARD's trainers laced together, hanging off one corner. TERRY enters with two mugs of tea and gives one to RICHARD.

> RICHARD
>> Ta.

TERRY walks to the sofa and clears a space in the *Autotrader* and *Classic Car* magazines which cover it in loose piles. He sits down, looks at RICHARD and grins. RICHARD grins back.

> RICHARD
>> What?

> TERRY
> You can't live with 'em . . . and
> you can't live with 'em.

They both laugh.

INT. FRONT ROOM. MORNING.

The sofa is crumpled, all the cushions are bunched at one end and it clearly looks slept on. The magazines are neatly piled on the floor, next to a plate with the remains of a fried breakfast, an empty mug, and RICHARD sitting in last night's boxer shorts and a clean, unironed T shirt. The clothes rack is bare, and RICHARD is sorting the now dry washing from a pile on the floor. TERRY sits in the comfy chair, reading the *Sunday Mirror*. Next to his chair is similar breakfast debris. RICHARD is pairing the socks.

> RICHARD
> You gonna give me a hand?

> TERRY
> I never was any good at that
> kind of stuff.

> RICHARD
>> And I am?

RICHARD runs out of pairs and is left with two odd socks. He holds them up for TERRY to see.

> TERRY
> Always happens like that.

> RICHARD
> If you took the trouble to sort
> them out before sticking them in
> the wash it wouldn't.

> TERRY
> Probably.

TERRY goes back to his paper. RICHARD drops the socks and starts to straighten a shirt.

FADE OUT.

There are many things to admire in the writing of this piece. First and foremost the piece does strike that important balance between literal and symbolic. We are offered a very credible scenario in which, first of all, we imagine that Richard has been chucked out of his home. The fact that he has a bundle of clothes and that some of them are muddy suggests he was more than given a helping hand on his way. To begin with, however, we are still only guessing, just as we are about the exact relationship of these two men.

By the second scene, it's clear Richard is free to make himself more than welcome here, and we are assuming they are either close friends, or far more likely father and son. That weak grin of Richard's as Terry opens the door on him suggests this is not an unfamiliar situation, that explanations are unnecessary, and that the young man expects to find automatic safe-haven here.

All of this is supported by their jokey interchange. With an ironic twist on the standard deprecating line about men and women they laugh it off, and collude in the implication that women are just impossible to live with. Note that it's the older man, Terry, who initiates placing the blame on the other sex, and invites his son to happily settle for that 'fact'. It's crystal clear from the look of the house that Terry is on his own and what's more the state of the sofa, with its piles of car magazines, suggests indifference to this state of male solitude.

The final section incorporates both metaphor and more subtext, as Richard ends up trying to sort pairs of socks, asks for help and is first fobbed off with a line which subtextually explains very well what a woman may have become impatient with; for that 'good' in Terry's rebuff, let's read in 'willing to make the effort'. Richard's reply also suggests he was brought up to do no better. Let's also notice what Richard is asking his father for help with – getting things sorted, and specifically into matching pairs.

When the crunch moment in the script arrives, and Richard holds up the odd socks, we are presented with some very clever writing. Terry can only manage doomed resignation in the face of what he sees as a natural phenomenon. Richard's response is enlightening. These are, after all, *his* socks and yet he chooses to take his father to task on the matter. It's as though Terry is responsible for this particular pair, and the illogicality of the moment brings us up short. Because of this, we look at that moment more closely, and as it works on us we can access the symbolic level of what these socks stand for as well as the literal. These odd socks can stand for a man unsuccessfully looking after himself. They also demonstrate unsuccessful pairings, and here those comically dangled socks – which at one level invite a knowing smile from us, and are an invitation to accept Terry's philosophy of life – at another level stand for the unsuccessful pairing Richard's currently involved in, as well as the unsuccessful pairing(s) his father may have been involved in, and finally for the 'odd coupledom' of this (presumed) father and son situation right now. It's with all this going on that Richard's parental injunction to Terry to sort out socks before putting them in the machine carries a definite poignancy. On one level they're definitely just talking about socks, and Richard's doing no more than challenging his father's victimhood. On another he's highlighting his own limited capacity to care and relate, and blaming the poor model he's been offered up by his father. After all they *are* Richard's socks, so why else is he lecturing Terry? Again that unconvinced 'probably' ending the piece, underlines its poignancy: father and son making the best of it, cheerfully sticking together, and at the same time very 'probably' destined to do no better. *A Right Pair* puts me in mind of the saying 'It'll all come out in the wash', meaning that all difficulties will be resolved in the natural way of things. In fact, the opposite has happened with this wash. Ironically we see exactly where the problem has come from.

I think some of the fine detail of Ian Mayor's writing is worth noting. The fact that Richard is sorting out his washing from a pile on the floor is significant. It underlines a sense of uncaring ineptitude, and echoes the loose piles of magazines on the sofa. It's interesting to note the way Richard tidies them. Perhaps simply a show of trying to do better, perhaps an act of nurture. The unspoken relationship, the subtext in what is going on, partly functions through this attention to detail.

To summarise, at the surface level of meaning we have a short drama in which a young man is thrown out of his home and turns up, dirty washing and all, to seek sanctuary with his father, who is happy to laugh his son's crisis off with him. Richard is offered a roof over his head for the night, but little more. He does his washing, gets irritated that he has ended up with two odd socks, and also with his father's seeming indifference, and reluctantly settles for it. At the deeper level, Ian Mayor astutely spotted the potential a pair of odd socks could have to carry the undertones about the father's victimhood around women, if not life in general, both men's deficient upbringing, and Richard's anger and disappointment with where he has been failed by his father. The piece also captures both men's limited capacity to communicate with each other at a meaningful, emotional level.

The socks are a well-chosen metaphor, a simple image which carries complex meaning and supports it all without feeling like an extraneous device; it is firmly located in the literal world of the story.

When Terry jokily observes, 'Can't live with 'em, and you can't live with 'em', what we are seeing is a combination of defence and avoidance at work. Terry is looking to save his son's feelings about his recent hurt, and probably his own past hurts as well: he is not bidding to open a talk about the situation. He would rather avoid that, quite simply dumping Richard's and his problems on womankind in general; implicit in this is a refusal to admit, if not a downright denial of any level of personal responsibility for relationship difficulties.

And when Richard snaps, 'If you took the effort to sort them out properly before sticking them in the wash it wouldn't,' he is clearly denying his deeper feelings of disappointment and anger, and avoiding open conflict with his father on that score by keeping the conversation all about socks.

When subtext is installed in a piece, there are two levels of meaning at work, the apparent and the real. When both are grasped and combined, they amount to an overall meaning. This springs from a combination of the pretext or apparent level of meaning, and the subtext – what is really going on. In addition, from studying the context of any given moment or scene, we will also understand the reasons why a character is speaking or acting indirectly, and this character motivation also becomes a part of the overall meaning.

The relationship of any given moment in a drama to the bigger picture, of the parts to the whole, is something the sharp-witted dramatist will always pay close attention to. Those parts all help to build the overall meaning and, in turn, also derive some of their particular meaning from it.

A masterful example of how to weave both sense and imagery to create potent subtext can be seen in *Shooting The Past* by Stephen Poliakoff. Here the story concerns the fate of the Fallon picture library, a huge collection of old photographs housed in an erstwhile stately home and run by a small team of eccentrics passionately committed to their work. The library is suddenly threatened with imminent decimation due to the building being bought by Americans for conversion into the American School of Business for the twenty-first century; immediately we can see that fundamental value systems are being brought into conflict. When Christopher Anderson, CEO of the new enterprise, arrives to supervise building work he is as shocked to find the library carrying on as usual as Marilyn Trueman, its chief librarian, is to realise that they are supposed to be out of there within twenty-four hours. What has happened is that her second in command, Oswald Bates, determined to resist the take over and keep the library as it is, has intercepted all the earlier correspondence from America, deluding the new owners whilst hiding the news from his boss. After both sides have skirmished and adjusted to reality, Anderson reluctantly agrees to see the collection simply to appease Trueman who is adamant that she will not see the collection broken up. He is equally adamant that the development work must go ahead, with only the really valuable pictures in the collection being salvaged before that happens.

However, Oswald has craftily dispersed these valuable pictures throughout the collection, so against his will and in order to get his hands on those pictures Anderson agrees to Trueman's request to see the collection. Part of the way she prevails on Anderson to get more leeway and eventually be granted a week to try and find a buyer for the entire collection is to get him to listen to a story constructed using photographs from the collection. Reluctant at first he is quickly then drawn in, fascinated and deeply moved by the story she tells about the Katzmans, a Jewish family in Germany in the run up to the Holocaust. To escape persecution the family scatters, the parents going into hiding, and the daughter extraordinarily finding safe refuge with a non-Jewish family. Using photographs taken by Lily's father, a doctor who was also an amateur photographer, as well as Nazi archive shots brought together from all over the collection to illustrate the facts, Trueman relates how the Katzman family at great risk met up for the last time, Lily's father meeting her in town and shopping and then taking her on to a public park to see her mother. The meeting is cut short, the parents leave and Lily is left alone. Returning home her journey is held up by a Nazi parade, an image of Lily watching having been caught by an official photographer. That very afternoon her adoptive family is arrested and Lily taken too. Another Nazi archive shot shows her being transported to the camps.

By this stage in the story Anderson is visibly moved and also clearly amazed by Oswald's acuity, expertise and commitment in scanning the library to gather these additional photographs, which supplement the Katzman family's shots donated by Lily's son-in-law, and complete the story. But the *coup de grace* comes in the shape of a shot taken in modern-day London near the Elephant and Castle showing the crazy, raddled old vagrant Lily was to become, her sanity shattered by the Holocaust experience. Working from a passport photo supplied by Lily's son-in-law, Oswald had scoured the collection of contemporary London street life till he had found her. Without the rest of her particular story being known, simply an anonymous vagrant; with it a special someone in particular whose story then also has universal importance. At first Anderson refuses to believe it is Lily in the photograph. Trueman tells him it has been confirmed.

This deeply affecting sequence in the drama generates resonant layers of metaphorical subtext. Suddenly the existence of a collection of millions of photographs is threatened, just as was true for the millions of European Jewry with their ancient history and tradition in the face of the Nazis coming to power. More than that, the story Trueman relates centres on the disinteg-ration and destruction of one specific family, the Katzmans. The library team at Fallon is shown to be very much a small, tightly bonded family also now threatened with dispersal and destruction. (In fact the unfolding drama is occasionally narrated by one-man-memory-machine Oswald in his flat while, ironically true to form, and feeling there is no purpose left in his continued existence once the collection has gone, he tape-records and occasionally photographs his own journey towards a serious attempt at suicide.) Moreover, as with the ill-fated Jews, the members of the library team are guardians of a rich and extensive historical resource, source of countless stories all holding significance, particular, general or both. To destroy that 'collective memory' actually enshrined in and also symbolised by the library is, the drama argues, neither a progressive nor an arbitrary act. Subtextually we are told it is as criminal and barbaric as Nazism itself. After hearing the story Andersen offers a compromise deal; Trueman can pick out whatever she wants in the very brief time available. He is, in his way, also only following orders and urges her to 'save what really matters'. However 'what really matters' to Trueman is all of it, the interdependent 'community' of images, every single one potentially as important a part of the story as all the rest. The parallel with placing equal value on all human life is clear.

That photograph of crazy old Lily Katzman speaks not only of the individual, personal devastation wrought by the Holocaust but also symbolises the madness of splitting up both this collection and its 'family' of keepers. Beyond that level of meaning, as the well worn saying goes 'those who ignore history are destined to repeat the mistakes of the past', and the challenge Trueman has in this story is to get Anderson to live up to the implicit injunction in that maxim, keep the collection together and - metaphorically speaking - *not* shoot the past.

Another, rather different example of subtext at work will also help illustrate the point about disguised layers of meaning. It is taken from *The English Patient*

(Anthony Minghella from the novel by Michael Ondaatje) and is related to the central spine of the piece, the burgeoning love affair between Almásy and Katharine. Here are the second and third in a run of three scenes which are all about the developing passion between the couple. In the film, these scenes are not immediately adjacent, but do build directly on each other:

Int. Shepheard's Hotel. Night.
The ballroom. A dance finishes. ALMÁSY takes over from D'AGOSTINO to partner KATHARINE. The others remain on the terrace, deep in conversation.

> KATHERINE
> *(as they dance)*
> Why did you follow me yesterday?

> ALMÁSY
> What? I'm sorry?

> KATHARINE
> After the market, you followed me
> to the hotel.

> ALMÁSY
> I was concerned. A woman in
> that part of Cairo, a European woman,
> I felt obliged to.

> KATHARINE
> You felt obliged to.

> ALMÁSY
> As the wife of one of our party.

> KATHARINE
> So why follow me? Escort me, by
> all means. But following me is
> predatory, isn't it?

ALMÁSY, by way of answer, bears down on her. They dance, fierce, oblivious to everything.

Anthony Minghella has created a brilliantly appropriate and effective subtextual scene. On the surface, Katharine Clifton's words suggest she is annoyed with Almásy. She accuses him of improper behaviour, and he rebuts the accusation by telling her he was only showing gentlemanly concern for her welfare. This is certainly an example of a character disguising his real goal, and at the same time the lie is perfectly in character and consistent with the level at which Almásy is in conflict between doing the right thing, and following his passion. Perhaps he also fears exposing his true motive before he knows whether or not it's safe to do so. What is even more interesting is Katharine's response to his answer. She could just tell him she thinks his behaviour after their meeting was predatory and leave it at that. Instead she *asks* him whether it's predatory; it's as though his answer has left her in doubt, and her question is checking out what is not being openly expressed between them, but what she clearly hopes is true. There's almost an unspoken ('I hope') hanging in the air after her question, a green light to Almásy which he is quick to obey. The tension between them is not really about propriety or social niceties, it is the sexual tension between would-be lovers.

ALMÁSY, *by way of answer, bears down on her. They dance, fierce, oblivious to everything.*

This scene is followed up with a superlative example of subtext at work when Katharine's husband is about to fly off to Cairo leaving Katharine behind.

Ext. Base Camp at Pottery Hill. Morning.
As CLIFTON prepares to leave in the Steerman, ALMÁSY approaches.

                    ALMÁSY
          Clifton, safe journey.

                    CLIFTON
          You too. Good luck!

                    ALMÁSY
          Clifton – it's probably none of my
          business – but your wife, do you think
          it's appropriate to leave her?

                    CLIFTON
          Appropriate?

                    ALMÁSY
          Well, the desert is – for a woman – it's
          very tough, I wonder if it's not
          too much for her.

                    CLIFTON
          Are you mad? Katharine loves it here.
          She told me yesterday.

                    ALMÁSY
          All the same, were I you,
          I would be concerned –

                    CLIFTON
          I've known Katharine since she was three,
          we were practically brother and sister before
          we were man and wife. I think
          I'd know what is and what isn't

too much for her. I think she'd
know herself.

                    ALMÁSY
Very well.

                    CLIFTON
        (laughing it off)
Why are you people so threatened
by a woman?!

ALMÁSY watches him walk toward the plane, then turns to see KATHARINE, a distant figure watching. He doesn't move. She doesn't move.

This scene works off the banner headline 'None so blind as those who will not see'. Almásy cannot say what he really means by 'All the same, were I you, I would be concerned': he is at once avoiding the unpalatable truth and so saving Clifton's feelings, and at the same time trying to assuage his own guilt: but this attempt to do the right thing here, to put Katharine out of harm's way, is a futile and ironic gesture. In the book of gentlemanly conduct, it amounts to Almásy giving Clifton a sporting chance. He is also saddling Clifton with responsibility for his destructive behaviour, and is tantamount to telling himself, 'What could I do? I tried to warn him'. Except of course, he didn't. He portrays himself as merely concerned about the welfare of another man's wife, when, in fact, he's anything but. Given that he knows full well the decision is already made, and that Clifton will have no qualms at all for Katharine's general well-being, there is only one person whose interests are really being served here – and that's Almásy's. He is no gentleman. He is at some level trying to manipulate Clifton into believing here, at least, is one man who'll be looking out for his wife: a cruel deception and one which only serves to bolster Clifton's delusions of marital bliss and security. But then, as the saying goes, and this scene demonstrates so clearly, 'All's fair in love and war'.

It is a scene dripping with irony. Clifton declares he and Katharine were practically brother and sister whilst growing up (in itself a subtextual give away about what kind of passion may well be missing from their marriage – a passion Almásy is only too ready to supply), and then goes on to assert how well he knows his wife, and even more ironically how well she knows herself, when even now she's in the midst of discovering herself in ways she couldn't have imagined, whilst her husband is blind to it all. There is a final savage irony in that throwaway put-down at the end; only one man has got reason to feel threatened here, and he's about to get on the plane. And the final action detailed at the very end of the scene makes that very clear. Katharine has made no move to say her final farewells to her husband, but has hung back watching the two rivals for her love. The look between Almásy and herself, exchanged behind her husband's retreating back, says it all.

So, in itself, the scene carries lots of subtext and works most effectively. It does so partly because of what else we know that Clifton is not a party to. But this scene also carries a subtext linking it to one of the most famous scenes in cinema and derives a whole extra layer of irony from that reference. You must remember this:

> ILSA
> (turns to Rick)
> You're saying this only to make
> me go.

> RICK
> I'm saying it because it's true. Inside
> of us we both know you belong
> with Victor. You're part of his work.
> The thing that keeps him going.
> If that plane leaves the ground and
> you're not with him, you'll regret it.

> ILSA
> No.

> RICK
> Maybe not today, maybe not tomorrow,
> but soon, and for the rest of
> your life.

It is, of course, from *the* scene in *Casablanca* (Julius and Philip Epstein, Howard Koch), in which Rick selflessly ensures Victor Laszlo's happiness by letting go of Ilsa. In *The English Patient*, Almásy does the opposite. Rick tells Ilsa, 'I'm not good at being noble', whilst he shows us the exact opposite, that given the chance of stealing Ilsa's love away from her husband, in the end he cannot do it, and ensures she does get on the plane. Part of the context we are invited to put Minghella's scene in includes its famous precursor. While Rick's famous 'Here's looking at you, kid,' heralds the end of their affair, Almásy's look at Katharine heralds the beginning of theirs. And yet, although the scenes present us with reverse sides of the same coin, there is a fateful truth in the unspoken echo Minghella's scene carries over from *Casablanca*. If Clifton gets on the plane and Katharine is not with him, they're *all* going to regret it. And so it turns out; later in the film, after he has discovered the truth, he dives that same plane (now *with* Katharine in it as well) directly at Almásy, and in so doing crashes, killing himself and fatally injuring Katharine.

The link with *Casablanca* is one of calculated intelligent irony and it serves only to enrich the impact and meaning of *The English Patient*. Nowadays there can be an almost epidemic tendency to drop cinematic references and parallels into scripts in an attempt to pull off impressive feats of intertextuality. Where quoting or nodding towards another film is neither intelligent homage nor appropriate, crafty layering of resonant content, it most usually amounts to nothing more than crass faddishness at work and provides an unwelcome level of interference. A clear exception to this school of gratuitous ostentation however is the comedy *Spaced* (Simon Pegg, Jessica Stevenson).

Revolving around a curious mix of misfits lodging at 23 Meteor Street and centred on Tim Bisley and Daisy Steiner, a pair of singles pretending to be a couple so as to get the flat, the fourteen episodes of the two series made simply burst at the seams with references to pop-culture. The house and household itself summon faint memories of that 1960s series *The Addams Family*, much more recent echoes of 28 Barbary Lane in Maupin's *Tales of The City*, and besides those there is also an amusingly dysfunctional nod towards *Friends* as well. Beyond that, as the stories of each episode unfold, there are numerous, clear cinematic references to pertinent films all along the way. So, for example, when Tim and Daisy are faking coupledom ('Beginnings', series one) to become tenants in (the somewhat Morticia-like) Marsha Klein's

Figure 9.1   Spaced © Channel 4 Television Corporation

house, *Green Card* is the film which gets referenced and entertainingly paro-died. A list of all of the films and TV programmes referenced, parodied or both would be very extensive, but they range from *Fight Club, Close Encounters, Star Wars, The Matrix, An Officer and a Gentleman* and *One Flew Over the Cuckoo's Nest* to the tv programmes *Grange Hill, Doctor Who, Robot Wars* and *Scrapheap Challenge*...to name but a few. However, *Spaced* is stylistically assured and the cinematic style it is shot in helps lend a fluency and fit to all its borrowed inclusions. Moreover the fact that its essential aim is to be enter-taining and funny also supports the magpie approach to its making. But above all and crucially, it is Tim and Daisy's characterisation which makes the imaginative flights of fancy seem nothing more than natural: he a fanatical video games playing science fiction devotee and would-be comic-book artist (destined eventually to land his dream job as graphic artist with Dark Star Comics), and she an aspiring writer with a definite leaning towards self-dramatisation. So when in 'Mettle' (episode three, series two) she is forced to take a menial job in a fast-food outlet, it actually fits perfectly that feeling oppressed she suddenly sees herself as McMurphy in *One Flew Over The Cuckoo's Nest*, casts her boss as the evil Nurse Ratched and other fellow workers as vulnerable Billy and Chief. *Spaced*'s Director, Edgar Wright, summed it up this way in the interview he gave in the documentary *Skip To The End* - that title itself one of Tim Bisley's catch phrases. Asked about the references and homages he said it wasn't just 'a case of let's do a five minute riff on *The Matrix*...the characters' lives are so governed by pop-culture they can only think in those terms...so breaking up with a girl-friend is as enorm-ous to Tim as The Empire Strikes Back'.

And as I've briefly illustrated that statement from Wright isn't just special pleading to excuse some severe bouts of self-indulgence; overwhelmingly the fantasy element works subtextually, both informing as well as being supported by the characters' inner worlds.

From a simple one-liner, carefully loaded with an additional level of meaning, to a whole scene carrying several additional layers of intent, right through to the scene or the sequence doing the same whilst also resonating with other moments or references lying completely outside the whole drama – subtext can really enrich your writing. Observe its skilful use wherever and whenever you can, and as and when you feel confident and ready to, have a go at creat-ing some yourself.

Exercises

1   A long-standing, close friend is getting married and has invited you to the wedding. You don't want to go. The real reason is that you also had a brief relationship with their fiancé, and you know she (or he) has kept this a secret. You care about your unsuspecting friend, and yet still harbour special feelings towards their intended. Obviously you can't tell your friend this is the reason you don't want to be at the wedding. So what do you tell them instead? Write a scene in which you meet one or both of them by accident, not having got round yet to responding to the invitation.

2   A teenager's mother (or father) discovers her son (or daughter) hasn't yet posted their application for university. The deadline is in two days' time. The parent has their real reason (which they cannot share) for wanting their teenager out of the house and away – they want their lover to move in. The son (or daughter) is reluctant to go to college, because they want to stay close to their girl (boy) friend. Neither can tell the other the truth. Write a scene in which the parent is doing their best to get that letter posted, and the son (or daughter) to resist.

10
Pulling it all together

The first script example in this book was for a very short film. The last example is from a considerably longer piece (over 100 times as long!) *Our Friends in the North* (Peter Flannery) which started life as a stage play way back in 1982 and was first commissioned by the BBC as a TV series in the same year. Passing through its own saga of changing fortunes, and initially projected to be 20 hours of drama, *Our Friends in the North* finally reached the screen 15 years on, at just half that length, winning awards as well as enormous popular acclaim.

The story of four friends from Newcastle unfolds over three decades, mid-1960s to mid-1990s, against a background of major political and social upheaval. It weaves the microcosmic and macrocosmic together, following the friends' individual and collective stories and outlining the context in which they play out their hopes and fears in such a way that we can see how the socio-political pressures impinge on and shape their personal destinies, and how those in turn contribute to the broader sweep of history in its making. It's an enormously ambitious piece whose success is a measure of its creator's skill and commitment. Picking up on that idea quoted early on from Robert McKee, that writers need to find their natural address on the story tellers' map, it's clear Peter Flannery never deserted his natural leanings as a politically and morally aware writer, and displayed every ounce of tenacity required to get that project through to completion.

I find Peter Flannery's integrity inspiring, and in an increasingly hard-nosed world which often sees dramatists' work, especially screenwriting, as a commodity geared to making big profits, the fact that he and the BBC did see it through, I also find quite reassuring. That isn't just because the story delivers political punch, or because it's a big and expensive project; it's because it grew out of a writer's personal background, experience and vision, clearly speaks with his voice, and is written and crafted to the highest standards.

Figure 10.1   Daniel Craig in *Our Friends in the North* © BBC

Writers aiming to work for film or television, if they succeed, will often find themselves creating work to pre-existing ideas, or in line with many pre-conceived notions of what will hold mass appeal, and are ever more subject to the widespread practice of draconian and sometimes seemingly endless revisions dictated by a commercially driven editorial machine. Room for individual authorship has diminished considerably, and despite the fact that there are lots more hours of popular drama series on many more channels needing to be filled, for the majority of writers looking to get their individual voices heard, all this 'more' has most definitely ended up meaning 'much less'.

So why bother doing anything other than learning how to be a writer who can copy the model – whatever it happens to be at the time – and then just slot in as a smoothly-running cog? Well, I'm going to suggest several good reasons. Firstly, in my opinion, you will never write drama to the best of your abilities until you've discovered your own voice – that's to say in the particular way you naturally have of telling stories, based on those passions which drive you and the strengths which you can bring to the craft. Secondly, again in my personal opinion, there has never been more of a crying need than there is now for writers who are ready and able to hold the line against a flood of mediocre melodrama, and at least offer a better alternative. Thirdly, despite everything I've said to the contrary, if you equip yourself to write well and believe in what you're doing, there's a chance that good, individually authored work will get through and be picked up for production. In any case, if you've discovered what you're about as an individual writer, if you are invited to write formulaic or formatted drama, and should you choose to take up that invitation, you will be able to deliver satisfactorily, and yet still produce work of distinction.

The extract from *Our Friends in the North* concerns itself with Geordie's story. Geordie has fled an unhappy history in Newcastle to try his luck in London. We have seen the difficult relationship with his alcoholic father back in Newcastle and how that has brought them to blows and the way he also abandoned his pregnant girlfriend. Now he is living in a tiny flat in Soho and working for porn-king Benny Barratt, who grateful for a warning from Geordie about imminent betrayal, has made him his right-hand man.

> INT. GEORDIE'S FLAT. DAY.
>
> GEORDIE SITS IN TROUSERS, NO SHIRT YET, WATCHING RACING ON TELEVISION. HE HAS A CUP OF TEA AND IS READING A LETTER WHICH HAS ATTACHED TO IT A PHOTOGRAPH OF ANTHONY COX. HE LAUGHS AT PART OF THE LETTER. HE GETS UP, REALISING THE TIME.
>
> 13. EXT. SOHO STREETS. DAY.
>
> GEORDIE WALKING BRISKLY THROUGH BUSY SOHO STREETS. HE KEEPS A KEEN EYE OUT FOR SIGNS OF POLICE. SMART SUIT. NICE WATCH. GOOD SHOES. WELL GROOMED. A BRIEFCASE HANDCUFFED TO HIS WRIST.
>
> 14. SOHO PORN SHOP. DAY.
>
> TWO CUSTOMERS ARE BROWSING IN THE RACKS OF WHACKING MATERIAL, WATCHED IDLY BY THE MANAGER MICHAEL FRISCH.
>
> THE DOOR OPENS.
>
> FRISCH AND THE CUSTOMERS LOOK UP.
>
> GEORDIE ENTERS.

GEORDIE TAKES IN THE SCENE AS HE GOES TO FRISCH'S COUNTER.

FRISCH: Hello, Mr Peacock.

GEORDIE: Hello, Michael. Everything okay?

FRISCH: Yes, if you like being bored out of your skull.

GEORDIE: Quiet again?

FRISCH: Well who wants to get arrested in his lunch hour?

GEORDIE OPENS HIS BRIEFCASE AND FRISCH PUTS HIS MEAGRE TAKINGS INTO IT.

A CUSTOMER ENTERS.

THEY BOTH LOOK UP TO CHECK THAT IT'S NOT POLICE.

GEORDIE: Yeh. Well. Is that it?

FRISCH: Hardly worth opening. When's Barratt going to do something about it?

GEORDIE: I'll pass on your comments, Michael. He'll also be interested in where you were last night. I called in here at eight o'clock and it was shut.

HE CLOSES THE BRIEFCASE.

FRISCH: Yeh, I had to sort something out. Sorry.

GEORDIE: Sorry?

FRISCH: I've got a few problems.

GEORDIE STARTS TO GO. SHAKING HIS HEAD.

Geordie?

GEORDIE LOOKS AT HIM, EYEBROWS UP.

Mr Peacock. You couldn't lend me 50 quid could you?

GEORDIE: What?

FRISCH: Bit desperate, actually. I'll pay you back.

GEORDIE HESITATES BUT GIVES HIM MONEY.

GEORDIE: You better. There's twenty.

GEORDIE ATTACHES THE BRIEFCASE TO HIS WRIST AND HEADS FOR THE DOOR VIA A CUSTOMER IN THE CORNER.

GEORDIE: (DISCREETLY) Put it back.

THE MAN HESITATES THEN TAKES A PACKET OF PHOTOGRAPHS FROM HIS POCKET AND PUTS IT BACK ON THE RACK.

On your way.

THE MAN GOES.

GEORDIE LOOKS AT FRISCH, WHO SHRUGS AND LOOKS EMBARRASSED.

GEORDIE LEAVES.

15. INT. FLAMINGO CLUB. SOHO. DAY.

THIS IS THE CLUB WHICH IS TO SUPERSEDE THE KING CLUB AS THE CENTREPIECE IN BARRATT'S EMPIRE.

IT IS A LARGE CLUB CREATED OUT OF A CELLAR. ABOVE IT ARE OFFICES AND AN APARTMENT. BOTH ARE ALREADY IN USE. THE CLUB IS ALMOST READY TO OPEN. DECORATION WORK IS IN PROGRESS.

A BABY GRAND PIANO IS BEING DELIVERED.

GEORDIE PASSES THROUGH THE CLUB, CASTING AN EYE OVER WORK IN PROGRESS. HE GOES THROUGH A DOOR AT THE SIDE AND UP SOME STAIRS TO THE OFFICES. THERE IS A LARGE OFFICE AND A SMALL OFFICE WITH A CONNECTING DOOR. IN THE SMALL OFFICE, WITH THE CONNECTING DOOR WIDE OPEN, SITS BARRATT'S SECRETARY, BRENDA, TYPING.

GEORDIE ENTERS.

GEORDIE: Hello, Brenda.

HE GOES THROUGH INTO THE LARGE OFFICE. NOBODY THERE. HE GOES BACK INTO BRENDA'S OFFICE.

Is Mr Barratt upstairs?

BRENDA INDICATING LETTERS TO BE SIGNED.

BRENDA: Haven't seen him. Miss Allen's there. She came in an hour ago.

GEORDIE: Any idea when he's coming back?

BRENDA SHRUGS.

GEORDIE PONDERS FOR A MOMENT HIS NEXT MOVE. HE HANDCUFFS THE BRIEFCASE TO A

FILING CABINET IN THE LARGE OFFICE AND
LEAVES. HE GOES UP A FLIGHT OF STAIRS TO
THE APARTMENT. HE LETS HIMSELF IN WITH A
LATCH KEY. HE GOES INTO THE LIVING-ROOM.
THERE IS A LARGE OIL-PAINTING OF BENNY
BARRATT ON ONE WALL.

(CALLING OUT) Benny?

HE GOES INTO CORRIDOR. HE HEARS THE
SOUND OF A SHOWER FROM DOWN THE WAY.
THE SHOWER IS TURNED OFF. HE WALKS DOWN
THE CORRIDOR TO THE MASTER BEDROOM
WHICH HAS AN ENSUITE BATHROOM.

THE BEDROOM DOOR IS AJAR. HE LOOKS IN
AND SEES RUSTY. SHE HAS JUST COME FROM
THE SHOWER AND IS ABOUT TO DRESS. SHE
STANDS FACING A LARGE WALL MIRROR.

GEORDIE GLIDES INTO THE ROOM BEHIND HER
AND GRABS HER BREASTS. SHE SEES HIM IN THE
MIRROR AND LOOKS PANICKY.

BARRATT: (FROM THE BATHROOM)

Towel. Where's the towel?

16. INT. APARTMENT. DAY.

LIVING ROOM.

RUSTY SITS UNDERNEATH THE PAINTING WITH
A DRINK. SHE IS IN A DRESSING-GOWN AND
HER HAIR IS WRAPPED IN A TOWEL.

GEORDIE SITS ACROSS THE ROOM WITH A
DRINK.

SILENCE.

ENTER BARRATT CARRYING HIS SHOES AND
TRYING TO DO UP HIS TIE.

BARRATT: What fettle, bonny lad?

GEORDIE: Canny fettle, Benny.

BARRATT: How's business?

GEORDIE: Bad.

BARRATT: Oh, why is my life full of problems?

HE DOES UP HIS TIE IN A MIRROR.

GEORDIE: One of Winters' shops got done on
Tuesday apparently. That's the first actual bust
anybody's had since March.

BARRATT: Did it? What happened?

GEORDIE: They confiscated the Danish stuff. No arrests.

BARRATT: The filth don't know where they are, do they? A load of arrests one day. Then nothing for months. Then one. Then nothing. I think they'd go away and leave us in peace if these bloody Maltesers like Winters would stop putting hard stuff in the windows. It's provocative, isn't it?

HE'S PUTTING ON HIS SHOES.

Old Bill's got to stop that, hasn't he? Can't turn a blind eye to bloody nuns and dogs. I've tried to tell them. But will they listen? Greedy foreign bastards.

HE PUTS ON HIS JACKET.

I've got to go. I'm taking Terri to a dinner party. Bloody neighbours. (TO RUSTY) Behave yourself, you.

RUSTY: I'll see you later.

BARRATT: No, I'll have to stay the night. It'll be expected.

BARRATT GRIMACES. HE KISSES RUSTY.

I'll see you both tomorrow.

HE PAUSES AND LOOKS AT GEORDIE.

What are we going to do, eh?

GEORDIE LOOKS AT HIM.

BARRATT: Let's talk tomorrow, yeh?

HE GOES.

SILENCE.

RUSTY AND GEORDIE LOOK AT EACH OTHER.

GEORDIE: Did he see?

SHE BURSTS OUT LAUGHING.

RUSTY: Your face!

THEY LAUGH. THEY STOP.

Come and do it again.

SHE OPENS HER DRESSING GOWN. HE JOINS HER ON THE SOFA.

SHE LEADS HIM INTO THE BEDROOM. THEY FALL ONTO THE BED, BECOMING PASSIONATE.

I love you, Geordie. I love you.

RUSTY STARTS TO REMOVE GEORDIE'S
CLOTHES.

IN THE LIVING ROOM: BARRATT RETURNS
SILENTLY. HE LISTENS. HE FINDS GEORDIE'S TIE
ON THE SOFA, UNDER THE PORTRAIT. HE
HOLDS THE TIE AND LOOKS INTO HIS LIKENESS
ON THE WALL.

IN THE BEDROOM: THEIR PASSION CONTINUES.

That first scene, brief though it is, sets up a couple of important elements.
The letter links him back to the close friends he has left behind in the North-
East, the photo being of Tosker's and Mary's son Anthony. That difficult past
he has left behind reverberates when we see him at the end of the sequence
on the bed with Rusty. She passionately declares she loves him, and he pointedly is unwilling to say anything in return. Also in that first scene the racing
is on the TV, at the literal level completely in character for Geordie and also
a reminder that in a broader sense he is a chancer, an opportunist not afraid
to take a gamble, or even play things dangerously; and let's face it, gambles
don't come much bigger than to mess around with a psychopath's mistress
right under his nose.

The central section of the sequence shows Geordie visiting one of Barratt's
sex shops to collect the takings. We find out three things of importance in
this scene: business is under pressure because potential customers are in fear
of the police; Frisch is quite subservient to Geordie who is very much
in control now, a complete turn-around of their first encounter, since
when Geordie did Barratt the big favour; and finally, in the way he spots the
pilfering, we see that not much escapes Geordie's eagle eye – ironically, the
same is true of Barratt as Geordie will shortly discover.

The background which this smaller drama is played out against is referred to
in the conversation Geordie and Barratt have about 'business'; the 'Swinging
Sixties' in London was a time when the porn trade was booming, its success
shored up by corruption amongst officers in the Metropolitan Police, who
were taking a slice of the action in return for turning a blind eye. So Barratt's
disapproval aimed at those 'greedy foreign bastards' who were leaving the
police no alternative but to act is richly ironic. Seizing the moral high
ground, in an activity which just hasn't got any, wittily points up the dangerous level of delusion Barratt and company are prey to: peddling sleaze could
never be a respectable business, and yet that oil painting tells us a different
story about how Barratt sees himself. Where is he off to now but back home
to take his wife to a dinner party? He is aiming to remake himself in the

image of a 'successful man of the world' entrepreneur, a pillar of club-land. The grand piano and the refurbishment going on down below is another reminder of the entertainment empire Barratt is aiming to build and rule over.

Then there is also a very interesting tension between the theme of sexual exploitation as a business, and what is going on between these three characters right here and now. Benny is cheating on his wife. Rusty is about to cheat on him, though we know she has only just been in bed with him, and from that 'I'll see you later' she offers him, we can guess she'd have been quite happy to fall back into his arms again later. Geordie is betraying Benny and using Rusty. It's altogether not a very nice picture. It is, in fact, a picture of use, abuse and unfeeling self-interest. That last shot of Barratt looking at his likeness is carefully calculated, as is the reference to the large wall mirror in the bedroom. It conjures not just voyeurism but also narcissism. These men of the world who can see no further than themselves, and that is a fatal limitation.

In fact when this episode was screened, several changes had been made from the final draft – a reminder as I pointed out early on in this book that the script is *and is not* a finished product. Rehearsal and pre-production periods offer opportunities for second thoughts. The first scene had Geordie adjusting his appearance before going out, looking in a mirror as he did so and then handcuffing himself to the case. The racing was on the TV in the background. You can see how that image of him looking at himself neatly bookends the scene with the moment when Barratt looks at himself in the painting, both moments underlining this idea of self-absorption. That preening in the mirror helped emphasise Geordie's smart appearance. And once the director and designers got their hands on this sequence, they really did capitalise on this aspect of image. Geordie was given a smart suit and expensive coat, Rusty a fetching kimono and Barratt an expensive Italian suit. Success and worldliness were to the fore. Rusty's drink was an exotic liqueur, blue curaçao, and in the recorded version Barratt's parting shot to them both is the Japanese 'sayonara'. These embellishments built on the parody of international businessmen's chatter we have in Barratt's slighting reference to Danish material and 'bloody Maltesers'. The portrait is deliberately tacky and, to my mind, works very well at several levels; beyond the ostentatious narcissism, it's also 'lord of the manor' material, pointing out graphically just who's in charge, and when we see Rusty sitting beneath it the image is ironically proprietorial too – she belongs to him, except, of course, she doesn't.

Visually underpinning the thematic concerns of the drama in this way raises the question of how far a production team can go before they overplay their hand. As the earlier chapter on metaphor suggests, that really is quite a long way, and the writer does well to realise this too. Just as the writer in this case ends with that great moment of Barratt gazing at himself ominously fingering Geordie's tie, so the addition of Geordie checking the look of that same tie in the mirror does nothing but extend and enhance the writer's idea. Geordie is aiming to fly high, his smart, new appearance essential to playing the part; but, just as in the Greek myth, where Icarus flew too close to the sun and melted the wax in his wings, so Geordie's flight is about to end in disaster. The intimations of a 'hanging' yet to come are clear enough in that final gesture of Barratt holding his tie.

Dramatically Geordie's kept journeying. There's a reminder of his roots in that first scene and, in any case, is ever present in the guise of his name. A character busily on the make, we see the city businessman he is intent on becoming. And finally, through a deliciously dangerous moment of dramatic irony, the self-destructive chancer is seen to put everything at risk.

There's a way in which the sequence also operates at three or four levels, all of them bouncing off each other. There's the level of social corruption being pointed up in the shape of the porn racket. Then there's the level of interpersonal corruption and vice in what we see going on between these three. After that we are invited to look at the intra-personal level of what these people are doing to their souls, and in particular Geordie. He may feel he's in seventh heaven right now, but we know that hell is just around the corner. Finally, and related to this, there's a way in which this sequence carries overtones of a morality tale, very much in the spirit of the medieval plays I mentioned earlier in Chapter 4. In those plays the virtues and vices were explicitly named. Here we have a character called George 'Geordie' Peacock. Pride is a deadly sin and comes before what we all know is just round the corner for our hero. His *hubris* (the classical tragic flaw of overweening pride) will be Geordie's undoing and eventually we will see him end up (quite literally) down and out in the gutter.

The whole sweep of *Our Friends in the North* demonstrates quite clearly that the playwright has a moral standpoint, picking the major examples of real life corruption as the models for episodes in his drama, through which he can put his central characters to the test. Along the way he gives them a universality with which we can thoroughly empathise. When Geordie handcuffs himself to that money we are being shown a moment which is about not just this character, but the potential we all have to be bought.

As I suggested earlier on, the ability to construct effective and moving sequences is key in the business of writing drama for the screen. Here we are offered an example of a brilliant piece of writing, creating a powerful, self-contained sequence which entertains and enthrals us at the level of simple story, whilst carrying verbal and visual images and subtext which allow the deeper meaning to work on us and so see ourselves in relation to the drama.

There are dramas which show us 'the world as it is not'; many soap operas fall into this category. Then there are dramas which try to show us 'the world as it is'; they convey a level of realism aimed at copying life with the intention that we will believe what it's about all the more. In fact, since drama is an artifice, a way of distilling truths and making metaphors out of life, then perhaps the most powerful way a script can operate is by showing us 'the world as it is, *seen through drama*'. And that, I think, is precisely what Peter Flannery has done here. It looks deceptively like a slice of life, yet in fact has the carefully crafted substance to reach out beyond its immediate context and carry deeper meaning and impact.

SOME FINAL TIPS

In learning to develop any art, there is great value in studying the work of accomplished practitioners. Screenwriting is no exception to that rule. I have tried to include excerpts from some work I admire in this book, and which I feel rewards close attention. I strongly recommend that you watch lots of screen dramas and then watch again those you have liked and really admired several times. (In fact try stage plays and radio plays as well, and don't overlook the importance of actually reading screenplays and scripts; this allows you to take time for reflection in a way you may not if you're wrapped up in just watching.) If you are on a relevant course of study and have co-students interested in developing their writing, or if you have informally formed a group to support your writing practice, then make viewing and discussion of what you've seen a regular part of your activity together. The ability to analyse and express what you think and feel about others' and your own work is an essential part of honing your critical abilities, and these, in turn, can really support your writing. Learn to be specific in what you say to each other, and get into the habit of offering the reasons for why you think and feel what you do. Feedback can be a really invaluable aid to your development. Sometimes what people have noticed in your work may surprise and please you: at other times the group's response to what you may have felt certain you were conveying with clarity can usefully make you think again; what's more there may be helpful suggestions from them as to how you might make changes.

Another important reason for taking part in discussion is that, in looking at a variety of work, you can't help but discover what it is you really do and do not have a passion for, and that too will help clarify what you want to try writing.

So don't hang back. However, do make a ground-rule in the group that anything anyone says about each other's work is offered in a supportive and constructive manner. There's no point in being part of a demolition team. Confidence plays an enormously important part in developing as a writer, and if you've not gathered people around you who are interested in nurturing that vital asset (and I don't mean just flattering each other) then I suggest you go elsewhere until you do find what you need. If it's just a rogue individual who enjoys throwing bricks, then perhaps he's the one who should go.

If not a group then finding a person whom you trust and who is genuinely interested in looking at your work, can also be a great support mechanism from time to time. Also consider doing some courses. Adult education centres, local education authorities, and organisations like the Arvon Foundation all offer courses in writing, and with increasing frequency scriptwriting in particular. These vary in length from day-schools to week-long, residential intensive courses. A benefit of finding a course or two to go on, above and beyond the experience itself, will be the opportunity to come into contact with other enthusiasts and perhaps become mutually supportive to each in the future.

Experiment with different kinds of writing. Don't just see yourself as a screenwriter. In writing poems or short stories, you may discover an activity you really love, and one which will complement and feed your drama writing.

Read widely. Both as a means of experiencing different ways with the pen, and also as a source of ideas and inspiration. *Our Friends in the North*, as I mentioned, had its basis in police and planning corruption cases. But don't confine yourself to looking at news stories which feel like they'd make a good drama. Perhaps you'll be inspired by a setting, or a character will be born out of reading something: maybe you have a leaning towards historical events, maybe you enjoy the fantastic. The knack is to keep interested in everything, and as I suggested in Chapter 1, learn to recognise those moments that are telling you they want you to write them. Keep practising your day-dreaming. When sequences of pictures start to roll in your imagination, let that happen. The more you practise visualising your stories unfolding, the easier it becomes.

If you give your favourite screenwriters particular attention don't neglect to watch more widely. Educate yourself about comedy, soap-opera, drama-documentary, short films; watch anything and everything with a keen eye as to how it has been put together and discuss these thoughts with others.

In particular, start noticing the broad differences between TV drama and film. Notice how cinema uses the soundtrack as a far more intrinsic part of the process, how very often a film can and does take its time to unwind, letting the pictures lead and using far less dialogue to supplement and support the story telling. Notice the fact that TV works better in close up and see what that means. Listen to radio plays and see what pictures these conjure in your mind. Try writing examples of each kind of drama. Try a bit of radio drama and see how well you can use sound. Try writing a short TV drama with the emphasis on dialogue and the focus thrown heavily on the characters' relationships to one another. Try writing short films. Move to and fro between the different forms, always concentrating on making images, verbal and visual, work for the audience.

Try your hand at different forms and styles you might not feel immediately drawn to. Perhaps you've never thought of yourself as a comedy writer. Have a go; and that doesn't necessarily mean sitting down to try and produce a half-hour sitcom. Maybe you have an idea for a funny short film script, or perhaps a poem. Explore your ability to be funny, is what I'm saying, then think about how that untapped ability might find its way into your scripts.

If you should want to try placing your work professionally, then do make sure that you have studied the demands and constraints the industry makes on writers, in regard to different areas of drama writing and the consequent expectations they will have on would-be writers in particular areas. There is nothing to say your work couldn't be different from the norm, or that it might even be found all the more interesting, but a sound knowledge of the general field will help you to know what to get in line with if you choose to do so, and just what you're taking leave of if you choose to do that.

If you are intent on originating material, then an established soap with its own in-house storyliners is unlikely to offer you all the elbow room you're looking for. However, writing an original radio drama will do just that, and many a good screenplay started life as a piece written for and broadcast on radio. Don't be afraid to branch out and experiment. The only way writers ever got better is by practising and trying out different ideas. Always keep looking to *author* your work. Listen out for *your* voice and whenever you get the feeling that your writing is going really well, nurture it and try to notice specifically what in your writing is exciting that sensation.

Be a writer for yourself first and foremost. Don't set about consciously copying others or offering them what you think they want. Please *yourself* with your work, safeguarding your individual abilities; alongside this process, develop your craft and your critical skills, and understand why different conventions have evolved and exactly how they work.

Every book on screenwriting will tell you to believe in yourself, so I don't see why I should be left out. Writing is an important means of self-expression. In itself that can be a joyful and creative process, even though it may feel like hard work – and sometimes most definitely will! In choosing to write, you are honouring a valuable, creative part of yourself and I believe that can be a most important, fundamentally life-enhancing activity. Give yourself credit for doing this, take care of yourself in this process as well as your work, and remember to celebrate your progress. Best of luck.

Bibliography and suggested reading

Aristotle, *Poetics* (Translation by Malcolm Heath), Penguin 1996
Ball, Alan, *American Beauty*, FilmFour Books 2000
Bennett, Alan, *The Complete Talking Heads*, BBC Consumer Publishing (Books) 1998
Blum, Richard A., *Television and Screen Writing*, Butterworth Heineman 1995
Boal, Augusto, *Games For Actors and Non-Actors*, Routledge 1992
Booker, Christopher, *The Seven Basic Plots*, Continuum 2004
Brady, John, *The Craft of the Screenwriter*, Touchstone 1982
Campbell, Joseph, *The Hero with a Thousand Faces*, Paladin 1988
Chayefsky, Paddy, *Collected Works, the Screenplays*, Applause Books 1981
Connaughton, Shane and Sheridan, Jim, *My Left Foot*, Faber and Faber 1989
Cooper, Pat and Dancyger, Ken, *Writing the Short Film*, Focal Press 1994
Egri, Lajos *The Art of Dramatic Writing*, Touchstone Books 1960
George, Terry and Sheridan, Jim, *Some Mother's Son*, Grove Press 1996
Goldman, William, *Adventures in the Screen Trade*, Warner Books 1983
Hodge, John, *Shallow Grave*, Faber and Faber 1996
Horton, Andrew, *Writing the Character Centred Screenplay*, University of California 1994
Johnston, Chris, *House of Games*, Nick Hern Books 1998
Johnstone, Keith, *Impro*, Methuen 1981
Johnstone, Keith, *Impro for Storytellers*, Faber and Faber 1999
Kübler-Ross, Elizabeth, *On Death and Dying*, Macmillan 1969
LaGravenese, Richard, *The Fisher King*, Applause Books 1991
Lucey, Paul, *Story Sense: Writing Story and Script for Feature Films and Television*, Mcgraw Hill 1996
Mamet, David, *On Directing Film*, Penguin 1992
McKee, Robert, *Story*, Methuen 1999
Minghella, Anthony, *The English Patient*, Methuen 1997
Parker, Philip, *The Art and Science of Screenwriting*, Intellect Books 1999
Proulx, Annie, McMurtry, Larry and Ossana, Diana, *Brokeback Mountain, Story to Screenplay*, Harper Perennial 2006
Seger, Linda, *Making a Good Script Great*, Hollywood: Samuel French 1987
Shakespeare, William, *Hamlet*, New Penguin Shakespeare
Swain, Dwight V. and Swain, Joye R., *Scripting for the New AV Technologies*, Focal Press 1991
Vogler, Christopher, *The Writer's Journey*, Pan Books 1988
Watts, Harris, *On Camera*, Aavo 1997

Index

References to figures/photographs are shown in *italic*